Advancing Learning Within an Classroom

This insightful book sets out five core elements of good practice that will lead to great teaching and learning both within and beyond the classroom. It looks in detail at the learning process and how teachers can support this through a rich mix of teacher-led direct instruction and collaborative and online learning, both flipped and blended.

Covering five major themes to reset our pedagogy, *Advancing Learning Within and Beyond the Classroom* presents the key evidence about 'what works' alongside practical activities to adopt or adapt to enhance your own practice. The chapters cover:

- the application of precise curricular **knowledge**
- the presentation of key **questions** to guide, check and deepen learning
- **elaboration** to build deep understanding
- personalised **feedback** to accelerate progress
- the introduction of regular **challenges** to drive high learning outcomes and relevant commercial and world-class standards

Including a comprehensive overview of evidence-based practice and a wealth of practical strategies to drive engagement and productive learning, this is essential reading for all teachers working in secondary schools or further education.

Bradley Lightbody has enjoyed a long career in education teaching history at all levels and holding senior management posts across sixth form, quality, adult education, learning resources and teacher training. He was appointed as an additional inspector with Ofsted and founded and led the educational consultancy Collegenet. He has written extensively on education and history in seven previous books and regularly presents at staff training events across the UK.

Advancing Learning Within and Beyond the Classroom

Resetting Pedagogy for the Online Era

Bradley Lightbody

Routledge
Taylor & Francis Group

LONDON AND NEW YORK

First published 2022
by Routledge
2 Park Square, Milton Park, Abingdon, Oxon OX14 4RN

and by Routledge
605 Third Avenue, New York, NY 10158

Routledge is an imprint of the Taylor & Francis Group, an informa business

© 2022 Bradley Lightbody

British Library Cataloguing-in-Publication Data
A catalogue record for this book is available from the British Library

Library of Congress Cataloging-in-Publication Data
Names: Lightbody, Bradley, author.
Title: Advancing learning within and beyond the classroom / Bradley
    Lightbody.
Description: Abingdon, Oxon ; New York, NY : Routledge, 2022. |
    Includes bibliographical references and index.
Identifiers: LCCN 2021024523 | ISBN 9780367677770 (hardback) | ISBN
    9780367677787 (paperback) | ISBN 9781003132783 (ebook)
Subjects: LCSH: Effective teaching. | High school teaching. | College
    teaching. | Experiential learning.
Classification: LCC LB1025.3 .L555 2021 | DDC 371.102—dc23
LC record available at https://lccn.loc.gov/2021024523

ISBN: 978-0-367-67777-0 (hbk)
ISBN: 978-0-367-67778-7 (pbk)
ISBN: 978-1-003-13278-3 (ebk)

DOI: 10.4324/9781003132783

Typeset in Bembo and Helvetica Neue
by Apex CoVantage, LLC

For my very own Generation Alpha, Isabelle, James, Eleanor and Ralph, who are all taking their first steps on their learning journey. May they find and gain the freedom to pursue their individual passions.

Contents

Acknowledgements

Standing on the shoulders of giants by drawing on the research of Professor John Hattie, Dylan Wiliam, Robert J. Marzano, Barack Rosenshine, Daniel T. Willingham and Professor Robert Coe in particular. Taking inspiration from Ross Morrison McGill's Five Minute lesson plan to design the Big Picture lesson plan. The enthusiasm of teachers like Sam Barnes for taking the concept forward. The practical guidance provided by Charlotte Danielson's Framework for Teaching (www.danielsongroup.org). Battelle for Kids for their permission to reproduce their deep learning and rainbow curriculum graphics. CBI/Pearson for their comprehensive surveys and statistics on employability skills and online learning trends. The research findings of the Organisation for Economic Co-operation and Development (OECD) and the World Economic Forum (WEF). The permission of JISC to quote the outcomes of survey reports in relation to online activity. UK government documents and strategies quoted under HMSO core licence C02W0007193. The impressive focus on oracy developed by School 21 in East London and the positive oasis of inspirational goals and learning support provided by the Kensington Aldridge Academy in the aftermath of the Grenfell fire tragedy. Ellie Chick for drawing attention to the largely forgotten underachieving third of each cohort. Aftab Hussain's highlighting of the potential of artificial intelligence (AI) with the pioneering development of Ada as a digital assistant in Bolton College. The following publishers, in particular, as a source of 'fair use' key quotations: Routledge, Solution Tree Press, Jonathan Cape, Jossey Bass and CEP Press.

Every attempt has been made to contact copyright holders and to gain responses, but any omissions will be corrected and addressed upon notification.

Finally, my continuing debt to Carol for her support and understanding over many years of research and writing.

Preface

After two hundred years of the primacy of the classroom, our education system stands on the threshold of fundamental change as learning beyond the classroom becomes as significant as learning within the classroom. The rising generations are comfortable online. They conduct and manage most aspects of their lives online, and as artificial intelligence (AI) transforms everything it touches, education cannot stand still. Opinion surveys conducted by Pearson and the Organisation for Economic Co-operation and Development (OECD) have revealed that most students worldwide endorse and expect a blended learning future following the closure of schools from 2020 to 2021. The impact will not be a retreat from the classroom, but rather a refocussing of class and teacher time to take advantage of online resources, digital tools and learning platforms. The future will not be a choice between classroom or online, but rather a beneficial fusion with a focus on high instructional standards. The chapters in this book reflect five major themes to reset our pedagogy. First the application of precise curricular **knowledge**; secondly the presentation of key **questions** to guide, check and deepen learning; thirdly **elaboration** to build deep rather than surface understanding; fourthly personalised **feedback** to accelerate progress; and finally, the introduction of regular **challenges** to drive high learning outcomes and relevant commercial and world-class standards. This book carries forward the earlier publication *Great Teaching and Learning* (2019) but fully updated as a second edition. Finally, please discover a wealth of practical strategies to support the creation of stimulating and inspiring sequences of learning within and beyond the classroom.

Bradley Lightbody
April 2021

Knowledge

1

The purpose of education

What is the purpose of education? Answering this question reveals a fault line that has divided society since ancient times between those who emphasise the importance of liberty and freedom of choice over what and when to learn and those who promote conformity in relation to school attendance and adherence to a prescribed curriculum. This fundamental division has returned to the forefront of educational debate as the choices afforded by online learning question the primacy of the classroom.

Liberty versus conformity

The liberty versus conformity debate is firmly rooted in ancient Greece and particularly associated with the teachings of Socrates, Plato, Aristotle and Protagoras. Socrates (470–399 BCE) is perhaps the most well-known and widely quoted of the Greek philosophers. He was born in Athens, and after a period as a stonemason and a soldier he began to closely observe and question the world around him. He gained a significant following because he was not afraid to question the ruling elite or to raise significant questions like 'what is justice?' or even to question the existence of the gods. The latter led to his arrest for what in the modern age we would refer to as heresy, and after a trial he was found guilty and sentenced to death in the spring of 399 BCE. He accepted the verdict of the court and was offered and drank hemlock without protest. It was his personal acceptance of the common good and the importance of conformity i.e. an acknowledgement of his offence, the considered verdict of his peers and his obligation to the state as a citizen. Socrates never wrote anything, and so we are primarily dependent upon the writings of his pupil Plato for our knowledge of how he guided petitioners by a process of ever-reducing dialectical reasoning to arrive at answers to their own questions.

DOI: 10.4324/9781003132783-2

After Socrates's death Plato founded a school in Athens known as the *Akademia*, or Academy, circa 385 BCE – the origin of the term academic – and carried forward the Socratic spirit in many of his publications, most notably *Apology* and *Republic*. The archaeological remains of the *Akademia* are located in an olive grove on the outskirts of Athens and are a fixture on the modern-day tourist trail. Plato's *Republic* specified the ideal curriculum for 'virtuous' rulers and the wider role of education in reinforcing the common values of parental authority, belief in a beneficent God and the responsibilities of citizenship. Ancient Greece also gave us the term pedagogy, arising from the slaves or Paidagogues (Pedagogues), who were retained by wealthy families to educate their children in all aspects of good manners, health, morality and wider citizenship. They were empowered to chastise and to discipline, but they were also close mentors and confidants and ultimately charged with guiding the transition from dependent child to independent adult. The *Paidagogue* essentially educated for life and responsible citizenship. Subject teachers, known as *Didaskalos*, were also retained but for specified periods of time and with a much narrower remit to impart their specialist subject knowledge. Those underpinning tenets and values are being re-affirmed as the world's leading nations re-evaluate the impact of universal education and increasingly aver personal development as the primary purpose of education, as detailed in Chapter 11.

Universal education

Universal education dates from 1 May 1802 when Napoleon (1769–1821) in a personal decree declared educational reform as a national priority and a key function of the new post-revolutionary French state. His decree introduced a network of secondary schools devoted to either civil or military careers, with Lycées for the academic elite and mandatory teacher training to improve the quality of instruction. He also took the significant step of removing the church's influence over education by enforcing the adoption of a strictly secular school system. Napoleon's motive was not simply altruism. The Industrial Revolution was raising a need for a literate and numerate workforce as the rise of science, mechanisation and the emergence of global trade fuelled economic growth and prosperity. Liberty was redefined, with school attendance no longer cast as a limitation on personal liberty, as famously articulated by Rousseau, but rather an enhancement; a universal right of citizens to learn how to read and write. It was an arm of France's revolutionary zeal which alarmed many nations in relation to what people might read and write, and consequently it was not until 1870 that Great Britain endorsed and introduced universal education. In contrast Prussia carried forward Napoleon's reforms and introduced the world's first fully comprehensive system of education in 1810. It is a system that has defined the structure and organisation of schools worldwide for the past two centuries.

Prussian school system

The Prussian school system, developed by Wilhelm von Humboldt (1767–1835), embraced a standard curriculum framework, a formal end of school examination the *Arbitur* and a requirement for all teachers to pass a state-approved certificate of practice. Humboldt was a leading academic and diplomat. He first elaborated his vision for education in an article entitled, *'On Public State Education,'* published in 1792. The article formed part of a much wider treatise, *'The Limits of State Action,'* published after his death and reflected Rousseau's philosophy of strict limitations on the reach and authority of the state, 'The government is best which makes itself unnecessary.'[1] However, Humboldt also believed that the first and foremost duty of the state was to improve the lives of its citizens, and he regarded universal education as central to personal development and fulfilment. His philosophy echoed Plato's concept of a benevolent and responsible state and reflected the humanistic ideals emanating from the French Revolution, but his immediate and practical motivation was to improve the Volksschule, a loose network of primary age schools established in 1763 by the Royal Decree of Frederick the Great. The schools were largely staffed by ex-soldiers with a reputation for strict obedience to the point of brutality and a curriculum that was dominated by little more than basic literacy and the recitation of the Catechism. In contrast Humboldt's guiding philosophy was *'Allgemeine Bildung,'* or the concept of a well-rounded education, "to inquire and to create; – these are the grand centres around which all human pursuits revolve"[2] and to open schools to girls as well as boys at a time when few girls had access to education. His approach was focussed upon individual choice and carried forward the broad foundation studies of the medieval Trivium rather than narrow subject disciplines. The *limits* envisaged by Humboldt were limits on state influence over the curriculum in favour of individual rather than state educational goals, "The sole purpose of education must be to shape man himself . . . Education of the individual must everywhere be as free as possible, taking the least possible account of civic circumstances."[3] Humboldt also turned his attention to the moribund university sector and encouraged universities to fuse and to blur the distinction between the arts and sciences and to support students to follow their personal research interests. This was *inquire* and *create* in action. Humboldt also successfully campaigned for the creation of a new University of Berlin, and by the 1830s German universities under his leadership enjoyed a worldwide reputation for advanced scientific and technological research. In 1949 the University of Berlin was renamed Humboldt University in honour of Humboldt's contribution to education and that of his brother Alexander von Humboldt, who was a renowned naturalist and explorer who gave his name to the Humboldt penguin. The success of Humboldt's school system in extending education to all children attracted delegations from around the world to study his reforms. It was the Finland of its day. Foremost among them was Horace Mann (1796–1859) who was secretary of the board of education for the US state of Massachusetts. Mann travelled to Prussia in 1843 and was impressed by the scale of the reforms and the movement towards a fully literate and well-educated workforce. On his return to Massachusetts, he successfully lobbied for the adoption of the Prussian system. New York State followed suit, and by degrees the Prussian tripartite system was introduced across the whole of the United States and by the end of the century by most of Europe, Scandinavia, Japan and Great Britain. The Monitorial system which had successfully extended education to millions of children was swept away.

The Monitorial system

The Monitorial system, originally known as 'mutual instruction,' was the most common form of mass education before the introduction of the Prussian school model. It was pioneered and developed by Andrew Bell in the late 1780s when he found himself responsible for the education of over 100 boys across different age groups in an orphanage in Madras, India. With no other teachers to call upon, Bell subdivided each subject into hierarchal levels, and once he had taught the first few lessons at each level he selected the most able students (with the incentive of a small payment) to step back to coach and support students in the lower levels, hence mutual instruction. The students advanced at their own pace, and once they were able to demonstrate a positive command of the relevant knowledge and/or skills, they stepped up a level. The system soon became self-sustaining and successful because the pupils were all regularly tutored in small groups with individual support, as required, rather than in the mass. The more able students also benefited because they returned to topics they had previously studied, and by coaching others, they consolidated their own understanding. Bell's students were engaging in what we know today as spaced practice and the Protégé Effect i.e. placing more able students into coaching and/or teaching roles. Bell returned to England in 1796 and published *An Experiment in Education* in 1797 to promote his system. In an age with a shortage of qualified teachers, his system was widely adopted and further amplified by the educational reformer Joseph Lancaster in a pamphlet entitled, 'Improvements in Education' published in 1803. Lancaster designated the student tutors as monitors, and the Monitorial system, as it became known, expanded worldwide and became the most common form of education for fifty years (1790–1840). However, as a steady stream of qualified teachers emerged from the universities to underpin the expansion of state school systems, the role of students in tutoring small groups and individuals faded away. Time may have forgotten the Monitorial system, but today the benefits of the Protégé Effect has been confirmed by multiple evidence-based research studies, with the most recent being Koh et al (2017).[4]

Teaching as a profession

Humboldt's requirement for all teachers to gain a licence to practice prompted the University of Konigsberg to establish the first professional study of pedagogy.

Johann Herbart (1776–1841) was appointed professor of philosophy and pedagogy in a position previously held by Immanuel Kant. Earlier in 1803 Kant had contributed to the debate by carrying forward the philosophy of ancient Greece in terms of the distinction between a pedagogue and a teacher:

> Education includes the nurture of the child and, as it grows, its culture. The latter is firstly negative, consisting of discipline; that is, merely the correcting of faults. Secondly, culture is positive, consisting of instruction and guidance (and thus forming part of education). Guidance means directing the pupil in putting into practice what he has been taught. Hence the difference between a private teacher who merely instructs, and a tutor or governor who guides and directs his pupil. The one trains for school only, the other for life.[5]

Kant was emphasising the importance of education for life. Herbart's publication *Universal Pedagogy* (1806) carried forward the concept of education as a preparation for life rather than the acquisition of a specified body of knowledge. He believed the latter would build dependency on instruction and regulation, whereas the former would build independence and self-direction. Herbart identified five significant principles to guide effective teaching and learning:

1 **Preparation** – to connect new learning with what is already known
2 **Presentation** – to use concrete references and examples or actual experiences
3 **Association** – to consider similarities and differences between new and old ideas
4 **Generalisation** – to extend from the concrete into the abstract or general principles
5 **Application** – to demonstrate new learning by utilising and putting into practice

These principles reflected the concept of apperception i.e. new information is assimilated with what is already known or understood or may be discarded if there is no relevant pre-existing conceptual framework. Herbart sought to resolve the division between proponents of discovery learning and teacher-directed lessons by highlighting flaws in both approaches. He reasoned that the application of discovery learning was unrealistic and false in situations where things were clearly known and understood, whereas overreliance on teacher-led instruction would simply repeat what was already known and stifle and inhibit new developments and creativity. His conclusion was a process of '*absorption*' and '*reflection*'. First, known facts and established knowledge should be presented via teacher instruction with checks for *absorption* followed by encouraging *reflection*, questioning and testing propositions with a view towards reforming or extending what was known. Humboldt's educational philosophy of encouraging questioning and Herbart's guiding pedagogy resulted in friction with both the church and the Prussian authorities. Their principles of enquiry and promoting individual autonomy were increasingly diluted and distorted in favour of national values.

National values

The shift towards promoting national values and loyalty to the state was primarily influenced by the writings and public lectures of Herbart's old mentor, Fichte. Prussia, the largest German state, had been defeated by Napoleon in war, and Fichte regarded education as an instrument of the state to rally national pride. In a series of *Addresses to the German Nation* he specified instilling national unity as the primary purpose of education: "They propose that you establish deeply and indelibly in the hearts of all, by means of education, the true and all powerful love of fatherland."[6] He regarded the cultivation of a common German identity as an essential first step for the thirty-eight separate German states to begin a process of unification and to ultimately unite as a single powerful nation. With this aim uppermost Fichte advocated that schools should inculcate unquestioning obedience to those in authority, "Education should aim at destroying free will so that after pupils are thus schooled they will be incapable throughout the rest of their lives of thinking or acting otherwise than as their school masters would have wished."[7]

Fichte's influence was significant, and his encouragement to overt nationalism and strict obedience to those in authority is often regarded as a factor in the later rise of extreme nationalism in 20th-century Germany. Fichte was not alone in identifying how schools could contribute to building and promoting national unity. Most countries imbued their curricula with a national colour to a greater or lesser extent. It became commonplace for schools to promote respect and loyalty towards the relevant head of state and in many cases to display the national flag and to reinforce adherence to a particular religious creed or set of political or religious values. For some, this is benign and no more than the fostering of a cohesive society by reinforcing relevant national traditions, customs, festivals and values. For others, it is at best social control and at worst overt indoctrination designed to enforce acceptance and obedience to a particular religion, political system or political ideology. By the late 19th century mounting criticism of the authoritarian leanings of the school system prompted a renewal of Herbart's five principles. Herbertian societies and 'schools' mushroomed across Europe and the United States along with a reaffirmation of the values espoused much earlier by Comenius (1592–1670).

The great didactic

The first significant consideration of how to teach, or *didactics* i.e. practical steps to build active participation, was written by the Czech philosopher John Amos Comenius who published *The Great Didactic* in 1648. The subtitle of *The Great Didactic* was *The Whole Art of Teaching All Things to All Men* and it reflected Comenius's quest to improve teaching and learning by defining 'how' rather than 'what' to teach. Comenius was strongly influenced by the theories of Socrates, Plato,

Aristotle and Pythagoras in terms of encouraging pupils to question and explore opinions, ideas and related evidence. Plato had advised teachers, "Do not train a child to learn by force or harshness; but direct them to it by what amuses their minds."[8] Comenius applied Plato's prescription and was highly critical of schools that made their focus obedience, conformity and discipline rather than fostering exploration, creativity and a love of learning. He also questioned the value added by a school compared to self-education:

> The examples of those who are self-taught show us most plainly that man, under the guidance of nature, can penetrate to a knowledge of all things. Many have made greater progress under their own tuition with oaks and beeches for teachers than others have done under the irksome instruction of teachers.[9]

His greatest concern was that schools enforced rather than inspired participation:

> This art of teaching and of learning was in former centuries to a great extent unknown . . . schools were so full of toil, weariness of weaknesses and deceits . . . education shall be conducted without blows, rigour or compulsion, as gently as possible and pleasantly as possible.[10]

He encouraged teachers to improve their presentation skills to in order to secure interest and engagement

> at the commencement of any new subject he should excite the interest of pupils, either by placing it before them in an attractive manner or by asking them questions . . . introduce something that is entertaining as well as of practical use; for in this way the interest of the scholars will be excited and their attention will be arrested.[11]

Starting a lesson with a motivational hook was just one of the many recommendations made in *The Great Didactic* for improving lessons. Comenius also raised the importance of parental support, peer support, reciprocal teaching, independent learning, questioning techniques, mastery learning and visual stimulation all recognised today as significant aspects of good practice. In terms of the latter Comenius published the first illustrated school textbook for children in 1658 entitled *Orbis Pictus* well in advance of modern-day awareness of the significance of dual coding. The book contained illustrated chapters, with the pictures rather than description presenting key information, across nature, the animal kingdom and sciences. It was regularly reprinted across Europe. Comenius's *art* of teaching was essentially the first teacher training manual and established the distinction between knowing something and knowing how to teach it. This is an important distinction because today it remains possible to be appointed to a teaching position in higher education, further education and many of our schools solely on the basis of subject knowledge.

Shifting values

The Prussian school model was first significantly challenged in 1872 by Francis W. Parker, a teacher from New Hampshire, who travelled to Berlin to study the system first-hand following its introduction into the United States by Horace Mann. He returned to the United States highly critical of the extent of teacher direction, and after his appointment as superintendent of schools in Quincy, Massachusetts, in 1875 he developed what became known as the Quincy method. This introduced a pupil-centred curriculum with a focus on electives, creative and interdisciplinary pursuits. His approach was adopted by schools across Boston, Cook County and Chicago, and today many schools are named Francis W. Parker in his honour. Parker was an outlier but far from alone. Many other progressives and alternative curricula have emerged over the past 200 years, including in more recent years the International Baccalaureate Organisation (IBO), which has now been adopted by 5,400 schools across 158 countries. The German educationalist Kurt Hahn was one of the founding fathers of the IBO, but he is most well-known for founding Gordonstoun School in Scotland attended by the late Prince Philip, Duke of Edinburgh. However, the Prussian model has endured as the mainstay of educational provision because it is measurable. The standard curriculum and standard summative examinations offer a yardstick for each cohort and permit subdivision into above-average, average and below-average performance. These measurements are interwoven into society as a modern-day rite of passage and by extension the sum of individual achievement. However, over the past decade the value of five or more hermetic examination grades (as discussed in Chapter 11) has been increasingly questioned as a qualification and preparation for living and working in the digital era with its emphasis upon innovation, creativity and entrepreneurship. In parallel, the core structure of the Prussian model has been undermined by self-access online resources i.e. teachers as sole gatekeepers and purveyors of knowledge. Those twin forces are propelling a shift from teacher-centred to learning-centred curricula along with a renewal of the original principles of *enquire and create* as espoused by Humboldt and equally Herbart's *absorption and reflection*. The current mission statement of the Francis W. Parker high school in Chicago (www.fwparker.org), evinces those values:

> Parker provides our students, and our society, with a specific, invaluable and sustainable resource: Educated people who identify themselves as creative citizens capable of thinking for themselves and listening to others – especially to those who with whom they may not agree – in ways that inspire them to apply their idealism in pragmatic ways as they think critically and act collaboratively to solve problems facing our world.[12]

More directly and succinctly, the Gordonstoun website offers the sentiment, "The role of a school is not only to prepare you for exams, it's to prepare you for life."[13] This is an echo of the original Socratic vision, and over the last decade a similar consensus has emerged across the world's leading education systems and global policy making forums, as detailed in Chapter 11. The era of mass education is giving way to a focus on personal development as the significant purpose of education.

Core elements

This global shift from teaching-centred to learning-centred practice does not herald a retreat from the classroom, but rather the application of high evidence-based instructional standards to advance learning within and beyond the classroom. Those standards are epitomised by the following five elements which form the core of effective teaching, learning and assessment practice.

Knowledge	Applying scholarship, curricular knowledge, evidence-based practice and online learning resources to create stimulating sequences of learning designed to stir curiosity and stretch students' interest beyond their immediate study goals.
Questions	Setting unit-by-unit pre- and key questions to clarify study goals, guide thinking and investigation, promote metacognition and self-assessment.
Elaboration	Planning a rich mix of direct instruction, peer tuition, one-to-one coaching and online pre- and post-learning extensions to build a learning dialogue to develop and elaborate key subject knowledge from the factual to the conceptual.
Feedback	Providing personalised mentor guidance across all aspects of personal development and well-being with the aim of mitigating disadvantage, raising ambition and assisting each individual to set and achieve their own study and life goals.
Challenge	Promoting creativity, innovation and entrepreneurship by drawing attention to real-world 'big questions,' world-class research and developments with a look to the horizon and considering what our students might help to solve, design, improve, create or invent if future years or even before they leave school or college.

Image 1.1

These elements are fully developed across the relevant chapters of this book and embrace a rapidly evolving education landscape as the rise of neuroscience, AI, mastery learning and collaborative practice reshape how we teach and learn.

References

1 von Humboldt, Wilhelm, www.brainyquote.com/quotes/quotes/w/wilhelmvon153628.html

2 von Humboldt, Wilhelm, https://en.wikiquote.org/wiki/Wilhelm_von_Humboldt

3 von Humboldt, Wilhelm, Prospects, *The Quarterly Review of Comparative Education*, vol. XXIII, no. 3–4, 1993, pg. 613–623, UNESCO, International Bureau of Education.

4 Koh, Aloysius Wei Lun, et al., *The Learning Benefits of Teaching: A Retrieval Practice Hypothesis*, 2017, https://profile.nus.edu.sg/fass/psylimwh/koh,%20lee,%20&%20lim%20(2018).pdf

5 Kant, Immanuel, *On Pedagogy*, 1803, para 21, https://oll.libertyfund.org/titles/kant-kant-on-education-uber-padagogik

6 Fichte, Johann Gottlieb, *Addresses to the German Nation 1807–08*, pg. 151, https://archive.org/stream/addressestogerma00fich#page/150/mode/2up/search/free+will

7 Fichte, Johann Gottlieb, www.azquotes.com/quote/698788

8 Plato, www.goodreads.com/quotes/tag/education

9 Comenius, John Amos, *The Great Didactic: The Whole Art of Teaching All Things to All Men*, 1648, para 11.

10 Ibid, para 8.

11 Ibid, para 32.

12 F W Parker High School Chicago, *Website/About*, www.fwparker.org

13 Gordonstoun School, *Website Title Page*, www.gordonstoun.org.uk

2

Resetting pedagogy

Prior to the pandemic, traditional classroom-based education was changing and evolving in response to the speed and scale of socio-economic change and the rise of the internet. Those trends were sharply accelerated by the experience of self-paced and remote learning during the closure of schools from 2020 to 2021. The hiatus introduced many more teachers and students to the benefits of online personalised learning programmes (PLPs), neuroscience-based strategies and the application of mastery learning principles involving online peer-to-peer coaching and one-to-one learning opportunities. Those positive experiences have stimulated a marked expansion in blended leaning curricula and learning centred mastery learning and neuroscience-based strategies. All three elements are resetting pedagogy as the locus of education shifts from effective teaching to effective learning and highlights the limitations of traditional classroom practice.

Classroom limitations

The Prussian model of education as detailed in the last chapter introduced classroom-based mass education as memorably caricatured by Harari:

> In the middle of town there is a large concrete building divided into many identical rooms, each room equipped with rows of desks and chairs. At the sound of a bell, you go to one of these rooms together with thirty other kids who were all born in the same year as you. Each hour some grown-up walks in and starts talking.[1]

Harari was writing in 2018 prior to the pandemic, and his blunt description highlighted a frustration, shared by many academics, at the slow pace of change. Most teachers today are aware of and apply adaptive teaching strategies, and few would operate in such a didactic manner, but his description accurately captured the

DOI: 10.4324/9781003132783-3

long-standing reality of the Prussian model of mass education. The daily norm for most students during the 20th century was for long periods of dictation and/ or copying notes from a roller chalkboard because the overriding focus was on the transfer of subject information. The result for most students was tedium rather than stimulation arising from too many dull lessons dominated by lengthy teacher exposition. For every teacher who inspired, far too many more were insipid. Time for discussion and analysis or to assist those who were clearly struggling or to stretch those who were insufficiently challenged was squeezed out by the weight of the curriculum. Questions or misunderstandings were all too often taken as evidence of impertinence or a lack of concentration, and the answer, in both cases, was the liberal application of the cane. In the United States the state of New Jersey outlawed corporal punishment as early as 1867, but it remains legal in a significant number of American states. In England corporal punishment was not outlawed until as late as 1987. By age fourteen many young people were eager to leave school or fell into regular truancy because their experience of school was largely one of a sense of personal failure arising from daily correction and often corporal punishment. Benjamin Bloom (1968) highlighted the high personal and social cost of the 'system':

> The system creates a self-fulfilling prophecy . . . it reduces motivation for learning in students; and it systematically destroys the ego and self-concept of a sizable group of students who are legally required to attend school for10 to 12 years under conditions which are frustrating and humiliating year after year. The cost of this system in reducing opportunities for further learning and in alienating youth from both school and society is so great that no society can tolerate it for long.[2]

The well-known TV presenter Michael Parkinson published his autobiography in 2008 and reflected upon his school days at Barnsley Grammar School:

> I didn't like the place. For one thing I had previously been taught by women in the main, caring and nurturing. Now I was in an all-male world, instructed by short-tempered brutes, who when all else failed, would try to beat information into you. The specialist at this form of teaching was our German master, Goodman an angry-looking man. whose favourite form of instruction was to emphasise a point by drilling his knuckle into the top of a boy's head. Alternatively he would raise you to your feet by hoisting you up by your hair. If he considered a boy to be particularly stupid he would make him stand by the blackboard and belittle him by asking questions he knew he couldn't answer.[3]

During the early 1970s opposition to the Prussian model increased, and critics compared the school system to a factory conveyor belt i.e. fixed chronological progression (regardless of actual progress), fixed curriculum content, fixed lesson times and fixed summative examination dates. The terms 'factory system' or 'factory model' were frequently referenced as disparaging descriptors of the lack of choice over what and when to learn. Hattie commented as recently as 2014 that too many students were reduced to passive observers rather than participants: "students seem to come to school to watch teachers working."[4]

Mastery learning

Bloom's treatise 'Learning for Mastery' (1968) produced a major challenge to the Prussian model by observing that conventional classroom practice only benefited the top third of the ability range:

> Each teacher begins a new term (or course) with the expectation that about a third of his students will adequately learn what he has to teach. He expects about a third of his students to fail or to just "get by." Finally, he expects another third to learn a good deal of what he has to teach, but not enough to be regarded as "good students." This set of expectations, supported by school policies and practices in grading, becomes transmitted to the students through the grading procedures and through the methods and materials of instruction. The system creates a self-fulfilling prophecy such that the final sorting of students through the grading process becomes approximately equivalent to the original expectations.[5]

As indicated in the last chapter, this subdivision of each cohort was the hallmark of the Prussian model. Bloom proposed a significant pedagogical shift by recommending that the curriculum should be presented in short individual units with each student demonstrating 'mastery' of each unit (defined as 90% plus) before moving forward. He elaborated his thesis in 1971 with the more succinct title 'Mastery Learning' and promoted the use of formative assessment to pinpoint and respond to individual student misunderstandings long before today's concept of adaptive teaching,

> One useful operating procedure is to break a course or subject into smaller units of learning. . . . For students who lack mastery of a particular unit, the formative tests should reveal the particular points of difficulty the specific questions they answer incorrectly and the particular ideas, skills, and processes they still need to work on.[6]

Mastery was achieved by stepping back to coach those who were finding difficulty and raising their performance to the relevant standard as indicated.

Mastery learning model

Bloom's model addressed the inescapable flaw at the heart of whole class teaching i.e. teachers advanced from unit to unit in line with the pre-determined pace of

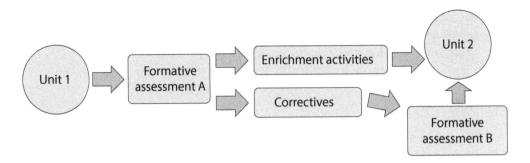

Image 2.1

their scheme of work rather than the actuality of student progress. It was a flaw acknowledged much earlier in 1904, by the British Board of Education:

> The characteristic note of recent educational doctrine or practice has been the insistence on the importance of the individual as distinct from the class. . . . Education consists in dealing with individual children and not with children in the mass . . . either the brighter children have to mark time while the teacher endeavours to help on the slower ones, or, if the work is planned so as to give full scope to the powers of the brighter children, the rest are dragged along in their wake in a confused and disheartened condition.[7]

The mastery model was widely endorsed but it presented the difficulty that once students moved out of step with each other, it raised a requirement for small group and/or one-to-one tuition. The latter was confirmed by Bloom's research as the most effective form of tuition with advances in individual progress calculated as two standard deviations or 2 Sigma. Bloom challenged educators to identify instructional and/or organisational methods to permit more students to benefit from one to one tuition: "can researchers and teachers devise teaching-learning conditions that will enable the majority of students under group instruction to attain levels of achievement that can at present be reached only under good tutoring conditions?"[8] His 2 Sigma challenge was never resolved because the costs of providing one-to-one tuition were prohibitive. Bloom also promoted peer-to-peer coaching as a means to advance individual progress in an echo of the Monitorial system as detailed in the last chapter,

> In our own experience we have found that small groups of students (two or three students) meeting regularly to go over points of difficulty in the learning process were most effective. . . . In the group process, the more able students have opportunities to strengthen their own learning in the process of helping another person grasp the idea through alternative ways of explaining and using the idea.[9]

This, too, failed to have an impact because most teachers prioritised keeping pace with their scheme of work and information transfer over allocating time for questioning and discussion, but recent developments in neuroscience have highlighted the importance of the latter for assimilating new information.

Applying neuroscience evidence

Advances in magnetic resonance imaging (MRI) technology have revealed how the brain receives and processes information, and the findings are transforming pedagogy as science fact increasingly eclipses psychological theory. The importance of neuroscience was recognised in 2007 by the Organisation for Economic Co-operation and Development (OECD) report, 'Understanding the brain: the birth of a learning science': "Today, it is useful, even essential, for educators and anyone else concerned with education to gain an understanding of the scientific basis of learning processes."[10] Harvard University was the first to respond to this challenge with the development of a new master's degree programme, 'Mind, Brain and Education,' described as a focus on "the intersection of biology, cognitive science and education."[11] John Hopkins University took it a step further and established an interdisciplinary 'Science of Learning' institute to investigate and develop evidence-based practice.[12] In a similar initiative the 'Deans for Impact' consortium of US universities regularly collates and shares cognitive science research in terms of its potential 'impact' on classroom practice.[13] Most university departments of psychology are similarly responding and incorporating neuroscience into their degree pathways. The OECD (2017) has recommended that teacher training should also make similar adjustments: 'make it [neuroscience] a fundamental part of teachers' pedagogical knowledge both through pre-service teacher education, as well as through on-going professional development."[14] The influential publication *Nature* has joined this growing field of applied neuroscience with the introduction of a new *Science of Learning* journal[15] to join the long-established Neuroscience journal. The common research goal of those initiatives is to explore how individual development is shaped by the interplay between our genetic inheritance, our 'environment' and our 'chance environment' of unique experiences. Unpicking the overlapping influence of those three factors is the focus of the new 'learning science' of neuro-education with significant implications for not only how we learn but also how we teach. The nature or nurture debate still divides, but it would appear from the research conclusions published in *Blueprint* (2018) by the leading geneticist Professor Robert Plomin that the debate may be at an end. Nature rather than nurture holds the dominant edge in our cognitive development but either realised or repressed by environmental influences. However, the lessons from Dunedin as detailed in Chapter 14 highlight the positive and negative impact of environmental influences. Weisberg et al. (2008) have also introduced a note of caution. They warn against 'the seduction of neuroscience' whereby we may unquestioningly accept a teaching and learning strategy if neuroscience research is referenced.[16] To avoid adopting so–called neuromyths (e.g. learning styles), check the context and conditions attached to a research study for peer review and importantly guard against confirmation bias i.e. citing research that confirms and supports a personal preference while ignoring contrary research.

Applying neuroscience

The following neuroscience findings have significant implications for effective teaching and learning practice.

Neuroscience has illuminated the process of information assimilation and retrieval and forms a vital knowledge base for teachers. These considerations are developed and illustrated by a range of practical teaching, learning and assessment strategies in later chapters.

• Neuroplasticity	Our brains are not static but continue to grow and develop deep into adulthood in response to everyday environmental and learning experiences. Genetic inheritance is the dominant factor governing our cognitive and personal development, but as Plomin has confirmed in his ground-breaking study (Blueprint 2018) genes are probabilistic not deterministic. Repetition of any activity produces physical changes in the relevant brain region(s). Black Cab drivers in London have an enlarged hippocampus centre responsible for spatial awareness. Studies on musicians and jugglers have revealed observable expansion of the neurons governing fine motor control. Ghosh (2016) demonstrated that using both thumbs to text increases synaptic links within the somato-sensory cortex. Learning anything produces a physical imprint within the brain.
• Sensory memory	Our senses notice a bird swooping down to the ground, a person crossing the street, a strong smell, a loud sound, a gust of wind stirring paper, etc. Those are fleeting memories measured in fractions of a second i.e. 200 to 500 milliseconds and processed without conscious thought. Without further attention or significance, they are gone. However, all stimuli build our personal schema and over time influence our attitudes and behaviours.
• Working memory	Our working memory is short i.e. 2 to 3 seconds before the relevant stimulus fades away. Without 'rehearsal' i.e. multiple repeats or an action to record the information, it is forgotten, although Cowan observed, "everything gets encoded into long-term memory almost immediately, but it gets encoded in a way that may not be distinct enough to be retrieved."[17] The capacity of working memory to hold and recall information is also strictly limited. Cowan (2008) recorded an average of just four items with implications for classroom practice. However, within popular culture, our comfort zone is just three items and we regularly apply the 'rule of three' i.e. three little pigs, granting three wishes, three branches of government, three social classifications, three Olympic medals, three-course meal and, of course, the three-part lesson.

• Long-term memory	Our lifetime store of knowledge and experiences is formed from implicit memory i.e. unconscious absorption of information and explicit memory i.e. conscious learning or 'rehearsal' of new information. Activating the former can 'nudge' opportunities, positive behaviours and consolidate learning, while the latter should identify and build upon existing schema. To remember information and understand information well, we have to pay attention to it, repeat it, retrieve it and use it. Those processes should regularly inform our selection of teaching and learning strategies.
• Cognitive Load Theory (CLT)	The limitations of working memory gave rise to the theory of CLT articulated by Sweller (1988).[18] Keep within the limits of working memory by introducing new learning one small step at a time to avoid cognitive overload. Essentially too big a step(s) can produce confusion and often result in withdrawal and reluctance to engage with a task because it is perceived to be too difficult. The key is to judge the level of difficulty for each student i.e. what is currently known and understood i.e. their existing schema and to connect with the new knowledge in small steps. Less is more.
• Dual coding	Visual and spatial stimuli and written and auditory stimuli are encoded in two separate but linked memory stores – hence dual coding. The former has a high memory impact. Activate with appropriate visuals, diagrams, charts and infographics to support and summarise key information. Ensure any labels are embedded within diagrams and charts to avoid the need for the eye to track between the image and a remote legend. Also note that reading and listening are recorded by the same cognitive centre (phonological loop). We can either listen or read, but we cannot do both successfully so ensure time for reading to avoid cognitive overload. The theory of dual coding is most associated with Paivo (1971), but Comenius got there much earlier with the publication of the Great Didactic (1648): "subjects that are taught should not merely be taught orally and thus appeal to the ear alone but should be pictorially illustrated, and thus develop the imagination by the help of the eye."[19]
• Spaced practice	Ebbinghaus's 'forgetting curve' (1880) revealed how quickly new information fades from memory and is forgotten. He demonstrated that retention of new information drops to 44% within an hour, 33% by the end of the day, 25% by the end of a week and 21% by the end of a month. His original research has been regularly replicated, with the most recent being Murre et al. (2015).[20] The counter is to apply regular spaced or retrieval practice by returning to information falling out of memory i.e. quiz, test or recap. In practice step back to topics covered four to five weeks in the past, and the regular retrieval will strengthen the memory store. Bjork recommended, "you should space your study sessions so that the information you learned in the first session remains just barely retrievable. Then, the more you have to work to pull it from the soup of your mind, the more this second study session will reinforce your learning. If you study again too soon, it's too easy."[21]

• Interleaving	Interleaving is similar to spaced practice but with a focus on switching between sub-topics /concepts/key facts during the process of new learning, whereas spaced practice is a focus on stepping back to retrieve and strengthen past learning. Rather than presenting new information ABCDE, introduce mini retrievals e.g. ABCADBEC. This interleaving involves 'reloading' information multiple times and will strengthen memory. The regular switch of focus makes the brain work harder, boosts concentration and often reveals misconceptions for correction.
• Humour	A sense of enjoyment and laughter is known to trigger a dopamine surge and reduce anxiety. The more students are relaxed, the greater the gain in levels of participation, concentration and interest, which in turn stimulates higher recall and memory. This is not about cracking jokes, but rather building warm, supportive, positive relationships.
• Behaviour	The orbit frontal cortex which regulates impulses and risk taking is the last part of the brain to fully develop at age 14+ and produces a perfect storm as teenagers try to balance reasoning with impulse, and more often than not impulse wins. This is reflected in the higher rates of death from accidental injury among fifteen- to nineteen-year-olds. It is six times greater than the age group eleven to fourteen. It is not until post twenty-five that the ability to process consequences and apprise risks is fully developed. It is perhaps unfortunate that those significant brain developments coincide with the modern 'gateway' into adulthood: the preparation for and sitting of major examinations at ages sixteen to eighteen. Davidson (2016) commented, 'teens are hard-wired to seek immediate rewards.'[22] It highlights the need for schools and colleges to offer outlets for excess energy via sports and leisure activities and to offer opportunities for recognition and improving confidence and self-esteem to help moderate and control choices. Offering a simple 'time out' to permit reflection is often the most effective response to poor behaviour.

Image 2.2

Blended learning

Prior to the pandemic, online learning was expanding but at a glacial pace and still very much as a 'bolt-on' extension to the classroom rather than as an integral part of an overall sequence of learning. In comparison with wider society, schools and colleges were very modest users of information technology, with subject knowledge still primarily presented in timetabled lessons via teacher exposition as caricatured by Harari. In addition, the social media channels routinely used by students for personal messaging and collaboration were largely underexploited by schools and colleges. Academic opinion tended to circle the wagons around the superiority of teacher-led lessons, but during the pandemic teachers in all settings took huge strides forward in planning and conducting remote lessons. The experience was often frustrating and stressful for both teachers and students alike, but it also introduced the benefits of learning anytime and anywhere, showcased authoritative online learning resources and spotlighted the boon of self-paced learning support and/or acceleration. In England, pupils in the primary sector became familiar with websites like topmarks.co.uk and bbc.co.uk/bitesize, and their parents were increasingly drawn into learning partnership via apps like tapestryjournal.com and classdojo.com High school students signed-up to websites like thestudybuddy.com and uplearn.co.uk and took advantage of the expanded Oak Academy, while Jamie Frost took charge of maths via drfrostmaths.com. Frost was named a Covid Hero in the Global Teacher Prize awards in 2020 for his contribution to remote learning. At the university level futurelearn.com and openlearn.com and many other massive open online courses (MOOCs) recorded an upsurge in enrolments. Worldwide students discovered a wealth of beneficial learning resources. Those positive experiences of online learning platforms were reflected by respondents in the Pearson Global Learner Survey, August 2020:

> There is no returning to a pre-COVID-19 education world. Globally, more than 3 in 4 people believe that education will fundamentally change as a result of the pandemic. Online learning will be a key part of experiences for learners of all ages, and economic uncertainty will drive more people to upskill and reskill for job security.[23]

In addition a global average of 79% of the respondents predicted that many more students will enrol on wholly online college and university courses over the next ten years,[24] and 83% believed that future learning will involve more "do it yourself-self-service" learning."[25] This trend was confirmed by OECD research January 2021 which revealed that just 22% of schools expected to restore traditional classroom lessons, with over 50% set to pursue hybrid or blended learning approaches post lockdown.[26] Wholly online universities like arden.ac.uk and online high schools like interhigh.co.uk are already experiencing a sharp rise in applications because of the benefit of lower fees and the opportunity to work and earn money while studying. Finally, largely unnoticed and unremarked artificial intelligence (AI) is steadily cataloguing and transforming access to open education resources (OER) and introducing intelligent tutoring systems (ITS) to not only monitor but to support Personalised Learning Programmes. The United Nations Educational, Scientific and Cultural Organization (UNESCO) (2021)[27] has detailed the scale of AI developments worldwide and predicted the widespread application of AI-assisted learning by 2030. The rise of PLPs will reset our pedagogy in five significant ways:

1 **Role of the teacher**
   The role of the teacher will be less a gatekeeper of knowledge and more a gateway: coaching, explaining, supporting and challenging.
2 **Anywhere and anytime**
   Education will no longer be bound by location, age or the time span of timetabled lessons.

3   **Mastery learning**
    AI-enhanced PLPs and ITS will support self-paced and one-to-one tuition
    and finally resolve Bloom's 2 Sigma challenge.

4   **Personal development**
    Personal development will become a primary rather than a secondary goal of
    education along with a focus on the 4Cs of personal competency: Communi-
    cation, Collaboration, Critical thinking and Creativity.

5   **Human intelligence**
    Personalised feedback and mentor support to guide personal development
    will build metacognitive and metasubjective intelligences and promote human
    intelligence (HI) capabilities i.e. enhance what humans do best rather than
    competing with AI.

The future is a fusion between the classroom and online learning with a focus on
high-quality personalised learning.

References

1   Harari, Yuval Noah, *21 Lessons for the 21st Century*, Jonathan Cape, 2018,
    pg. 266.
2   Benjamin, Bloom S., *Learning for Mastery*, Chicago University, Department of
    Education, May 1968, pg. 1.
3   Parkinson, Michael, *Parky, My Autobiography*, Hodder and Stoughton, 2008,
    pg. 31.
4   Hattie, John and Yates, Gregory, *Visible Learning and the Science of How We
    Learn*, Routledge, 2014, pg. 47.
5   Benjamin, Bloom S., *Learning for Mastery*, Chicago University, Department of
    Education, May 1968, pg. 1.
6   Ibid, pg. 9.
7   Board of Education, *Handbook of Suggestions for Teachers*, 3rd edition, Board of
    Education, 1927, pg. 53, 59.
8   Benjamin, Bloom S., The 2 sigma problem: The search for methods of instruc-
    tion as effective as one to one tutoring, *Educational Researcher*, vol. 13, no. 6,
    July 1984, pg. 4.
9   Benjamin, Bloom S., *Learning for Mastery*, Chicago University, Department of
    Education, May 1968, pg. 5.
10 OECD, *Understanding the Brain: The Birth of a Learning Science*, OECD, 2007,
    pg. 8.
11 www.gse.harvard.edu/masters/mbe accessed 17th February 2017.
12 http://scienceoflearning.jhu.edu accessed 17th February 2017.
13 www.deansforimpact.org accessed 17th February 2017.
14 Guerriero, Sonia, *Pedagogical Knowledge and the Changing Nature of the Teaching
    Profession*, OECD, 2017, pg. 30.

15 www.nature.com/npjscilearn accessed 17th February 2017.

16 Weisberg, D. S., et al., The seductive allure of neuroscience explanations, *Journal of Cognitive Neuroscience*, vol. 20, no. 3, April 2008.

17 Cowan, Nelson, *Journal of the Proceedings of the National Academy of Science*, vol. 105, no. 17, 14th April 2008.

18 Sweller, John, Cognitive load during problem solving: Effects on learning, University of New South Wales, *Cognitive Science*, vol. 12, pg. 257–285, April 1988, http://onlinelibrary.wiley.com/doi/10.1207/s15516709cog1202_4/epdf

19 Comenius, John Amos, *The Great Didactic: The Whole Art of Teaching All Things to All Men*, 1648, para 36.

20 Murre, Jaap and Dros, Joeri, Replication and analysis of Ebbinghaus' forgetting curve, *PLoS Journal*, 2015, www.ncbi.nlm.nih.gov/pmc/articles/PMC4492928/

21 www.science20.com/brain_candyfeed_your_mind/how_learn_robert_bjork_director_ucla_learning_and_forgetting_lab-86451

22 Davison, Juliet Dr., www.mprnews.org/story/2016/10/07/npr-teens-penchant-for-risk-may-help-learn-faster

23 Pearson, *The Global Learner Survey*, Pearson, August 2020, pg. 5.

24 Ibid, pg. 28.

25 Ibid, pg. 9.

26 OECD, *What Will Education Look Like in the Future*, Webinar, OECD, 28th January 2021.

27 UNESCO, *AI and Education Guidance for Policy-Makers*, UNESCO, 2021.

3

Great teaching

A habitual question posed at the start of a new teaching training programme is: 'what makes a good teacher?' often followed by the question, 'what makes a great teacher?' The distinction between good and great is widely acknowledged and regularly triggers discussion of childhood memories of inspiring teachers and stimulating lessons. The former tends to attract most discussion, but perhaps the latter is more significant, and our focus should shift from the teacher to the lesson by questioning, 'what makes good teaching?' and as a qualitative step-up, 'what makes great teaching? This is an even more significant question following the Coronavirus epidemic 2020–2021 and the expansion of Personalised Learning Programmes (PLPs). It is common for PLPs to define great teaching not in terms of the knowledge and skills of an individual teacher, but the combined knowledge and skills of a specialist team spanning different disciplines as illustrated by Century Tech:

> Century has been developed by an award-winning team of experienced teachers, neuroscientists and technologists. Together, we have combined the latest research in learning science, artificial intelligence and neuroscience to ensure Century is underpinned by evidence-based scientific and pedagogical techniques.[1]

Century emphasise a community of practice, whereas in contrast schools and colleges tend to invest in and celebrate great teachers rather than great teaching. Lesson observations tend to be skewed towards sifting for and identifying great teachers rather than a well-planned, stimulating curriculum.

Great teachers

The tendency to elevate individuals and personalise teaching is very common. Speaking at the Global Teacher Award ceremony in 2016 the late Professor Stephen

DOI: 10.4324/9781003132783-4

Hawking named and praised his maths teacher Dikran Tahta for his lively and inspirational lessons and commented, "When each of us thinks about what we can do in life, chances are, we can do it because of a teacher. Behind every exceptional person, there is an exceptional teacher. Today we need great teachers more than ever."[2] Hawking's warm praise for his 'stand-out' teacher from his school days was not unusual. It is a premise that underpins our inspection and national and international award systems to elevate individual teachers (although Ofsted is shifting its focus) as opposed to innovative practice. This tendency was overplayed by a British university in the Midlands in 2021 awarding a prize for a 'one in a million' lecturer when there are only 439,955 university lecturers in the whole of the UK. The distinction between great teachers and great teaching was raised by Professor Peter F. Drucker in 1992: "in teaching we rely upon the 'naturals' the ones who somehow know how to teach. Nobody seems to know what it is the 'naturals' do that the rest of us do not."[3] Drucker was writing at a time when lesson observations were rare and evidence-based research was largely unknown. Teachers closed their classroom doors and seldom shared or discussed their classroom practice with others. The classroom was consequently described by Black and Wiliam's in 1998 as a 'Black Box' in their seminal publication, 'Inside the Black Box' and prompted their question, "What is happening inside the box? How can anyone be sure that a particular set of new inputs will produce better outputs if we don't at least study what happens inside?"[4] Black and Wiliam's observation of the opaque nature of classroom practice was extended by Professor John Hattie to educational research. In his inaugural address as professor of education, University of Auckland, in August 1999, Hattie lamented the rarity of communication between teachers and educational researchers: "Both educational communities work behind closed doors, coming out to discuss kids, curricula, accountability, and each other, but rarely discussing the fundamental tenets about their teaching that leads to positive impacts on student learning."[5] Educational research tended to be published in obscure education or psychology journals and often behind high pay walls limiting access.

Great teaching

Hattie famously opened the black box of educational research in his celebrated publication, 'Visible Learning' (2009) by summarising and listing in rank order the major evidence-based influences on achievement followed in 2012 by a detailed analysis of effective teaching and learning strategies in 'Visible Learning for Teachers.' It would be a mistake to discount Hattie's work because of the reported flaws in his calculation of effect sizes. Hattie's strength remains the depth and clarity of his commentary on the major features of effective practice at each stage of a lesson. He has made often obscure educational research studies transparent. His eight 'mind frames' for schools and colleges (2012) offer a compelling summary of good practice considerations, and his later nine principles of effective learning (2014) provide a solid base for building good practice. Black, Wiliam and Hattie have formed the educational peloton, and over the past fifteen years the evidence from classroom observations and educational research has caught up with and demystified the key ingredients of effective practice. Central to this process has been the distillation by Barak Rosenshine of the evidence arising from neuroscience, teacher effectiveness and learning interventions research into seventeen principles of instruction as detailed in Chapter 7. We now know what other teachers do. We also know what great teachers do. Rather than continuing to try and capture the intangible stardust of Drucker's 'naturals,' we need to shift our focus from great teachers to great teaching. The significance of the latter is highlighted when a 'star' principal, manager or teacher leaves or retires. The evidence from Ofsted inspections of schools and colleges in England is not one of rising standards as refinement build upon refinement, but more of a rollercoaster experience. Data released by Ofsted in March 2019 revealed that 117 'outstanding' schools were re-inspected between September and December 2018 and of those only 27 retained the accolade 'outstanding,' 50 slipped to 'good,' 35 dropped to 'requires improvement,' and 5 plunged to 'inadequate.'[6] This equates to only 23% of schools maintaining their standards from one inspection to the next. A similar pattern of ups and downs is evident in the performance of individual curriculum areas as different managers and teachers come and go. The lack of consistency is testimony to the absence of a collective school or curriculum team pedagogy that is maintained regardless of staff changes. Online learning platforms, as indicated, harness team expertise and adopt common resources and processes to ensure a consistent, high-quality learning experience. As learning beyond the classroom becomes as important as learning within the classroom, collective rather than individual practice will be pivotal to ensuring uniform, high-quality learning experiences. In essence, the use of a highly effective resource, strategy or app in one classroom should not be unknown in the next.

Communities of practice

The promotion of collective practice is not new. It arises from the recommendations for developing communities of practice (CoPs) made by Jean Lave and Etienne Wenger in 1991 and as elaborated by Wenger in 1998. The benefits of collective practice were the subject of investigation and recommendation by the leading consultancy McKinsey & Co. In 2010 McKinsey & Co detailed the following four key steps underpinning teaching excellence in their report, *How the World's Most Improved Schools Keep Getting Better.*

The steps may be summarised as:

- Setting standards,
- Monitoring implementation,
- Relaxing control as standards become embedded and finally,
- Empowering autonomous curriculum teams to 'own' the standards with the freedom to innovate.

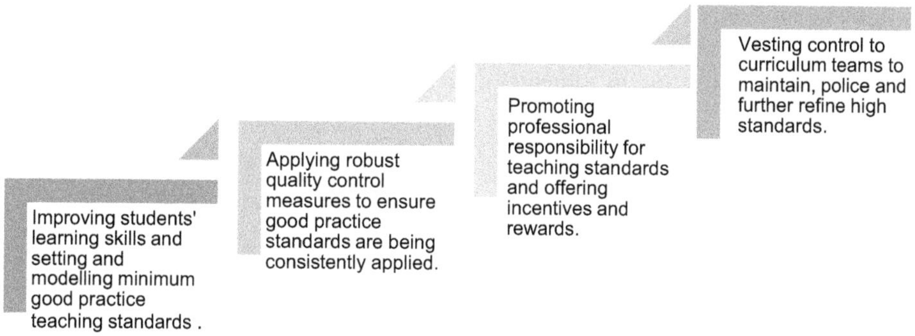

Vesting control to curriculum teams to maintain, police and further refine high standards.

Promoting professional responsibility for teaching standards and offering incentives and rewards.

Applying robust quality control measures to ensure good practice standards are being consistently applied.

Improving students' learning skills and setting and modelling minimum good practice teaching standards .

Image 3.1

The recommended process starts with high central control but ends with ceding control to curriculum teams by promoting evidence-based scholarship leading to self-governance of high standards akin to medicine or law. The standards identified and agreed to by individual curriculum teams should ideally be published in the form of a teaching and learning policy as the 'voice' of the team. The induction of new teachers should involve addressing the recommended policy but with encouragement to raise refinements to ensure that up-to-date research, innovation or new resources are not overlooked. Once a policy is embedded across a curriculum team, the departure of a manager or a teacher should not alter the high team standards adopted and thereby ensure consistency from one teacher to the next, one manager to the next and from one inspection to the next. The development of CoPs of this type promotes and sustains high standards because teachers pool their knowledge and experience. The process of collective investigation, trial and selection of effective teaching and learning strategies is even more of an imperative given the ever-expanding array of online resources and digital tools. Curriculum teams need to apply evidence-based scholarship to ensure the adoption of effective classroom and online strategies and resources.

Evidence-based scholarship

Many of the theories of learning which dominated the 20th century are in retreat following the rise of neuroscience, which has increasingly unravelled, if not cut, the Gordian Knot of how we construct, store and retrieve information. Many popular psychological theories have failed under the spotlight of evidence and been downgraded as myths, most notably 'learning styles.' Psychology's Achilles heel is replication, and many an attention-grabbing strategy has waned as the hyped advantages fail the replication test. It has produced a shift towards a more practical rather than theoretical pedagogy in relation to the evidence-based practice of 'what works.' This trend was charted within higher education by Kreber as early as 2002: "Over time, most faculty develop a repertoire of approaches and strategies that tend to work well."[7] The following organisations are rich sources of independent evaluations of 'what works' in relation to strategies underpinned by robust research:

- Clearinghouse.com
- Deansforimpact.com
- Education and Training Foundation
- Education Endowment Foundation
- The Sutton Trust
- Bestevidence.org
- ResearchEd.org.uk
- Society for Education and Training
- Chartered College of Teaching

In addition, the rise of teacher-bloggers has made a major contribution to the testing and sharing of effective teaching and learning strategies. In the UK the government minister Nick Gibb praised their commitment and the benefits of peer-to-peer guidance: "The flourishing online community of teacher-bloggers – who share their experiences, challenge received wisdom and critique evidence – are raising the status of the profession and improving the lives of pupils."[8] The scale of online interactions between teachers reviewing evidence, trialling and refining strategies was proposed as a new theory of learning in 2005.

Connectivism

The theory of connectivism asserts that the internet has become the arbiter of pedagogical knowledge through multiple interconnected forums presenting and commenting on worldwide educational research. The theory was first proposed in a paper written by George Siemens in 2004 entitled, *A Learning Theory for the Digital Age* and further developed in collaboration with Stephen Downes and detailed in *Knowing Knowledge* (2006). Siemens and Downes postulated that knowledge exists in a myriad of connections (referred to as nodes) across the internet and is constantly evolving in response to the interactions between practitioners, research organisations, theorists and academics. Pedagogical knowledge is essentially fluid and ever-extending as new research and data are released by organisations, universities, academics, companies, governments, bloggers, etc., inviting comments, modifications, refinements and further research. It is increasingly evident that pedagogy is tilting away from the entrenched ideological positions of the 20th century towards the evidence-based practice of what works. Over the past decade or more, teachers, without perhaps realising it, have embraced connectivism by engaging with online professional and social media networks and interacting with other practitioners to post comments. Many have also moved beyond commenting to contributing by sharing personal good practice suggestions and resources via online blogs, vlogs, personal websites, Twitter, Facebook, YouTube channels, LinkedIn, education festivals, conferences, Teach-Meet communities, ResearchEd events and in articles submitted to the educational press. Those forms of connectivism operate as supportive, interconnected CoPs questioning, exploring and arriving at an agreed consensus of 'what works.' Havant and South Downs College has taken this further by developing a website entitled the teacherstakeaway.co.uk to share good practice and to promote teacher-led pedagogical research. Slavin (2017) endorsed the practical approach of 'what works,' but with the firm rider of ensuring underpinning evidence:

> Use what works. . . . Recent developments in research and policy make it possible to finally put education on the road to genuine reform. With consistent support, proven, effective models of school and classroom reform can be developed, rigorously evaluated, and disseminated, benefitting hundreds of thousands of children.[9]

Connectivism has carried forward the CoPs theory from governing the actions of individual curriculum teams to worldwide exchanges of effective practice. The online discussions reflect today's changing educational landscape as artificial intelligence, neuroscience, evidence-based practice and the changing employment landscape alter perspectives not just on definitions of great teaching but on the overall scholarship of teaching and learning (SoTL).

Applying SEED

The acronym SEED spotlights four significant aspects of effective practice as education adjusts to those major influences and in particular the immersion into a digital age.

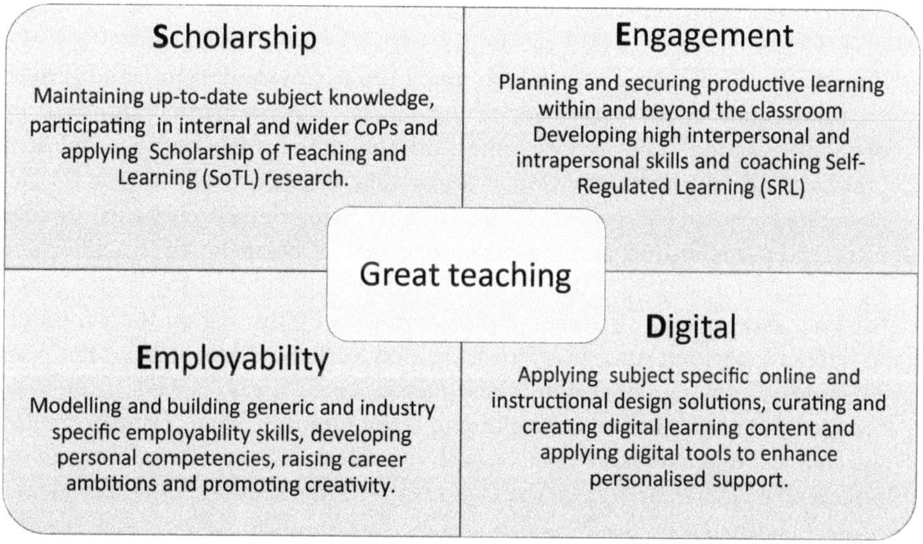

Scholarship

Maintaining up-to-date subject knowledge, participating in internal and wider CoPs and applying Scholarship of Teaching and Learning (SoTL) research.

Engagement

Planning and securing productive learning within and beyond the classroom Developing high interpersonal and intrapersonal skills and coaching Self-Regulated Learning (SRL)

Great teaching

Employability

Modelling and building generic and industry specific employability skills, developing personal competencies, raising career ambitions and promoting creativity.

Digital

Applying subject specific online and instructional design solutions, curating and creating digital learning content and applying digital tools to enhance personalised support.

Image 3.2

The term scholarship is most often associated with the university sector, but all teachers should identify as scholars in relation to engaging with evidence-based practice and seek to grow their expertise across the above four aspects of effective practice.

Scholarship of teaching and learning

In 1986 Professor Lee Shulman questioned the division between subject knowledge and pedagogy. He identified that in the late 19th century 90% to 95% of the requirements to be a teacher in a US school related to subject knowledge rather than pedagogy, whereas by the mid-to-late 20th century this had reversed: "Has it always been asserted that one either knows content and pedagogy is secondary and unimportant, or that one knows pedagogy and is not held accountable for content?"[10]

Shulman articulated that the most effective teaching and learning arose from subject-specific pedagogical knowledge referred to as pedagogical content knowledge (PCK). This recognised the need for teachers of different curriculum areas to qualify general pedagogical knowledge by selecting the most effective strategies to advance and secure learning within each specialist discipline e.g. English, science, mathematics and/or across a sector e.g. primary education as against secondary. Shulman established a research programme entitled *Knowledge Growth in Teaching* to examine from a teacher's perspective the key knowledge to underpin effective instruction. He identified three interlocking facets of teachers' knowledge: subject, pedagogical and curricular. Shulman's treatise contributed to a rising interest in recognising teaching as a subject of research investigation within higher education but also triggered a debate on whether his threefold definition was too narrow in scope. In 1990 Ernest L. Boyer (1928–1995) included the skill of teaching within a four-part redefinition of scholarship and coined the term 'Scholarship of Teaching.' Boyer regarded the traditional university interpretation of scholarship, meaning 'discovery' research, as much too narrow and championed effective communication skills: "the work of the scholar also means stepping back from one's investigation, looking for connections, building bridges between theory and practice, and communicating one's knowledge effectively to students."[11] Boyer re-defined scholarship as having four significant interlinked elements: discovery, integration, application and teaching. The new Scholarship of Teaching envisaged identifying strategies that work i.e. seeking an evidence-based link between teaching and learning by trialling, monitoring and reflecting on the effectiveness of different teaching strategies. Boyer defined learning as arising from developing a culture of learning between teachers and students: "great teachers create a common ground of intellectual commitment. They stimulate active, not passive, learning and encourage students to be critical, creative thinkers, with the capacity to go on learning after their college days are over."[12] The following three key elements of the Scholarship of Teaching first specified by Shulman were further developed and extended notably by Kreber and Cranton and more recently by Boshier and

Huang (2008) to embrace the importance of learning as an outcome of effective teaching, hence SoTL.

- *Pedagogical knowledge* – consideration of how we learn and how best to promote and assist the process of assimilating new learning. This involves knowledge of the key theories of learning across cognitivist, behaviourist and humanism perspectives. Within recent years the contribution of neuroscience research, evidence-based practice and online teacher-bloggers have significantly impacted on this debate as science fact, evidence-based studies and practical teaching experiences either confirm or contradict theoretical perspectives.
- *Instructional knowledge* – awareness of the relevant merits of different teaching and learning strategies and associated resources that might be employed to meet specified learning goals. Over the past five years the choices have expanded to include a wide range of digital tools, apps, social media and learning platform applications that teachers should be able to confidently select and apply.
- *Curricular knowledge* – displaying a close awareness of the knowledge and skills standards of a particular learning programme to inform adaptive teaching strategies and to address related cognitive, affective and psychomotor domains as appropriate.

The underpinning principles of SoTL raise an obvious but often overlooked point that a great teacher identifies as a teacher. A newly appointed teacher may have enjoyed a successful career as a physicist, an historian, an engineer, a hairdresser, an economist, an artist, etc., but from their first day in the classroom it is important that they embrace their new role as a teacher of physics, a teacher of art, etc. It is teacher first and subject expert second. As early as 1648 Comenius, in his publication, *The Great Didactic: The Whole Art of Teaching All Things to All Men*, raised the distinction between knowing something and knowing how to teach it. Or in other words not every expert makes a great teacher.

Teachers' knowledge

Knowledge is a teacher's bedrock. Clearly all teachers must possess a sound knowledge of their subject or skill to be judged competent let alone good or great. The Sutton Trust evidence-based review of the factors underpinning great teaching reported, "The most effective teachers have deep knowledge of the subjects they teach, and when teachers' knowledge falls below a certain level it is a significant impediment to students' learning."[13] However, there is no agreed-on definition of what constitutes 'deep knowledge 'whether measured by years of experience or by the possession of higher qualifications. Research published by Rivkin, Hanushek and Kain in 2005 concluded that the extension of subject knowledge to master's level produced no obvious gains in teacher effectiveness: "we find absolutely no evidence that having a master's degree improves teacher skills."[14] In addition, the same report noted that contrary to expectation teacher effectiveness reaches a plateau within three to five years: "there is little evidence that improvements continue after the first three years."[15] This developmental 'standstill' is not just an issue for teaching. It is observable across all sectors of employment and was first established by Bryan and Harter in 1899 based on a study of Morse code operators. Employees essentially reach a level of comfortable proficiency, and in the absence of incentives stand still and do not progress any further. However, recent research conducted by Anne Podolsky et al. (2019) identified not so much a standstill as a slow-down. Podolsky noted that teachers' effectiveness can improve over time but requires stability i.e. consistency of teaching the same programme and the nudge provided by collective practice.[16]

The highest performing nations in the Programme for International Student Assessment (PISA) international rankings of school effectiveness all specify above-average degree performance as the entry standard for teacher training. However, in areas of teacher shortage the Organisation for Economic Co-operation and Development (OECD) has reported that it is common for the entry bar to be lowered and/or for teachers to be assigned to teach subjects without apposite qualifications.[17] In 2017 26.3% of maths teachers in England's schools did not have a degree in the subject, nor did 38% of physics teachers or 25% of chemistry teachers or 33% of geography teachers or 25% of history teachers. It raises the question of how much knowledge is enough? Whether teachers need to be one step ahead or two or three steps ahead, etc., is a moot point. The former headmaster of Harrow School, Barnaby Lenon, categorised the skill set of effective teachers as follows:

- 30% subject knowledge,
- 30% personality factors,
- 30% high expectations and
- 10% classroom management.[18]

Lenon's recipe presents a personal rather than an evidence-based opinion. Many would place a much higher percentage on knowledge and depending upon the school and community served a much greater emphasis upon effective classroom management skills. In high-performing education systems like Finland, teaching is a tier one profession with remuneration on a par with law or medicine. This attracts well-qualified graduates and fierce competition for places, but it is a myth that Finnish schools only select and appoint applicants with either an upper second or first class degree classification. Professor Pasi Sahlberg, who was the director-general of Finland's Ministry of Education and Culture for four years, has detailed that Finland's teachers were not exclusively selected from the top 10% of graduates. The applicants also had to satisfy selection criteria linked to high interpersonal and intrapersonal skills, and those personal qualities were ranked above an applicant's degree classification: "Another myth about Finland is that academic ability would be the best predictor of teacher effectiveness. . . . But in reality, minority of those accepted to very competitive research-based academic programs come from the top quintile of the talent pool."[19] Sahlberg has emphasised that the success of Finnish schools relates to 'growing' great teachers rather than appointing great teachers. Time is allocated on a weekly basis for involvement in pedagogical research, and this is routinely linked to the completion of an in-service master's degree. The master's degree is not an entry qualification, as also widely misreported, but an in-service commitment to developing high instructional and curricular knowledge. Finland's flexible approach to entry qualifications acknowledges the lack of a correlation between high subject knowledge and learning outcomes. The limited evidence of a correlation was confirmed by the Sutton Trust as follows:

> the search for a relationship between characteristics such as academic qualifications or general ability and student performance has been rather disappointing: correlations are typically very small or non-existent.[20]

Creemers and Kyriakides's review of research literature dating back to the 1990s similarly concluded,

> teachers' subject knowledge, regardless of how it is measured, has rarely correlated strongly with student achievement. . . . A minimal level of knowledge is necessary for teachers to be effective, but beyond a certain point, a negative or even no relation at all may occur.[21]

Hattie also accorded a very low rank to teachers' knowledge: "teachers' actual depth of knowledge of the content of what is being taught bears little relationship to the attainment levels of their students."[22] Further he added that a high knowledge may actually present a barrier to effective teaching:

> possessing a high level of knowledge about a topic does not automatically bring with it the ability to teach the topic well. In fact, all too often, it is the reverse. The more you know about an area, the more difficult it can be to see the same area from another person's position.[23]

Essentially, what is obvious to an expert may be far from obvious to a novice, and the expert can often struggle to recognise and address a novice's learning difficulty. It appears that once knowledge passes a certain threshold, interpersonal and intrapersonal skills assume greater significance. This is in accord with student opinions and wider society. Teachers are expected to know their subjects, but great teachers can also find the words, metaphors and analogies to reach every student. Einstein expressed the opinion, "if you can't explain it simply you don't understand it well enough."[24]

Higher education reform

The introduction of the UK Teaching Excellence Framework (TEF) for Higher Education in 2017 appears to have acknowledged this reality with the introduction of Gold, Silver and Bronze awards for effective teaching and learning practice: "the emphasis is on teaching that provides an appropriate level of contact, stimulation and challenge, and which encourages student engagement and effort."[25] In the past whether the 'sage' could engage or not was very much a secondary consideration in comparison to their research despite Boyer's focus on communication. However, there is a growing recognition that world-class knowledge is of limited value if it cannot be presented in a way that students can grasp and, as the criterion states, offer *stimulation* and *challenge* and encourage *engagement and effort*. Whether or not the TEF can lead to improvements in university teaching may rest on the perceived rewards for investing time and effort in improving teaching and learning as opposed to a focus on research. Kreber confirmed that within higher education the rewards are stacked in favour of research rather than teaching:

> On the teaching side, external rewards for teaching are also present, but there are fewer than for research. Furthermore, effective teaching is generally considered good enough. It would follow that expertise in teaching, going beyond what is necessary, or "becoming even more effective," is not something that is externally rewarded. It matters little whether you receive a teaching award once, or twice, or ten times; but it matters a lot whether you publish one article or two or ten, and it matters a lot whether you receive one external research grant or two or ten.[26]

Universities will need to consider the career structure and recognition accorded to effective teaching and to establish and uphold high presentational standards.

Engagement

Great teachers draw their students into rich interaction through their tone of voice, enthusiasm, passion, body language, pace, rapport, humour, care and high expectations that all with suitable effort can achieve. This focus on personal attributes rather than knowledge should not be dismissed because at some point, knowledge as previously indicated, must be presented and developed and often with reluctant students. The attributes are not about charisma, but rather building and developing effective communication and engagement skills. Effective communication, like any other skill, can be taught as regularly demonstrated within the world of business. Companies regularly send their staff on training courses to improve their presentation skills, voice projection, 'soft' people skills and to discover how to design eye-catching PowerPoint presentations or similar that range well beyond text bullet points and increasingly, in this digital age to produce polished online video presentations. It is instructive to look at the business shelves of a major bookshop and to count the number of book titles relating to improving presentation and communication skills and to repeat the exercise in the teacher training section. There are often no similar books aimed at teachers, and it also instructive to ask an audience of teachers the last time they attended a training event entirely devoted to improving presentation and communication skills. All too often the answer is 'never' but there is a well-established correlation between warm, upbeat communication skills and positive student engagement. Research published by Guerrero and Miller in 1998 concluded, "the more warm and involved a student perceives an instructor to be, the more likely the student is to perceive the instructor as competent and likeable and to see the course content as valuable and enjoyable."[27] Essentially students respond well to teachers who build a 'feel good' factor by exhibiting warmth, passion and enthusiasm for their subjects and encouraging and welcoming every contribution. However, it is important not to accept engagement alone as evidence of learning.

Coe's proxies for learning

It is all too easy to be beguiled by cooperative students enjoying a lesson and to assume that learning is taking place, but as Fenstermacher has emphasised, "successful teaching is teaching that yields the intended learning."[28] Professor Robert Coe made the same point when he detailed common proxies for learning. Coe listed the following aspects of engagement which are often misconstrued as evidence of learning:

1   Students are busy: lots of work is done (especially written work)
2   Students are engaged, interested, motivated
3   Students are getting attention: feedback, explanations
4   Classroom is ordered, calm, under control
5   Curriculum has been 'covered' (i.e. presented to students in some form)
6   (At least some) students have supplied correct answers (whether or not they really understood them or could reproduce them independently).[29]

Neuroscience and especially our knowledge of the operation of our working and long-term memories have raised our awareness that classroom engagement is performance, whereas learning occurs over time. Soderstrom and Bjork (2015) warned against conflating engagement with learning and defined the latter as evidence of long-term retention and transfer. However, it is a question of qualifying rather than dismissing engagement because clearly active student participation and co-operation in receiving, questioning and recording new information are the most basic precursors to learning as highlighted by Wiliam: "The fact that someone can do something now does not mean they will be able to do it in six weeks but if they cannot do something now, it is highly unlikely they will be able to do it in six weeks."[30] To move beyond the proxies Coe suggested that "learning happens when people have to think hard."[31] Soderstrom and Bjork (2015) qualified this further in terms of introducing *desirable difficulties* to deepen and extend thinking about new information in order to strengthen retention within long-term memory. Teachers should reflect on their lesson plans and consider what aspects of the lesson would involve the students in thinking hard. The learning plan approach presented in Chapter 10 encourages the setting of higher-order questions and at least one challenge question per topic.

Inspire

The ability to hold attention and to exercise effective classroom management is an essential base engagement skill for all teachers, but the edge observed in the behaviour of great teachers is their ability to draw all students into productive engagement through their obvious passion and enthusiasm for their subjects. At its highest reach this extends to the accolade inspiring. The three words inspire, passion and enthusiasm are the top three personal attributes associated with great teachers in surveys of students' opinions, inspection criteria, teacher recruitment adverts, teacher award citations and professional standards. Duckworth et al. (2009) reported a correlation between higher levels of achievement and teachers' demonstrating a passion and a commitment to their subjects along with displaying a warm, positive outlook.[32] Marzano described the interpersonal skills of great teachers in the following terms: "the teacher uses verbal signals such as the volume and tone of voice, verbal emphasis on specific words or phrases, pauses to build anticipation and excitement, and the rate of speech to communicate intensity and enthusiasm to students."[33] Those personal qualities can be cultivated because ultimately all teachers are actors. During the recording of a live album by the singer Van Morrison a member of the audience shouted out during a long moment of silence, "Turn it on, turn it on man," to which Van Morrison replied after a pregnant pause, "It's turned on already." All teachers, as they set foot in the classroom, need to 'turn it on' and most do. The students of Woodside High School in London in a survey conducted in 2017 described their teachers as enthusiastic, supportive, inspiring, passionate, challenging, caring, respectful and motivational.[34] On a much larger scale a survey of 3,000 school children in the UK, published in July 2017, cited humour as the overall winning quality of the most effective teachers but also the personal qualities of being encouraging, inspiring, passionate, enthusiastic and notably the ability to be strict and to maintain order.[35] The latter is a fairly common outcome of students' opinion surveys. Students' welcome teachers who promote consistent rules and can keep order. Agasisti (2018)[36] confirmed the enforcement of high behavioural standards as a key factor in raising achievement and especially with underperforming students.

Within the United States the 'Great Schools' network answered the question, what makes a great teacher as follows:

> Teaching is one of the most complicated jobs today. It demands broad knowledge of subject matter, curriculum, and standards; enthusiasm, a caring attitude, and a love of learning; knowledge of discipline and classroom management techniques; and a desire to make a difference in the lives of young people.[37]

Perhaps the final word on the skills and attributes of great teachers should go to children. In 2000 the Hay McBer (now just Hay group) consultancy report entitled *Research into Teacher Effectiveness: A Model of Teacher Effectiveness* invited children aged eleven to twelve years to list the personal qualities of good teachers. The children commented as follows:

"A good teacher

is kind
is generous
listens to you
encourages you
has faith in you
keeps confidences
likes teaching
likes teaching their subject
takes time to explain things
helps you when you are stuck
tells you how you are doing
allows you to have your say
doesn't give up on you
cares for your opinion
makes you feel clever
treats people equally
stands up for you
makes allowance
tells the truth
is forgiving."[38]

The overall theme of the children's criteria places an emphasis upon a warm relationship with the teacher and ultimately 'caring' qualities. However, note that children are quite perceptive and have concluded that some teachers do not like teaching or even their own subject. This is a fundamental question for any teacher – do you love your own subject or is teaching just a job? Hattie emphasised that the most effective teachers "cared about teaching the students their passion for their subject, gave students confidence in themselves as learners and as people, treated the student as a person, and instilled a love of learning of their subject(s)."[39]

The Australian Society for Evidence Based Teaching has adopted Hattie's focus on passion as the first of seven key attributes of great teachers: "Their passion is contagious, and they infect their students with a love of learning."[40] This is perhaps the most significant hallmark of great teachers – a connection at an emotional level – a sense that your teacher not only wants the best for you but at its most basic that your teacher loves teaching and cares about you.

Addressing employability skills

During the Davos World Economic Forum (WEF) in 2016, the expansion of AI and the pace of automation was described as the onset of the Fourth Industrial Revolution.

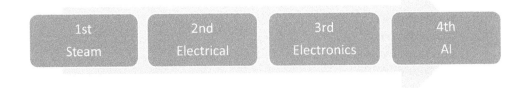

| 1st | 2nd | 3rd | 4th |
| Steam | Electrical | Electronics | AI |

Image 3.3

The First Industrial Revolution used water and steam power to mechanize production. The second introduced electricity with its myriad of life-changing applications, not least electric light banishing the dark. The third used electronics to transform all aspects of communication, and the fourth, the advance of AI, is busily creating a highly automated, interconnected society as highlighted by the WEF:

> The possibilities of billions of people connected by mobile devices, with unprecedented processing power, storage capacity, and access to knowledge, are unlimited. And these possibilities will be multiplied by emerging technology breakthroughs in fields such as artificial intelligence, robotics, the Internet of Things, autonomous vehicles, 3-D printing, nanotechnology, biotechnology, materials science, energy storage, and quantum computing.[41]

In 2021 the Chief Executive of Google, Sundar Pichai, speculated that AI will have a more profound impact on humanity than fire, electricity or the internet. Employment is global, and young people are in competition for employment with people from all corners of the globe, and it is changing quickly, as more and more jobs from the complexity of surgical procedures to flipping burgers in a fast-food restaurant are being undertaken by AI-enabled robotic technology. Japan's Henn-na Hotel near Nagasaki is the first to be fully staffed by robots. In 2014 the then British Secretary of State for Education Michael Gove highlighted the significance of the robotic revolution:

> Technology is poised to change the world of work in a manner as dramatic as the shift from a predominantly agricultural to a predominantly industrial

society which advanced nations underwent in the 19th century. . . . We are embarking on a second industrial revolution – a new machine age. . . . Cars which were once assembled by robotic technology are now being driven by robotic technology. . . . How can we prepare young people for jobs that don't yet exist in industries that haven't yet been invented in a world changing faster than any of us can predict?[42]

Jobs are being lost, but new jobs are also being created – jobs that demand a much higher level of skill and particularly the flexibility to adapt to new roles and to new technology as innovation builds on innovation. The governor of the Bank of England, Mark Carney, commented in a speech in December 2016 "that up to 15 million of the current jobs in Britain could be automated over time."[43] Any routine unskilled repetitive tasks are vulnerable to automation, as are any professional or semi-professional jobs that are largely focussed on data processing, although it should be noted that chatbots are also rapidly advancing into the field of customer service, receptionist duties, student support and care for the elderly. On the immediate horizon are automated ships, aircraft, trucks, trains and cars and the application of AI to manage all routine administration and data handling tasks. The world of medicine already has Babylonhealth.com with AI-enabled medical scanning capable of highly accurate diagnosis beyond that of experienced specialists. Beyond administration and data handling Amazon opened its first Amazon Fresh store in the UK in London on 4 March 2021. The store has no staff and no checkouts. Customers download an app, and as they shop an array of AI-enhanced surveillance cameras monitor and record every item selected, and as the customer leaves the store the bill is automatically charged to the app. The House of Commons investigation into digital skills commented, "The rise of the Internet of Things, Big Data and robotics means that 65% of children entering primary school today will be working in roles that do not yet exist."[44]

Consequently, great teachers do not simply focus on the knowledge to pass examinations but also address the skills and personal competencies valued by employers and of value to the individual within a competitive jobs market. The skills versus knowledge debate is a false dichotomy because we can have both. Past curricula often made the mistake of separating skills from knowledge. Ideally, employability skills should arise from and be firmly anchored within subject-specific domains by planning regular opportunities for students to practise and develop the 4Cs of employability, Communication, Collaboration, Creativity and Critical thinking, as detailed in Chapter 12. Consideration should also be given to opportunities to enhance Human Intelligence (HI) i.e. social, metacognitive, creative and emotional intelligences, as our unique human intelligence signature against the march of AI. Subject knowledge alone will be insufficient preparation for thriving and advancing within the rapidly evolving employment landscape of the Fourth Industrial Revolution.

Developing digital skills

In April 2019, the Department of Education published the strategy paper, 'Raising the Potential of Technology in Education' to promote the development and application of digital teaching and learning skills:

> EdTech is not a silver bullet. In the 21st century, it should be seen as an inseparable thread woven throughout the processes of teaching and learning. It's senseless to pretend it isn't something that every teacher and every learner uses, every day. What we should concentrate on is when and in which ways it is best deployed to support these processes.[45]

The strategy envisaged a step-by-step evolution of teachers' digital skills, but the closure of schools during the coronavirus pandemic in 2020 accelerated teachers' skills to the point that the foundation steps were surpassed by the close of 2020. The UK strategy is being supported by the Chartered College of Teaching with a range of free training modules. In addition, the Education and Training Foundation (ETF) has published a Digital Teaching Professional Framework to guide and establish national standards. The standards specify seven elements of digital competence as follows:[46]

A   Planning your teaching
B   Approaches to teaching
C   Supporting learners to develop employability skills
D   Subject- and industry-specific teaching
E   Assessment
F   Accessibility and inclusion
G   Self-development

Each element is subdivided into specific aspects of practice with a total of twenty different standards for teachers to attain and in each case measured against three stages of digital competence defined as *exploring, adopting* and *leading* i.e. stepping up from basic to advanced digital applications. Schools and colleges with a learning management system (LMS) hold the advantage because the LMS offers an intuitive supportive framework for the development and application of digital skills. However, the ability to share online resources and lessons is also possible through free platforms like Google Classroom, YouTube, Facebook, Ted Ed, Zoom, Teams, Meet, etc. Video is the primary method for sharing knowledge online and is included as a target within the ETF digital standards: "Visualise and explain new concepts in a motivating and engaging way using digital technologies e.g. by using animations or videos."[47] The ability to create and edit video is a digital skill most teachers will increasingly need to develop and refine. It is already a norm for most young people to post videos on YouTube or Tik Tok or to maintain a vlog as a routine part of their social lives, and for an increasing number a lucrative career path as an influencer. To hold attention, instructional designers emphasise the importance of addressing a single clear learning goal so that any resulting video instruction is ideally kept to around six to eight minutes, but many are much shorter i.e. two to three minutes. Each video can link to a task to absorb detail from an e-book, website, expert video, etc., coupled with the submission of related assignments or a direct instruction presentation. Simply recording a video and posting on You-Tube or an LMS is straightforward. Writing and sketching on a digital whiteboard like Microsoft Whiteboard is also popular or embedding video into a PowerPoint presentation or equivalent. To create a video, it can be as simple as using the video camera on a smartphone or laptop to capture a short overview of a particular task or topic, but during the Coronavirus pandemic, most teachers embraced Zoom, Teams or Google Meet for their ease of use. Those platforms primarily facilitate live teacher–student interactions, but a recording is preferable. A recording offers students the advantages of when and where to watch plus the ability to pause, rewind, and re-watch. A stimulating sequence of learning can also be created by embedding video into a PowerPoint slideshow interspaced with photographs, infographics, text and/or links to websites, expert video, e-books, etc. The latest Microsoft upgrade PowerPoint 365 gives the added advantage of video recording and editing directly within a slide rather than the need to import a video file.

Video recording with PowerPoint 365

Capturing video is straightforward and something that all teachers should practise and seek to perfect. The following long list of steps may be off-putting, but they are micro steps to ensure a frustration-free video recording experience.

- Highlight a slide and select slideshow on the top ribbon and the option 'record slideshow.'
- When the recording window opens, click on the microphone and video camera icons to turn on or off in the bottom-right-hand corner as appropriate.
- Adjust your position to get the optimum distance and camera angle and consider what is visible in the background. Remember to look directly at the camera and ensure the sound on your laptop is not muted.
- When you are ready click on the red record button at the top left of the screen and recording will commence after a three-second countdown. Imagine you are facing your class and present as you ordinarily would but keep arm gestures small and restrained.
- When finished click on the stop button in the upper-left-hand corner and click on playback to view your completed video. If you want another go, simply click on record and it will record over the initial video capture. Repeat this as many times as wished until you are satisfied with the recording. Few achieve success in one take.

- Once ready press 'escape' on your keyboard to exit the recording screen.
- Drag and position the video and resize as you wish. You can opt to make the video full screen or shrink to a small window and place it anywhere on the slide to integrate with text or graphics.
- To edit simply right-click and select trim. Drag the green slider forward to start the video from a preferred position and/or the red slider backwards to end at a preferred position.
- Note that when a video is highlighted 'video format' will pop up on the ribbon at the top of your screen. Here you can select a variety of borders to frame your video.
- If you wish to save the whole PowerPoint slideshow as a video you will first need to open transitions and use 'advance slide' to automatically advance to the next slide. Check the length of embedded videos by clicking on the bar below the video window, and enter the relevant minutes and seconds into the 'advance slide' box. For slides without video, enter the time you wish the video to pause on each slide before moving forward. Ensure that the advance on 'mouse click' is unchecked, and check the slideshow runs smoothly from start to finish before you opt to save it as a video.
- To save as a video select 'save a copy' from the file menu, click on the small drop-down arrow and select MPEG-4 video format. Remember to save to a location on your computer where you can easily find the video, or it may default to some obscure folder. Desktop is often easiest.
- Upload your video to your LMS or Google Classroom or YouTube.

Creating your own videos can be a highly creative and professionally satisfying task and especially in conjunction with colleagues across a curriculum team. The staff of Gloucestershire College have already developed an impressive online learning offering across many of their major programmes (www.gloscol.ac.uk). A growing number of teachers are creating a YouTube channel, a website or a blog. The maths teachers Colin Hegarty and Jamie Frost were both shortlisted for Global Teacher of the Year prizes for their development of online maths resources (HegartyMaths.com and drfrostmaths. com, respectively). Similarly, the business studies teachers Alex Norbury and Drew Chambers from Nottinghamshire have established the 'Two Teachers' YouTube channel, along with an associated website to cover all things business studies. Their videos set a high bar in terms of production and demonstrate the high value of short, snappy engaging videos on key topics. It serves to emphasise that digital skills and applications are fast evolving and raises the importance of developing digital skills as online learning becomes a norm rather than an exception. The development of digital skills along with the other SEED elements should ideally be a team rather than an individual endeavour to ensure consistency of high standards across a curriculum area and to build and sustain a supportive CoP.

Teaching is a craft

The OECD publication 'How to Build a 21st Century School System' commented, "Too many teachers believe that good teaching is an individual art based on inspiration and talent, and not a set of skills you can acquire during a career."[48] The former leans towards Drucker's 'naturals,' but in reality teaching is a craft which we can learn, practise, review and collectively perfect.

References

1 Century Tech, www.century.tech accessed 30th October 2020.
2 Hawking, Stephen Professor, *The I Newspaper*, 9th March 2016, pg. 17.
3 Drucker, Peter F., *The Age of Discontinuity, Guidelines to our Changing Society*, Library of Congress, 2008, pg. 338.
4 Black, Paul and Wiliam, Dylan, *Inside the Black Box: Raising Standards Through Classroom Assessment*, Delta Kappa International, 1998, pg. 1.
5 Hattie, John, *Influences on Student Learning*, University of Auckland, 2nd August 1999, pg. 2.
6 *The Times*, 29th March 2019, pg. 1.
7 Kreber, Carolin, Teaching excellence, teaching expertise, and the scholarship of teaching, *Innovative Higher Education*, vol. 27, no. 1, Fall 2002, pg. 12.
8 Gibb, Nick, Minister for educational standards, *The Power of Greater Freedom and Autonomy for Schools*, 2nd November 2017, www.gov.uk/government/speeches/nick-gibb
9 Slavin, Robert, *Evidence Based Reform in Education*, Taylor & Francis, pg. 33–38.
10 Shulman, Lee S., Those who understand: Knowledge growth in teaching, *Educational Researcher*, vol. 15, no. 2, February 1986, pg. 6.
11 Boyer, Ernest L., *Scholarship Reconsidered: Priorities of the Professoriate*, The Carnegie Foundation, pg. 16, https://depts.washington.edu/gs630/Spring/Boyer.pdf
12 Ibid, pg. 24.
13 Coe, Robert, et al., *What Makes Great Teaching? Review of the Underpinning Research*, The Sutton Trust, October 2014, pg. 2.
14 Rivkin, Steven, Hanushek, Eric and Kain, John, Teachers, schools and academic achievement, *Econometrica*, vol. 73, no. 2, March 2005, pg. 449.
15 Ibid, pg. 449.
16 Podolsky, Anne, et al., Does teaching experience increase teacher effectiveness: A review of US research, *Journal of Professional Capital and Community*, vol. 4, no. 4, 28th June 2019, pg. 286–308.
17 OECD, *Teachers Matter: Attracting, Developing and Retaining Effective Teachers*, OECD, 2005.

18 Lenon, Barnaby, You don't need a qualification to be a good teacher, *Daily Telegraph*, 15th January 2015, www.telegraph.co.uk/education/educationopinion/11347131/You-dont-need-a-qualification-to-be-a-good-teacher.html

19 Sahlberg, Pasia, *We Need More Than Just Better Teachers*, 2018, https://pasisahlberg.com/we-need-more-than-just-better-teachers/

20 Coe, Robert, et al., *What Makes Great Teaching? Review of the Underpinning Research*, The Sutton Trust, October 2014, pg. 18.

21 Creemers, Bert and Kyriakides, Leonidas, *Improving Quality in Education, Dynamic Approaches to School Improvement*, Routledge, 2012, pg. 24.

22 Hattie, John Professor and Yates, Gregory, *Visible Learning and the Science of How We Learn*, Routledge, 2014, pg. 11.

23 Ibid, pg. 11.

24 Einstein, Albert, www.brainyquote.com/quotes/albert_einstein_383803

25 Department for Education, *Teaching Excellence Framework: Year Two Specification*, Department for Education, September 2016, pg. 19.

26 Kreber, Carolin, Teaching excellence, teaching expertise, and the scholarship of teaching, *Innovative Higher Education*, vol. 27, no. 1, Fall 2002, pg. 14.

27 Gayle, B. M., et al., *Classroom Communication and Instruction Processes: Advances Through Meta-Analyses*, Lawrence Erlbaum Associates, 2006, pg. 267.

28 Fenstermacher, Gary D., *Richardson Virginia, on Making Determinations of Quality in Teaching*, National Academy of Sciences, 2000, pg. 6.

29 Coe, Robert Professor, *Improving Education: A Triumph of Hope Over Experience*, University of Durham, Centre for Evaluation and Monitoring (CEM), 18th June 2013, pg. 7.

30 Wiliam, Dylan, *Feedback, Performance and Learning: Putting the Research into Practice, Powerpoint Presentation*, www.dylanwiliam.net

31 Coe, Robert Professor, *Improving Education: A Triumph of Hope Over Experience*, University of Durham, Centre for Evaluation and Monitoring (CEM), 18th June 2013, pg. XIII.

32 Duckworth, A., Quinn, P. and Seligman, M., Positive predictions of teacher effectiveness, *Journal of Positive Psychology*, vol. 4, no. 6, 2009, pg. 540–547.

33 Marzano, Robert J., *The New Art and Science of Teaching*, Solution Tree Press, 2017, pg. 70.

34 www.theguardian.com/get-into-teaching/ng-interactive/2017/mar/31/what-makes-a-great-teacher-pupils-have-their-say

35 *Times Educational Supplement*, 21st July 2017, pg. 37.

36 Agasisti, Tommaso, et al., *Academic Resilience: What Schools and Countries Do to Help Disadvantaged Students Succeed in Pisa*, OECD Education Working Papers, No. 167, 2018.

37 www.greatschools.org/gk/articles/what-makes-a-great-teacher/Learner

38 McBer, Hay, *Research into Teacher Effectiveness: A Model of Teacher Effectiveness*, DfES, June 2000, pg. 3.

39 Hattie, John, *Visible Learning: A Synthesis of Over 800 Meta-Analyses Relating to Achievement*, Routledge, 2009, pg. 250.

40 Australian Society for Evidence Based Practice, www.evidencebasedteaching. org.au/makes-great-teacher/

41 www.weforum.org/agenda/2016/01/the-fourth-industrial-revolution-what-it-means-and-how-to-respond/

42 www.gov.uk/government/speeches/michael-gove-speaks-about-the-future-of-vocational-education

43 www.cbronline.com/4th-revolution/robots-automation-destroy-15-million-uk-jobs-mark-carney/

44 House of Commons, *Science and Technology Committee, Digital Skills Crisis*, Second Report of the Session, 2016–2017, pg. 7.

45 Department for Education, *Raising the Potential of Technology in Education, a Strategy for Education Providers and the Technology Industry*, Department for Education, April 2019, pg. 4.

46 Education and Training Foundation, *Taking Learning to the Next Level, Digital Teaching Professional Framework*, pg. 21, www.et-foundation.co.uk/wp-content/uploads/2018/11/181101-RGB-Spreads-ETF-Digital-Teaching-Professional-Framework-Full-v2.pdf

47 Ibid, pg. 20.

48 Schleicher, Andreas, *World Class, How to Build a 21st Century School System*, OECD Publishing, 2018, pg. 268.

Questions

Questions to guide and plan learning

Our education system from primary to higher education is underpinned by questions and answers, from sitting our first Standardised Assessment Test (SAT) at age seven through to a thesis at university level or an assessor visit within vocational programmes and perhaps the greatest questioning challenge of all – a successful viva voce to earn a doctorate. Questions are primarily associated with assessing progress within lessons, but questions underpin all aspects of effective teaching practice.

Question categories

The following categories of questions highlight the different roles questions can play at each stage of teaching, learning and assessment:

- 'Big' questions to stir curiosity and interest above and beyond immediate curriculum goals
- 'Thunks' to build confidence in speaking and engaging in discussion
- Pre-questions as well as narratives within advance organisers to cue and direct self-regulated learning (SRL)
- Questions in place of lesson objectives to chunk the lesson and provide learning-centred rather than task-centred progression checks
- Recap questions to prompt a summary of key learning points arising from the immediate past lesson to inform a learning continuum
- Recall questions involving 'spaced practice' to test retention of knowledge from more distant lessons i.e. four to five weeks in the past using 'all response' questioning strategies i.e. relevant apps, short multi-choice test papers and quick-fire quizzes

DOI: 10.4324/9781003132783-6

- Questions following each discrete learning episode within a lesson to check for factual errors and/or conceptual misunderstandings
- A decisive 'hinge' question to inform the direction of the lesson
- Socratic questions to probe and check reasoning and to prompt deep thinking
- Exit questions to provide a final check on the lesson outcomes
- Bridge questions as a bridge to the next lesson and/or to extend learning beyond the classroom
- Questions to guide flipped learning research as a preparation for the next lesson
- Self-assessment questions to prompt SRL and to encourage metacognitive thinking

The implementation of these different forms of questions is considered across this and the following two chapters.

Questions for planning

The 'backward design' planning process is perhaps the most well-established and widely applied method for planning robust and stimulating programmes of study, as well as individual lessons. The underlying principles were first articulated in 1949 by the educationalist Ralph Tyler (1902–1994). He specified a sequence of four key questions to prompt and guide curriculum development. Firstly, establishing the purpose i.e. the anticipated learning outcomes. Next selecting appropriate methods of instruction, thirdly the organisational steps to secure learning and fourth and finally, the format for evaluating student progress. Tyler's sequence was highly influential but in practice the overlapping instructional and organisational questions were merged to yield a more concise three-question format. The educational psychologist and 'father' of lesson objectives, Robert Mager, adopted the three-question format in his definitive guide to writing lesson objectives published in 1962:

"How often are educational units, whether, large or small, prepared in response to the questions:

- What is it we must teach?
- How will we know when we have taught it?
- What materials and procedures will work best to teach what we wish to teach?

Not only must these questions be answered to instruct effectively, but the order is which they are answered is important. The first question must be answered before the other two."[1]

These three questions raise a simple but significant set of core considerations to guide curriculum planning. Mager, like Tyler before him, emphasised the importance of the first planning consideration preceding the other two. The importance of closely establishing the purpose of a programme was later emphasised by McTighe and Wiggins in their 1998 publication 'Understanding by Design (UbD).' It was McTighe and Wiggins who introduced the term 'backward design' to describe the process of working backwards from the expected learning outcomes to inform the most appropriate teaching, learning and assessment strategies. The concept was a common design principle within the motor car industry in the 1980s. More recently in 2011 McTighe and Wiggin emphasised the importance of establishing a close alignment between the three stages: "A key concept in UbD framework is alignment (i.e., all three stages must clearly align not only to standards, but also to one another). In other words, the Stage 1 content and understanding must be what is assessed in Stage 2 and taught in Stage 3."[2] The significance of alignment as a planning device was first articulated by Professor John B. Biggs in the theory of constructive alignment 2003:

> In setting up an aligned system, we specify the desired outcomes of our teaching in terms not only of topic content, but in the level of understanding we want students to achieve. . . . When we teach we should have a clear idea of what we want our students to learn. More specifically, on a topic by topic basis, we should be able to stipulate how well each topic needs to be understood.[3]

Biggs emphasised the importance of specifying outcomes not simply in terms of the subject information to be developed but ensuring alignment with the relevant programme standards. In practice a lesson planned for a Level Three course should involve higher standards than for a Level Two or a Level One course, and those standards should be aligned with appropriate instructional and assessment methods. Biggs also re-ordered the planning process by shifting the assessment question from the second to the third key consideration. The planning cycle below illustrates how 'backward design' questions can promote precision in lesson and course planning.

The questions first direct consideration to the desired learning outcomes followed by working backwards to the selection of appropriate teaching and learning strategies and finally apposite methods of assessment to confirm achievement. The questions are deceptively simple but can spark significant and beneficial debate between teachers in relation to the selection of the most effective teaching, learning and assessment strategies. These three elements are evident within the Ofsted 2019+ Education Inspection Framework (EIF) with inspectors charged with appraising curriculum planning in relation to *intent, implementation* and *impact*. Marzano has also recommended questions as a planning tool, but orientated towards the student experience and presented as a checklist for improving student engagement.

"How will I communicate clear learning goals . . .

- How will I design and administer assessments . . .
- What strategies will I use to help students feel welcome, accepted and valued?

- What engagement strategies will I use to help students pay attention, to be energised, be intrigued and be inspired?
- What strategies will I use to help typically reluctant students feel valued and comfortable interacting with me and their peers."[4]

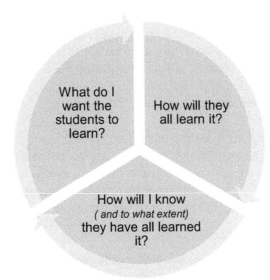

Image 4.1

Those questions raise valuable considerations because all too often planning can focus upon the transfer of subject information rather than, as Marzano indicates, how to *intrigue* and *inspire*.

Questions rather than objectives

The translation of these planning considerations into course and lesson specifications ordinarily involves writing objectives, but questions offer greater clarity and a direct link to assessment. Objectives are deeply embedded within our education system and teacher training programmes as the primary tool for course and lesson design. However, in practice objectives promote a task rather than a learning-centred curriculum and can generate an illusion of progress i.e. the students have completed the task, therefore learning has taken place. More directly we are aware from neuroscience evidence that learning happens over time rather than within the span of a single lesson and therefore the standard lesson opening 'by the end of the lesson you will be able to . . .' followed by a list of objectives is redundant. It is also instructive to observe the body language of students while teachers present and read aloud lesson objectives. The list of objectives is commonly received by students as a bureaucratic act i.e. a rubric the teacher is obliged to recite on a par with taking the register. Many teachers compound this impression by reading the objectives much too quickly and with often little in the way of any 'big picture' expansion or discussion around the learning intentions. Marzano highlighted the limited impact of objectives:

> one fairly stable finding in the literature on goal setting is that instructional goals stated in behavioral objectives format do not produce effect sizes as high as instructional goals stated in more general formats. . . . Perhaps they are simply too specific to accommodate the individual and constructivist nature of the learning process.[5]

In contrast introducing questions and particularly pre-questions with the prefix 'I would like you to be able to answer . . .' offers an open-ended learning agenda. The students are alerted not to a list of tasks for completion during the lesson, but rather to what they should know and be able to answer. Pre-questions can be posed in advance of a lesson to apply a flipped pedagogy or raised at the start of the lesson with an expectation of extension beyond the lesson to deepen classroom investigation and inform later spaced practice. By specifying questions to be answered, the planning focus shifts to identifying tasks and resources to provide the answers rather than vice versa. The questions raise a quest for answers, and as students process the questions, they are likely to flag-up common areas of difficulty. Individuals can also to pinpoint where they stall to inform teacher, classroom assistant and wider mentor coaching support. Willingham, in his celebrated treatise, *Why Don't Students Like School* endorsed starting lessons with questions:

> "it's the question that piques people's interest," and he advised, "When you plan a lesson you start with information you want students to know by its end. As a next step, consider what the key question for that lesson might be and how you can frame that question so it will have the right level of difficulty to engage your students and so you will respect your students' cognitive limitations."[6]

Carpenter and Totness (2012) demonstrated that pre-questions boost learning[7] by clarifying and making learning expectations explicit. They also promote a consideration of prior learning by inviting students to share how far they already know the answers. The importance of discussing and identifying prior learning was elaborated by Ausubel in the theory of 'subsumption.' His guiding principle was "the most important single factor influencing learning is what the learner already knows. Ascertain this and teach him accordingly."[8] The underpinning principle was first raised by Alexander Bain in 1879 in his influential book *Education as Science* and described as a process of helping students to move from the "known to the unknown." Overall questions prompt a learning dialogue, or as Willingham termed, it a conflict to be discussed and resolved: "the material we want students to know is the answer to a question – and the question is the conflict."[9]

Objectives are summative and are best left outside the classroom as a specification of the expected programme outcomes, whereas pre-questions and key questions to guide learning within and beyond the classroom are formative and provide an active learning agenda.

Ending all, most and some

The associated practice of subdividing lesson objectives into *all*, *most* and *some* is a commonly applied differentiation strategy, but in practice it can place an artificial ceiling on learning and promote low rather than high expectations. The basis for the divisions is rarely identified whether drawn from a teacher's curricular knowledge, assessment of individual prior learning or students' past assessment outcomes. It raises the danger of triggering the Pygmalion effect of unconscious low and high expectations of different students as detailed in Chapter 14. The aspects of new learning that individuals find difficult will emerge and become obvious during and by the end of a lesson. Great teachers closely monitor and react to differing levels of progress as lessons unfold and apply adaptive teaching strategies with the aim of carrying all forward rather than planning from the outset to leave some learners behind. Stepping forward one question at a time permits stumbling blocks to be pinpointed and corrected in real time.

Applying curricular standards

The questions selected should reflect the relevant curricular standards. If a programme has Pass, Merit and Distinction criteria or Grades A to E, etc., those standards should be reflected and applied as appropriate. However, associating grades with the questions should be avoided to guard against less confident students adopting a safe, self-limiting approach. Ideally, plan for three levels of questions, as illustrated, from a base of core knowledge stepping up to advanced knowledge and finally a challenge question(s) to stretch and extend the most able and/or most motivated.

Planning questions against the relevant curricular standards core (factual) and advanced (conceptual) knowledge is more manageable and realistic than trying to step through the six or more gradations of Bloom's Taxonomy or a similar cognitive hierarchy e.g. SOLO. Benjamin Bloom's cognitive hierarchy, *Taxonomy of Educational Objectives: The Classification of Educational Goals,* was not designed by Bloom as a universal differentiation tool. It was designed as a guide for course designers to differentiate summative assessment and final examination standards rather than a formative classroom assessment. Mager was critical of linking objectives to a cognitive hierarchy, "What in the world for? I don't know where such an idea originated, but I wish it would go away."[10] His preferred base was precise curricular knowledge. However, rather than 'go away,' Bloom's Taxonomy became synonymous with lesson planning and remains a feature of most teacher training programmes despite the absence of any academic research base.

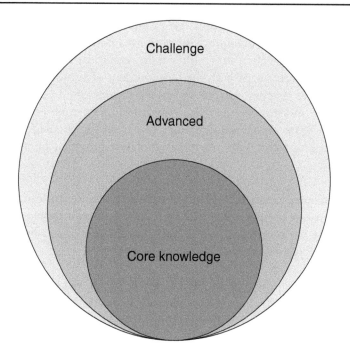

Image 4.2

The challenge category sits above and beyond the immediate programme standards to address Bjork's "desirable difficulties."[11] The aim is to promote deep
thinking and to encourage engagement with higher levels of subject knowledge
or mastery-level vocational skills. The highly successful Newham Collegiate
Sixthform Centre includes challenge extensions in all its programmes,

> students will spend time in small group sessions . . . exploring academic mate-
> rial that is beyond the A-Level syllabus. Students will need to come prepared
> ready to analyse, evaluate and explore key concepts, ideas and practices for their
> chosen area of interest.[12]

Some vocational courses are competency based with no grading scale beyond pass
or fail, but this should not prevent the introduction of challenge questions to raise
awareness of the highest commercial, industrial or world-class standards. Competency is one thing, but world-class expertise is another.

Redesigning course and lesson planning

Course and lesson planning tend to be teacher rather than student facing, but
to facilitate online learning and develop SRL, the latter is key. Chapter 10
presents student-facing advance organisers (AOs) to break the dependency on

lesson-by-lesson teacher direction and promote SRL. An AO provides the 'big picture' and along with pre-questions presents a clear learning agenda to scaffold learning across a specified unit rather than individual lessons. Lesson planning needs to be similarly recast with the development of a student-facing lesson plan and a simplified teacher version to reduce workloads. Lesson plans that seek to time, track and record every aspect of a lesson are time consuming to complete and an unnecessary requirement. The need for detailed individual lesson plans is also reduced by the overview guidance provided by an AO. Marzano commented,

> it is ineffective practice to plan one lesson at a time. Instead teachers should plan from the perspective of the unit, which should provide an overarching framework for instruction . . . teachers should be free to adjust daily activities as the unit progresses.[13]

As indicated earlier, progress should be closely monitored with the application of adaptive teaching strategies to adjust the pace as necessary. Essentially, experienced teachers are highly familiar with their subjects and can judge when to step back or step forward in response to students' questions and evidence of progress. In addition, 'lesson plans' are increasingly embedded within PowerPoint or equivalent i.e. a slide sequence can cue direct instruction, questions, assessment and collaborative learning tasks. However, in the early years of a teaching career, lesson plans are an essential tool for novice teachers to prompt, develop and refine effective sequences of learning.

'Big picture' lesson plan

The 'big picture' lesson plan provides a practical illustration of a student-facing lesson plan and with pre-questions replacing objectives. The starting point is to design a title page like the following example.

This title page is designed to be presented in A4 landscape format to create sufficient space for student notation. Once expanded to A4, the circles will expand with sufficient space for text to be entered. Start by entering an aim for the lesson, which should be a direct clear statement of the overall expected learning outcome. In the centre of the page select and paste a SmartArt image from Word or equivalent. There are a wide variety of shapes, diagrams and colour schemes to choose from and over time vary the images presented. Project the brightly coloured image via PowerPoint or equivalent to capture attention as the lesson is introduced. In this example the lesson title is placed in the centre circle and a series of pre-questions, in place of specific objectives, are placed in the outer circles. Circles can be added or taken away according to the number of planned questions but keep to three or four maximum in line with cognitive load theory (CLT). Less is more. The questions may advance from core knowledge to advanced knowledge or be entirely focussed on establishing and confirming

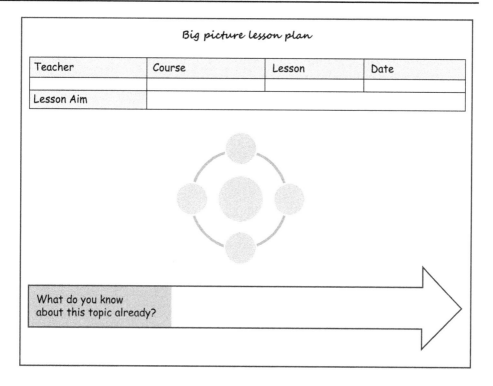

Image 4.3

key factual knowledge or a significant concept. There is no necessity for every lesson to rise from lower order to higher order. The key is to be clear on the purpose of the lesson and especially in the case of an observed lesson i.e. building factual information or consolidating understanding of a specified concept. At the bottom of the page insert space to capture discussion around prior learning as illustrated. Ideally each student should be issued with a copy, but if photocopying costs are an issue, invite the students to copy the diagram from the whiteboard or a PowerPoint slide. The act of writing and processing the questions can be an advantage rather than a disadvantage by promoting engagement and perhaps triggering points for clarification. Introduce the lesson in the style of I would like you to be able to answer . . . followed by expanding on the pre-questions and the learning strategies planned for the lesson. Address prior learning by granting the students time to jot responses to the prompt question: What do I know about this topic already? Invite feedback and encourage discussion in relation to how far the topic is new to everyone, being mindful of Ausubel's primary rule. As the lesson unfolds, use the pre-questions to punctuate the lesson and to check for progress and inform adaptive teaching strategies before advancing question by question. Summarise the key points as you advance and encourage the students to annotate the diagram with their own notes. The aim, by the end of the lesson, is for each student to have a single-page summary of the key learning arising during the lesson. The questions can be returned to in future weeks to facilitate spaced practice and inform future revision.

Active engagement

The blank reverse page of the big picture lesson plan can be used to present a wide variety of active reflective, key information and assessment tasks linked to the lesson:

- Appetiser – record details of one of the many appetiser suggestions presented in Chapter 7 e.g. a big question, an arresting image, a key quote, a key statistic
- Recall – apply an element of spaced practice by presenting multiple-choice questions, a short quiz or a task linked to an earlier topic.
- Present a Cornell note-taking template to capture and evaluate key notes as the lesson unfolds.
- Key knowledge – introduce a knowledge organiser by listing some of the key concepts, theories, people, events, specialist vocabulary, etc., that the lesson is going to cover.
- Print one of the SmartArt graphics presented in Chapter 8 to support a paired or group task.
- Present a self-assessment table as described in Chapter 5 to capture responses and to promote metacognitive thinking.
- Learning summary – place some note-taking/review subheadings and at the end of the lesson invite the students to capture a short summary of key knowledge.

The combination of the title page and the selected learning or assessment prompt on the reverse recast lesson plans as tools to guide and capture learning.

Teacher lesson planning template

The final element of the big picture lesson plan is the attachment of a lesson planning template for teachers as a simplified approach to lesson planning. The title page, as described earlier, is designed to be common to both teachers and students, but whereas students have learning or assessment prompts printed on the reverse, this is replaced for teachers with a learning development template as illustrated.

This approach adapts the famous 'five-minute' lesson plan concept developed by Ross Morrison McGill. The different shapes and labels are presented as an illustration of the approach rather than a fixed proforma. Curriculum teams can

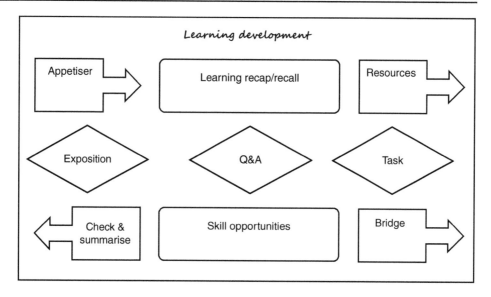

Image 4.4

apply their own creativity to design a template or template(s) best suited to their needs. The key consideration is to keep to one side of A4 landscape paper. The labels in the example are taken from the Diamond Lesson Plan, as described in Chapter 7, but curriculum teams may make their own choices. For instance, a science team may wish to have the label 'practical', a catering team 'demonstration' and an engineering team 'equipment.' Sam Barnes, a teacher on the Wirral, has created a whole range of jazzy templates which he shared with colleagues following his attendance at a big picture lesson plan Continuing Professional Development event. He is one of a growing number of teachers whose creativity spills well beyond the classroom. Once the template(s) are fixed, it is a matter of writing brief notes into each box or shape. The timings for each step of the lesson are indicated by writing the number of minutes at the base of each box or shape. For example, a planned appetiser to start a lesson might be expected to last for four minutes. A brief description of the activity would be placed into the box followed by the number 4 for four minutes.

Learning clarity

Replacing objectives with questions holds many benefits, but perhaps clarity is the most significant as we embrace the close integration of online learning with the classroom.

References

1 Mager, Robert F., *Preparing Instructional Objectives*, Fearon Publishers, 1962, Foreword.
2 McTighe, Jay and Wiggins, Grant, *Understanding by Design Framework*, White Paper ASCD, 2011, pg. 2.
3 Biggs, John, *Aligning Teaching for Constructing Learning*, The Higher Education Academy, 2003, pg. 2, www.heacademy.ac.uk/system/files/resources/id477_aligning_teaching_for_constructing_learning.pdf
4 Marzano, Robert J., *The New Art and Science of Teaching*, Solution Tree Press, 2017, pg. 6.
5 Marzano, Robert J., et al., *Classroom Instruction That Works*, Association for Supervision and Curriculum Development (ASCD), 2001, pg. 94.
6 Willingham, Daniel T., *Why Don't Students Like School*, Jossey Bass, 2009, pg. 20.
7 Carpenter, S. and Toftness, A., The effect of pre-questions on learning from video presentations, *Journal of Applied Research in Memory and Cognition*, vol. 6, 2017, pg. 104–109.
8 Ausubel, David, *Educational Psychology a Cognitive View*, Holt McDougal, 1968, pg. VI.
9 Willingham, Daniel T., *Why Don't Students Like School*, Jossey Bass, 2009, pg. 49.
10 Mager, Robert F., *Preparing Instructional Objectives*, 3rd edition, CEP Press, 1997, pg. 150.
11 Bjork, Elizabeth and Bjork, Robert, *Making Things Hard on Yourself, but in a Good Way*. Creating Desirable Difficulties to Enhance Learning, UCL, Bjork Learning and Forgetting Lab, 2011, https://bjorklab.psych.ucla.edu/wp-content/uploads/sites/13/2016/04/EBjork_RBjork_2011.pdf
12 https://thencs.co.uk/ncs-super-curriculum
13 Marzano, R. J., *The New Aer and Science of Teaching*, Solution Tree Press, 2017, pg. 107.

5

Questions to check and develop learning

Questions are the primary way we gauge students' progress as lessons unfold. The answers give us immediate feedback and in the most effective lessons prompt a mixture of restatement, reframing or extension of key learning points to help identify and correct misconceptions. Ideally, we seek to build a dialogue to help students to assimilate new knowledge and by probing assumptions and evidence promote reflection and deeper understanding. The positive impact of questioning within lessons was confirmed by the educational researcher Kathleen Cotton in a much-quoted review of thirty-seven research studies published in 1988:

- Instruction which includes posing questions during lessons is more effective in producing achievement gains than instruction carried out without questioning students.
- Students perform better on test items previously asked as recitation questions than on items they have not been exposed to before.
- Oral questions posed during classroom recitations are more effective in fostering learning than are written questions.
- Questions which focus student attention on salient elements in the lesson result in better comprehension than questions which do not.[1]

Questioning works, but Cotton also identified a series of key issues for improvement relating to an imbalance between lower- and higher-order questioning, support for less able students, 'wait' times, probing evidence, re-directing questions and extended elaboration of correct answers. Cotton concluded by recommending, "Better preservice training in the art of posing classroom questions, together with in-service training to sharpen teachers' questioning skills, have potential for increasing students' classroom participation and achievement."[2]

A decade later Professors Paul Black and Dylan Wiliam of the University of London reported similar issues arising from their research study 'Inside the Black

Box' particularly in relation to insufficient 'wait times', asking too many lower-order questions, teachers answering their own questions and evidence of low participation rates. Black and Wiliam identified the importance of developing a positive and supportive learning culture to improve not just questioning but the overall clarity of learning intentions and related feedback. The outcome was the Assessment for Learning (AfL) initiative which recommended improvements to four key aspects of classroom practice:

- Questioning
- Feedback
- Sharing criteria
- Self-assessment

Black and Wiliam adopted the term *Assessment for Learning* to counter the widespread interpretation of assessment as a summative procedure i.e. an exam or a piece of written work to be submitted, marked and graded, whereas AfL was identified as a formative procedure i.e. a developmental process of regular checks on understanding in 'real time' to uncover and correct misunderstandings as they arose lesson by lesson. Black and Wiliam described questioning along with feedback as 'pivotal' to improving learning. Following a small-scale trial involving six schools and thirty-six teachers AfL was widely adopted across the UK school sector, but the results were ultimately disappointing with no demonstrable improvements to overall learning outcomes. An Ofsted evaluation of AfL published in 2008 revealed confusion amongst teachers as to the most effective implementation strategies, but in particular it was concluded that too many teachers failed to sufficiently change their practice and shift the focus of their lessons from teaching to learning. Professor Robert Coe in commenting on the issue as director of the Centre for Evaluation and Monitoring (CEM), University of Durham, speculated that issues of robustness, scaling up and independence of reporting were probable factors but also "many of the most effective strategies are complex, open to interpretation and hard to implement. We do not know how to get large groups of teachers and schools to implement these interventions in ways that are faithful, effective and sustainable."[3] Coe quoted Wiliam's response in relation to the low impact of AFL as follows, "The last 30 years have shown conclusively that you can change teachers' thinking about something without changing what those teachers do in classrooms."[4] Wiliam was subsequently critical of how AfL had been implemented and regarded it as being skewed towards target setting and tracking outcomes rather than 'teacher responsiveness' i.e. reacting to in-lesson evidence of progress. However, AfL successfully focussed attention on the dynamics of question-and-answer interactions and spotlighted many aspects of poor practice to avoid:

- Teachers ask too many lower order-questions
- The more confident students dominate answers and the less confident remain silent.

- Teachers often interrupt and essentially answer and extend the answers to their own questions.
- Teachers give insufficient 'wait' or thinking time.
- Correct answers are interpreted as evidence of learning rather than performance at this point in time.
- Students are rarely asked to explain or justify their responses.
- Open questions to probe and extend into a dialogue are rare.
- Questions are often not clearly linked to the programme standards.

Effective questioning practice seeks to build full participation and to extend answers into a supportive learning dialogue to provide evidence of progress and to uncover and correct misunderstandings.

Core practice

The ability of teachers to apply effective question and answer strategies is an element of widely endorsed core practice. Charlotte Danielson introduced her hierarchy of questioning competencies with the statement: "Questioning and discussion are the only instructional strategies specifically referred to in the Framework for Teaching, a decision that reflects their central importance to teachers' practice."[5] Danielson's criteria for effective questioning practice are detailed in Chapter 6. Similarly, the Dynamic Model of School Improvement first outlined by professors of education, Bert Creemers and Leonidas Kyriakides in 2006 identified questioning as one of eight elements of core teaching practice involving three significant steps: "(a) raising different types of questions (i.e. process and product) at appropriate difficulty level; (b) giving time for students to respond; and (c) dealing with student responses."[6] Their distinction between product and process questions related to the difference between simple factual recall and higher reasoning in terms of the ability to articulate and explain relevant underpinning knowledge. More recently in 2014 the Sutton Trust's review of evidence-based practice entitled, 'What Makes Great Teaching' concluded:

The two factors with the **strongest** evidence of improving pupil attainment are:

- Teachers' content knowledge, including their ability to understand how students think about a subject and identify common misconceptions
- Quality of instruction, which includes using strategies like effective questioning and the use of assessment.[7]

In addition, the Sutton Trust found **good** evidence to support:

- Asking a large number of questions and checking the response of all students.[8]

The Sutton Trust's recommendations endorse the fifth principle of Barack Rosenshine's Seventeen Principles of Instruction i.e. *Ask a large number of questions and check for understanding.*[9] In addition, Rosenshine emphasised the need to question all rather than some students and offered the following guidance:

> questions allow a teacher to determine how well the material has been learned and whether there is a need for additional instruction. The most effective teachers also ask students to explain the process they used to answer the question, to explain how the answer was found. Less successful teachers ask fewer questions and almost no process questions.[10]

The focus on 'process' questions is an important rider as identified by Creemers and Kyriakides i.e. a check on the ability of students to elaborate and explain their answers and reasoning rather than simply parroting overheard or known responses.

Communication apprehension

Answering questions is a challenge. Monosyllabic answers from many of our students are not unusual. Even as adults we often shy away from the spotlight in meetings or conferences because we fear being wrong. Most of us have experienced the embarrassment of being 'wrong,' and it burns. Black and Wiliam raised this issue as a leading cause of underachievement in 1998:, "many [pupils] become reluctant to ask questions out of a fear of failure. Pupils who encounter difficulties are led to believe that they lack ability, and this belief leads them to attribute their difficulties to a defect in themselves about which they cannot do a great deal."[11] A whole variety of factors influence levels of personal confidence including self-image, home background, socio-economic pressures, peer culture and the often underestimated impact of making and securing friends. In some cases, communication apprehension (CA) is so pronounced that it can become a limiting factor because the student(s) will avoid answering questions and fear any form of public speaking. Many relatively straightforward aspects of communication, from personal introductions during an induction course, to reading aloud or being asked to give a report back from a group activity, can trigger excessive anxiety manifesting in physiological reactions of appearing red in the face, excessive sweating, hesitation, dry mouth and a tremulous voice. Those experiences can cause deep personal embarrassment and add to a memory store of negative experiences associated with speaking. As with any experience or aspect of learning, the repetition deepens and strengthens the associated memory store and those negative memories of previous embarrassment further inhibit participation. The answer is cognitive modification i.e. building an alternative memory store of positive experiences associated with speaking until eventually the positives outweigh the negatives. Or, as the cognitive scientists term it, the negative memory store fades and falls into disuse. The principal stepping-stones to achieve this are:

- Setting a warm supportive climate of welcoming every contribution.
- Using the 'all response' questioning techniques, as described later, to draw all students into participation so all become familiar with providing answers.
- Congratulating students by name for correct answers and ensuring CA students receive a warm positive. Confidence is built is micro steps.
- Avoid 'creeping death' i.e. moving along a row asking one student at a time to express an opinion. Waiting for the spotlight to arrive heightens anxiety. Instead apply 'popcorn' whereby you invite spontaneous contributions. However, watch for those who regularly choose not to 'pop' and ensure additional positive support to encourage participation.
- Ask regular fact-checker questions that only require a one-word answer using one of the random selection techniques described below in place of 'creeping death'. Again, issue warm praise for a correct answer.
- No hands up – select who will answer and for those exhibiting CA ask a question that only requires a brief answer, as noted earlier, and one they should be able to answer. This will engage the students who rarely 'pop' but it is fairly non-threatening and will promote participation. Again, warm praise for the answer.
- Introduce thunks as described later – the absence of a correct answer reduces the anxiety of being wrong. Give lots of positives for the contributions.
- Regular paired discussion – agreeing answers with a partner will increase and build confidence. Move pairs into fours (quads) to widen the discussion and agreement.
- Directly address CA with the class as a whole and coach how to develop the skills of public speaking as described in Chapter 11.
- Directly address extreme displays of CA because it may be the manifestation of significant underlying clinical anxiety. One-to-one counselling may be appropriate and beneficial to help the student to resolve related personal issues/triggers.

The regular overlapping and application of these strategies can, over a period of months, build personal confidence but in general the key is to create a positive learning culture. Acknowledge that some questions are challenging and that it is OK to be wrong. Remind all that learning something new is difficult. It is normal to have misunderstandings and therefore every student should expect to get some things wrong. In other words, make it easy for your students to say, "I don't understand." Encourage all to ask when they are uncertain. Take on the blame for any hesitations by apologising for speaking too quickly or for not explaining the point well enough, etc. – never imply they should know this or that something is easy. Overall, try and give positives to all. Ignore any minor silly behaviour and praise those participating in a positive manner to reinforce the behaviour you expect. Marzano recommends the term 'recognition' rather than praise because of the dangers associated with empty praise: "praise given for accomplishing easy tasks can undermine achievement. Students commonly perceived it as undeserved; further praise for accomplishing easy tasks might actually lower their perception of their ability."[12] Therefore attach the praise to the answer and explain why an answer was a good answer or a good example, etc. Recognising contributions in a positive way will encourage further participation.

Try a thunk

Thunks were first developed by the writer and presenter Ian Gilbert and are deliberately calculated to provoke a response. Here are some examples:

- Give me five uses for a brick?
- Would you rather fight a duck the size of a horse or 100 duck-sized horses?
- If I travel facing backwards on a train will I witness the past?
- If days were colours what colour would Wednesday be?
- If the answer was 'seven feet off the ground' what is the question?
- At 12 noon are you standing between the past and the future?
- Is a red sheet of paper blank?
- If the choice was between wings or four legs, which would you choose?
- Does lined paper inhibit creativity?

The thunks website (www.thunks.co.uk) offers further examples, including a daily thunk. Posing morally based questions can similarly help students to find their voice and to express opinions in front of the wider class.

- Should the smacking of children be made illegal?
- Should Gordon Ramsay curb his language?
- Should you flash your car headlights to warn fellow motorists of a police speed trap ahead?
- Should the ban on smoking be extended into homes where there are children?
- Is eating meat wrong?

Consider the age group of your students and pose appropriate opinion sharing questions. Current news items wrapped up as the three-minute debate of the day (or week) often work well. The benefit of open (even ridiculous) thunks lies in the non-threatening nature because there are clearly no correct answers. Although thunks may seem an odd proposition, they will often succeed in provoking responses, beneficial laughter and ultimately helping our students to express and defend their opinions and ultimately build their confidence.

Lesson introduction

Questions perform three key functions at the start of a lesson.

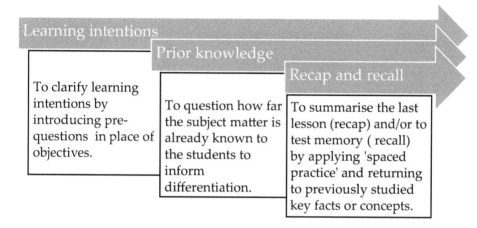

Learning intentions	Prior knowledge	Recap and recall
To clarify learning intentions by introducing pre-questions in place of objectives.	To question how far the subject matter is already known to the students to inform differentiation.	To summarise the last lesson (recap) and/or to test memory (recall) by applying 'spaced practice' and returning to previously studied key facts or concepts.

Image 5.1

The order of this sequence may be altered as thought appropriate, but all three aspects of questioning are important to build a continuum of learning and to ensure sufficient stretch. The 'big picture' lesson plan, as presented in the last chapter, is one way to address both the sharing of learning intentions, in the form of questions, and to capture prior knowledge. It is rare for a topic to be new to everyone, and most students will enter the classroom with some knowledge of the topic. Ausubel, as highlighted in Chapter 4, emphasised the importance of discovering and building upon what students already know. A stimulating way to discover what students already known is to design a story board to tease out prior knowledge in a step-by-step manner.

Storyboard question and answer

A storyboard can successfully engage and hold the attention of all students by posing questions linked to a sequence of PowerPoint or equivalent slides. The following example illustrates the approach for introducing a poetry lesson.

The questions are illustrative and can be extended or adjusted in response to the answers received. The idea is to draw out prior knowledge, to inform differentiation and to gain as much participation as possible. It is important not to confirm or deny any contributions as you move through the slides to extend the discussion.

	Have you ever seen this man before? Any guesses on who he might be? Which army do you think he served in? Why? Do you think he held a rank? Why? What age might he have been?
	Have you ever seen this poster before? Where? What does it represent? Who is the central character? Who is standing behind him? What do you think was the purpose of this poster? What time period are we discussing? Who is absent?
	Can you identify those flowers? Where do you think this field was? What is the significance of those flowers? What happened to this landscape?
	So, what war are we talking about? When did the war start and finish? Can anyone give the dates? Who was fighting? Where did most of the fighting take place? What is this war remembered for?
Dulce et Decorum est Pro Patria Mori	Have you ever come across those words before? What language is that? Can anyone translate into English? What are those words associated with? Do you think there is a link with the man in the first photograph?
	What sort of headstone is this? Where might we find this sort of headstone? Is that the date of the end of the war? When did the war end? So, what do you think that date signifies?

Image 5.2

The soldier is Lieutenant Wilfred Owen who enlisted in the British Army and fought in World War One (1914–1918). He was stationed in Northern France and like all soldiers was horrified by the immense human cost of the war. He wrote poetry as an expression of his grief. The person in the poster is the fictional patriotic Englishman John Bull whose image was used in recruitment posters across England. The words *Dulce et decorum est pro patria mori* are Latin and the title of one of Owen's most famous poems. The title is generally translated as, *It is sweet and right to die for your country.* However, within the poem the line is prefixed by the words 'the old lie.' It was an anti-war sentiment because Owen, like so many, was bitterly disillusioned by the high death rate and the immense suffering he witnessed. He was awarded the Military Cross for bravery 1 October 1918 but was killed in action on 4 November 1918, exactly one week before the end of the war 11 November 1918. He is buried in the military cemetery at Ors in Northern France close to where he fell.

Have you guessed what today's lesson is about yet?

Today we will be studying the war poetry of Wilfred Owen starting with 'Dulce et Decorum est Pro Patria Mori.'

Image 5.3

Use your own creativity to design a story board to introduce one of your topics using a mixture of photographs, quotations, diagrams, statistics, charts, etc. It rarely fails to build interest and engagement and can be followed by the pre-questions you would like the class to be able to answer by the end of the lesson or unit of study.

Recap and recall

Recap and recall are the third most significant element of the recommended lesson introduction and extend to the heart of effective practice by seeking to gain a positive check on learning as distinct from engagement. A recap offers a reminder of what was covered in the last lesson with links to the new learning to build connections and an opportunity to gauge how far the students have retained and understood the key points. If exit slips or some other form of lesson summary were employed in the last lesson, encourage students to refer to their notes and invite them to undertake the recap in the style of if someone was absent, what did they miss? Our strategy is to take one step back and only three or four steps forward every lesson with respect to CLT. If the recap raises clear evidence of misunderstandings, it is important to react and not to ignore the evidence. It is counterproductive to introduce new learning if students are still struggling to absorb aspects of a previous lesson. Lesson plans are *plans* and should be adjusted if feedback indicates that more time is needed to repeat or consolidate some key points. It is also important to move beyond summarising learning by testing the *recall* of key facts and key concepts by introducing retrieval practice.

All response questioning

The purpose of recall is to gain a precise check on learning by *all* rather than *some* students by employing some or more of Wiliam's 'all response' questioning techniques. The questions may relate to the last lesson but ideally, they should involve 'spaced practice' i.e. returning to a topic studied four to five weeks earlier to ascertain how far key knowledge can be accurately retrieved. Returning to topics at the edge of our memories significantly strengthens retrieval and storage strength within long-term memory. The following 'all response' questioning techniques work well to benchmark student progress and may be used at any part of a lesson rather than simply limited to recall.

Mini whiteboards	Display four multi-choice questions on a PowerPoint or equivalent and invite the students to record A, B, C or D as appropriate on their mini whiteboards. On the command 'show me' all students should hold up their answers. The result is an immediate overview of the extent of any incorrect responses. Alternatively ask a question that only requires a one-word answer or a calculation. In all cases before confirming the correct answers first 'work the room' by asking students to state why their answer is correct. Note the extent to which wrong answers are being displayed and check for common misconceptions for correction.
Traffic light cards	Experience has shown that it is best to dispense with the middle ground of amber and to restrict the response cards to green or red. Pose a key question and invite the students to hold up green if they are confident they know the answer or red if they do not know the answer. Question a selection of 'greens' at random to check for agreement and accuracy. Watch the body language of the other greens to gauge how far all seem to be in agreement or wish to add to the answer. A high level of red cards delivers a very powerful, visual message to review the topic. Seek agreement from the 'reds' that they now understand the answer and build some discussion around their misunderstandings. Alternatively invite greens to pair with reds to explain the answer and then re-ask the question to see if the whole room can go green but keep an eye open for 'passengers.'

Traffic light display	Present a list of key questions on a handout and issue the students small, coloured dots in the traffic light colours. Each student without discussion or conferring should work down the questions and colour code their responses by placing a dot in the margin: Green – I am confident I know the answer Amber – I think I know Red – I have no idea List the same questions on flip chart paper (by number if lengthy) with a large gap between each question and pin up along the classroom wall. Issue large-coloured dots for higher visual impact and invite the students to repeat their personal scores from their handouts onto the flip chart paper. This will generate a high impact colourful display of levels of confidence and should be used to facilitate a progress discussion and prompt re-teaching of questions dominated by 'red' responses. Some students may be tempted to post green when they do not understand but over time the key is to draw the students into a 'mature' learning partnership i.e. the benefit of being truthful because they gain a repeat explanation and can gain a measure of control.
Apps	There is an ever expanding array of apps for posing questions, creating multiple choice quizzes and live interactions with your students. Take a look at Microsoft Forms, Answer Garden, Plickers, Qwizdom, Quizlet, Quizizz, Socrative, Zeetings, Osmosis, Book Widgets, Menitmeter, Gimkit, Kahoot, Wooclap, Crowdsignal and Poll Everywhere to explore the different services. Most are free, but some will apply a monthly charge to access advanced functions. In most cases students will need a smartphone to log into the presentation. Google Classroom and Google Forms are entirely free services and offer quiz settings, question tools and polls among a much wider range of learning support services.
Thumbs	Our thumbs are a fast way to gain responses: Thumb up – I understand Thumb sideways – I am a bit uncertain Thumb down – I do not understand
True or False	Issue a card with a large capital T on one side and an F on the reverse and use for responses to a range of true or false questions. Alternatively, as noted earlier, employ a thumb up to signal true and a thumb down to signal false.
Fingers	The students should respond to a multiple choice questions by holding up one, two, three or four fingers to correspond with their choice of answer.
Raised hand	The students raise their hands as the teacher moves down through the multiple choice options to indicate their choice of answer.
ABCD cards	Issue the class with ABCD cards to respond to multiple choice questions.
Multiple choice question paper	Issue a question sheet with a list of multiple choice questions and give a strict time limit for completion. When time is up the students should swap papers for peer marking. The teacher should list overall scores on the board and use to facilitate discussion. The questions may be differentiated from straightforward factual recall to higher order conceptual understanding. Top Ten questions on a topic works well and generates instant percentages.

Post-it	Use large Post-it notes and invite all students to write down one aspect of misunderstanding or difficulty arising from the last lesson and post it on the wall. The teacher should group according to the 'issues' presented and re-teach as appropriate.
Cornered	Label the four corners of the classroom A, B, C and D and invite the students to move to the relevant corner in response to multiple choice questions displayed on PowerPoint or similar. Do not immediately reveal the correct answer but 'interrogate' the students standing in each corner as to why their answer is correct. Watch out for the 'herd' instinct whereby students follow those they think are more likely to get it right. Question anyone who appears to be regularly following the herd.
Stand-up	As a variation on the previous exercise, invite the students to stand up in reaction to each multiple choice question alternative. Ask the students to defend their choices and do not confirm right or wrong until all answers have been given.

Image 5.4

Multiple choice questions permit greater accuracy than other forms of questioning, but to avoid ambiguity they need to be well designed:

- Write a short, precise stem prompt.
- If the stem includes a particular instruction word e.g. 'which one of these choices is **not** an example of . . .' ensure that the key instruction word is in bold and/or underlined.
- Provide four choices i.e. one correct answer and three distractors.
- Ensure the distractors are all clearly wrong rather than being marginally different from the correct answer. We do not set out to confuse.

Quiz formats can also be usefully employed with *Blockbusters* and *Who Wants to Be a Millionaire* as perennial favourites. Many enterprising teachers and organisations have placed free templates to support both quizzes and free downloadable apps on the internet. Simply Google 'who wants to be a millionaire template' or 'Blockbusters template' and you will be spoilt for choice. Some downloads arrive complete with the music and graphics to generate the whole atmosphere of the TV programme.

The following questioning techniques develop active participation in pairs and small groups to review previous learning.

The regular introduction of these types of questioning strategies makes for lively, engaging classrooms and more importantly feedback on how far the students are following and understanding the lessons. This is highly significant for motivation and overall progress. If teachers ignore evidence of misunderstandings and advance to the next topic, the unspoken message given to the students is: 'you should be able to understand this, at this pace, and if you can't then this places a question mark over your ability.' There are flaws in all questioning techniques, but those techniques are far removed from the throwaway teacher enquiry, 'has anyone got any questions?' with few, if any, students ever responding.

Top ten learning review activities	
1 Alien/Earthling	Place the students into random pairs using one of the techniques described in Chapter 10. One student takes the role of the alien and the other the earthling. Display a key question relating to a key concept, event, process or theory from an earlier lesson. The alien asks: What is meant by . . . ? How does X work . . . ? How do I . . .? The alien must play the part of being completely ignorant of all concepts/knowledge and consequently the earthling must provide a detailed definition/explanation. The alien can ask further sub-questions to clarify the answer. Remember the alien does not know anything. This mimics the approach of Socratic question and answer as described in the next chapter. Consider issuing a prompt sheet with Socratic root questions to prompt more precise answers. Set a timer for one minute. This sounds very brief but it is a challenge for most students. When time is up 'work the room' and invite different pairs to explain the concept, etc. Ensure at least one further round but this time invite the students to swap roles. The alien becomes earthling and vice versa. Conclude by asking key questions of the whole class to confirm full understanding and as appropriate capture some notes. Oxford University applies the 'explain to an alien' form of questioning as one of its approaches in admission interviews. In 2018 a student reported that he had been asked to explain as if to an alien 'what is a cucumber.' It may seem an unusual approach but it is a significant test of knowledge, vocabulary and clarity.
2 One minute	This is a similar approach to the one noted earlier. Pre-print key topics on small cards for students to select at random and place into pairs. The students take turns to speak for one minute on a given key topic or question. They may pass and invite their partner to explain. Keep fast paced and offer lots of encouragement.
3 Cartwheel	Draw a large cartwheel shape on flipchart paper with a small centre circle and two concentric outer circles and as many spokes as there are sub-topics i.e. divide the cartwheel into segments like slices of a pizza. Place the topic in the centre. Place key sub-headings in the inner circle and invite the students in pairs or small groups take charge of one segment and to write a concise summary/explanation in the outer circle. It will work best if you take scissors and cut out each segment for each group to complete and then re-assemble on a noticeboard. Perhaps use different coloured pens for each segment for maximum visual impact.

(Continued)

Top ten learning review activities	
4 Concept bingo	Issue a handout containing a grid of nine squares. Use the whiteboard or PowerPoint to display twelve key concepts or headings. Each student selects nine and copies into his or her grid. The teacher should provide the twelve definitions at random and the first learner to shout bingo i.e. correct match of definitions and concepts wins. Select one student per concept to explain the concept and related facts. To produce bingo cards try the free resource https://myfreebingocards.com
5 Hesitation	Divide the class into teams. Ask each team in turn to define or explain a key concept, event, discovery, person, formula, etc. The team nominates someone to answer that question. If the person hesitates then a member of another team may challenge and take over the answer. If they complete the definition or explanation, they win a point for their team. Keep fast paced and aim to cover about ten key questions.
6 Knowledge tree	Place into groups of three or four with a sheet of flipchart paper and coloured pens. All are to draw a 'knowledge tree' as a summary of the topic under review. The trunk can be two vertical parallel lines and the branches can curve out of the top of the trunk to the left and right. At the end of each branch draw an oval for leaves. This is a mind mapping approach with the topic written on the trunk and individual facts written on the leaves. If the topic is major one, each branch could be labelled with the title of a subtopic and more leaves can be radiated off. Place a timer on screen and give five to eight minutes to complete a colourful learning tree for the topic. At the end pin these up and confirm and check learning by naming students to explain different points. You might identify other key visuals to 'hang' learning points from i.e. the eight legs of a **spider**, the tentacles of an **octopus**, rays of **sunshine**, the steps of a **ladder**, the bars of a **farmer's gate**, a row of **test tubes**, a **roundabout**, etc. This applies dual coding by associating a bright visual with a particular topic and can significantly boost memory. Build into note taking and flash cards for revision. Perhaps simplest of all (assuming five key learning points) is to invite all to draw around their **hand** on a sheet of paper and to write one key point per finger. You can add an extra hand to yield ten points or one hand for positive points and the other for negative points or other categorisation. Alternatively draw the hand in the thumb up position with the topic on the thumb and four key points on the fingers.
7 Truth	Place into teams of three and give each team a key concept, event, discovery, person, formula, etc. One person provides the correct definition or answer, the next a near version of the truth and the third student a more fanciful version of the truth. The students have to arrive at the different versions. In turn each team comes to the front of the room to form a panel and the class questions each team member and decide who is telling the truth.

Top ten learning review activities	
8 Match	Prepare index cards with a question on one side and an answer on the reverse side. However, the questions and answers should be mismatched. Start by selecting a student to read out their question. Someone in the room should have the matching answer and should confirm this by reading out the answer printed on their card. The student should then turn the card over and read out their question and wait for someone in the room to identify the answer, etc.
9 Line-up	Design four or five bright A4-sized title pages for different concepts, theories, people, discoveries, etc. Select volunteers to stand at the front of the classroom holding up the title pages. Next issue at least one key fact card (on index cards) to the rest of the students. The students link their fact to the relevant topic and line up behind the student holding the relevant topic title card. Once all are lined up each group must present their topic and link all the key facts into one fluid overview. Ask questions as they present to check for full understanding.
10 Flip	A variation on the bingo and match games. Prepare sets of twelve index cards with a question on one side and the correct related facts or information or definition on the other side. Place the class into pairs, and each pair places their set of index cards on the tabletop with the question uppermost. The first student asks one of the questions and their partner gives an answer. The student should turn the card over to check the answer given. If the answer is correct, turn this card over but if incorrect, it is returned to the tabletop question uppermost. The students continue to question each other until all questions are correctly answered and all cards are turned over.

Image 5.5

Lesson development

The presentation and development of new learning within a lesson will most often involve a mixture of direct instruction and collaborative learning. However, it is possible for one or the other to form the focus of an entire lesson. The key in either case is to punctuate the lesson with questions to gain feedback in 'real time' to gauge progress and to inform any adjustments to the lesson flow in terms of how far to step back or to step forward.

A common frustration in managing classroom question and answer is the tendency for more confident students to dominate the answers and for the less

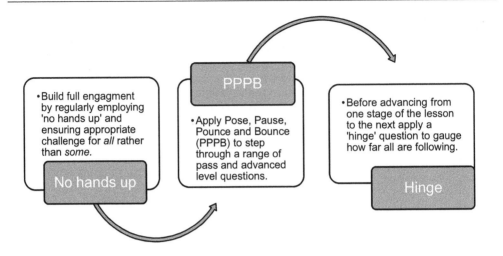

Build full engagment by regularly employing 'no hands up' and ensuring appropriate challenge for *all* rather than *some*.

No hands up

PPPB

Apply Pose, Pause, Pounce and Bounce (PPPB) to step through a range of pass and advanced level questions.

Before advancing from one stage of the lesson to the next apply a 'hinge' question to gauge how far all are following.

Hinge

Image 5.6

confident to acquiesce and over time to become increasingly disengaged. It is therefore important to develop a culture whereby all are expected to listen, follow discussion and to engage with answering questions. Raised hands are a useful gauge of confidence but also make it a regular habit to cold call i.e. select a student who has not raised their hand and issue the invitation, 'I would like to hear from.' On a regular basis apply cold call by specifying 'no hands up' and 'no shouting out' to promote full engagement and concentration. As Wiliam commented, "those who are participating are getting smarter, while those avoiding engagement are forgoing the opportunities to increase their ability. This is why many teachers now employ a rule of "no hands up except to ask a question."[13] Teachers should select a student to answer. This can result in challenges for the more able because whereas they do regularly provide correct answers there are also some things they do not know. The more able, like all students, will only raise their hands when they feel certain they know the answer. Teacher selection and the introduction of random selection techniques will introduce a challenge for all over time.

Wait time

Research originally published by Mary Budd Rowe in 1974 identified that teachers ordinarily waited just 0.9 seconds between asking a question and intervening and similarly after gaining a student response, "when teachers ask questions of students, they typically wait 1 second or less for the students to start a reply; after the student stops speaking they begin their reaction or proffer the next question in less than 1 second."[14] A wait time of less than one second gives insufficient time to process a question and essentially closes down rather than opens up student engagement. Teachers tend to be unnerved by silence and all too often fail to allow for the necessary thinking time to absorb a question and the time to consider an answer. Rowe identified that a wait time of 2.7 seconds, generally rounded up to 3 seconds, significantly improved the quality and depth of student answers. Importantly this applied to both immediately after posing the question and after the student response. The former gives sufficient thinking time to answer and the latter time to add further points of detail to support and extend the initial answer. Rowe also discovered that the introduction of the second wait time prompted other students to join in and to contribute further points in the 'popcorn' style of spontaneous contributions. Further studies by Stanford University distinguished between lower- and higher-order questions and recommended a wait time of eight to ten seconds for higher-order questions to help students marshal their thoughts. The significance of 'wait time' was confirmed by AfL research undertaken by Black and Wiliam in 2003. A teacher in the study reported "increasing waiting time after asking questions proved difficult to start with due to my habitual desire to add something almost immediately after asking the original question. The pause after asking the question was sometimes painful."[15] When teachers waited and gave more thinking time, the following benefits were observed:

- Answers were longer
- Failure to respond deceased
- Responses were more confident
- Pupils challenged and added to or improved the answers given by other pupils
- More alternative explanations or requests for clarification were made[16]

Pose, Pause, Pounce and Bounce (PPPB)

This highly effective questioning technique was attributed by Dylan Wiliam to an anonymous middle school teacher and summarises good practice within a memorable phrase. First express 'no hands-up' and *pose* a question. Apply 'wait time' and *pause* for either three or up to ten seconds in terms of the level of challenge before a *pounce* i.e. naming a student to answer. Listen to the answer and employ positive, encouraging body language and wait for a further three seconds to give space and time for any additional thoughts. Next *bounce* to another student to see if they can extend or add further detail to the answer given. Equally if a student is clearly stuck and struggling to find an answer, then intervene and *bounce* the question away to another student. Thank the student(s) for their answer and follow up by inviting wider contributions from anyone, popcorn style, in relation to agreement, correction or extension. PPPB promotes involvement and ensures that students stay on their toes because it might be their turn next to answer. Applying the bounce is a key part of the strategy because it permits the spotlight to be shifted away if a student is clearly uncomfortable. Rowe incorporated sensitivity to discomfort into her guidance by inviting students to opt for a 'pass,' although today we might consider substituting the familiar options of 'phone a friend' or 'ask the audience.' Those options offer the recognition that it is OK not to know something. This is a powerful message which feeds into a 'have a go culture' and will over time encourage participation. Rowe also noted that students who opted for a pass often re-engaged with the question after another student's contribution had prompted their memory. If this is not the case teachers should 'rebound' the question back to the original student for agreement and an invitation for 'anything to add' or to ask a related supplementary question. The aim is to remove any sense of embarrassment from the original hesitation and inability to provide an answer and to draw into participation. Warm praise for any contribution is important, especially for those exhibiting CA, to promote a positive rather than a negative feeling from the interaction.

Plan your questions

Beyond the significant questions that may be presented in a big picture lesson plan as described in the last chapter, aim to enter the lesson with a set of pre-planned questions to consolidate and deepen the new learning. Apply your curricular knowledge to generate two sets of questions, taking care to align with the relevant grading hierarchy and programme level as detailed in Chapter 4. The questions should address core knowledge i.e. the minimum knowledge and skills required to achieve a pass and advanced knowledge i.e. the knowledge required to achieve a high learning outcome. Entering a lesson with pre-prepared questions will permit a brisk Q&A pace to be maintained rather than relying upon spontaneity. It also facilitates a planned balance between core and advanced level knowledge checks or a tilt either way as appropriate.

Random selection

When selecting a student to answer a question, teachers tend to gravitate towards students who they identify as confident and more likely to answer. Students within a teacher's immediate field of view are also more likely to be selected than those seated on the periphery. This can lead to low expectations and an unspoken agreement between teachers and some students that their participation is not expected. There is a distinction between coasting and CA. We need to challenge coasters or over time they will drift and not achieve as well as they might. We also need to build the confidence of students exhibiting CA so that they over time find their voice. Without support and steps to draw into participation, a student displaying CA in September will still be reticent in June. Help all to find their voice by applying the following random selection methods:

- **Table numbers** – identify each table with a letter and if more than one student is seated at a table add a seat number e.g. Table A - Seat 3, Table D - Seat 2.

- **Lolly sticks** – this is a Dylan Wiliam favourite. Write the name of each student on a lolly stick and stand in a holder e.g. a mug. Select a stick and when the student has finished answering the question set the stick to one side so that over the course of the lesson every student is selected. Alternatively return the stick to the mug to maintain engagement; otherwise, each student questioned might sit back having answered 'their' question. A wise teacher would also write the names close to one end of the lolly sticks and return to the mug 'upside' down.

- **Photographs** – If you have photographs of your students paste into PowerPoint slides or equivalent and set the transition command to rotate and then freeze frame. Alternatively enter the students' names.

- **Random name generators** – Google random name generators and you will discover a wide selection to download. Most involve a subscription, but classtools.net is free and gives you a 'spin a wheel' generator among other choices.

- **Soft ball** – throw a soft ball to a student and invite them to answer a question. The student in turn throws the ball and whoever catches it answers the next question. Toyshops have a wide collection of soft balls, including more quirky choices like a rubber brick for construction or a teddy bear for childcare, etc. You might consider dividing the class into two teams.

- **Snowball** – write questions on individual sheets of paper and squish together into a ball. Throw the ball to a student and invite to peel off the outermost sheet and read and answer the question. The 'snowball' is then thrown in the air and whoever catches it reads and answers the next question, etc. The questions can be differentiated so they become progressively more demanding as the core is approached and like 'pass the parcel' why not place a wrapped chocolate within the last sheet?

- **Numbered worksheets** – place a number in the top right-hand corner of any handouts planned for use during the lesson or alternatively a coloured dot. Call out a number or a colour.

- **Question chain** – give all the students three to four minutes to write down a question about the topic being studied. The teacher should start the question chain by selecting a student and asking the student a question. After answering the student should name a classmate and ask the named student their pre-prepared question and so on. The initial task of thinking of a question is often as difficult as answering one and will engage all with the curriculum.

The questions posed should involve regular 'fact checker' questions relevant to the topic and occasionally a spelling and/or a definition of a key term to build specialist vocabulary over time. Cotton's guidance is for a 50/50 balance between lower-order and higher-order questions, but there may be a planned imbalance according to the purpose of the lesson as a whole or an episode within the lesson. Ensure this planned imbalance is communicated to an observer in situations of an observed lesson.

Hinge questions

Monitoring progress in real time is highly important to inform a decision whether to move forward or to take a step back. Our aim is to carry everyone forward rather than leaving any students behind because over time this will build a sense that the subject is too difficult and reduce personal confidence. Wiliam recommends introducing a 'hinge' question at the mid-point of a lesson to inform a decision whether to move forward or to take a step back. To be effective the hinge question needs to be narrowly focussed on a single, key learning point central to understanding and to involve all by using one of the above 'all response' questioning techniques. Over time a bank of hinge questions can be developed and aligned with common misconceptions as a standard 'test' of understanding.

Lesson summation

Often the first clue that a teacher receives that the end of the lesson has arrived is the sound of chairs being pushed back and files being packed away. If control is not immediately asserted, some students will be out of their chairs and walking towards the classroom door before the teacher can even say, "See you next week." It is a natural tendency to be tired towards the end of any lesson or any presentation no matter how engaging. Consequently, care must be taken to manage the end of a lesson and, to paraphrase T.S. Eliot, end the lesson with a bang rather than a whimper. Aim to end exactly on time but with sufficient time reserved for a final check on learning by introducing a learning summary and/or exit tickets and finally a bridge to the next lesson. In each case questions are the significant tool.

Summarise

The word precis appears to have disappeared from the educational lexicon, but a short, sharp summary or precis of the key knowledge gained during a lesson provides a powerful check on understanding. Research published by Peper and Mayer

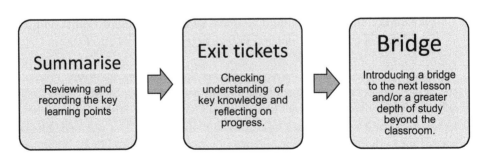

Image 5.7

(1986) revealed that recall was 15% to 17% higher when students summarised key learning points at the end of a lesson rather than simply taking notes during a lesson.[17] The process of writing a summary promotes deep thinking about the information in terms of evaluating, discarding and selecting the key information to record as well as raising questions for clarification. Marzano specified 'summarising and note-taking' as one of his central tenets of effective practice because of the positive impact on memory and retrieval. Allied research into pen and paper note-taking as opposed to note-taking on a laptop has revealed that we should encourage the former. Muller and Oppenheimer's (2014) research[18] revealed that students who took notes on a laptop tended to make verbatim notes because they could type faster than they could write. However, students using pen and paper tended to listen and every few minutes selected and summarised the key points. The significant difference lies between recording rather than processing information. The latter has a higher impact on memory and understanding. The additional negative for laptops is simply the distraction opportunities with too many students observed straying onto social media. Ideally laptops and phones should be switched off in our lessons unless directed for a specific purpose. Follow up the summary task by confirming the key points via question and answer to guard against misconceptions being locked into notes. If you issued a big picture lesson plan at the start of the lesson as described in the last chapter, use the visual template to capture the learning summary. Alternatively, you might consider:

- Capturing a summary of learning as a mind map. At its simplest level, a spider diagram works well.
- Invite all to write a precis of key learning within a single paragraph and to raise any questions that the activity provokes. As a writing prompt suggest that they are writing a summary for someone who was absent and missed the lesson. What did they miss? In real incidences of absence select a student to share their summary with the student(s) who missed the lesson.
- Invite the students to write three key things they have learned during the lesson and compare with their neighbour.
- Place four facts, concepts, photographs, quotations, statistics, etc., drawn from the lesson material on PowerPoint or equivalent but include an odd one or something entirely incorrect. Ask the class to identify the odd one out and to explain the other three.
- Display a single key question and invite all to write an answer in a single paragraph. Select a few students at random to read out their answers and seek agreement and suggestions for addition or correction from the other students.

Exit tickets

An exit ticket can provide feedback on a single targeted aspect of the lesson or more generalised reflection on personal progress. Either way the exit tickets facilitate an easy and quick scan of progress. Exit slips do not have to be applied at the end of every single lesson. They are at their most effective targeting feedback on a specific aspect of learning akin to Wiliam's 'hinge' questions.

Exit tickets can be easily created by using index cards or designing on A4 cards. A single sheet of A4 stiff white card can be used to generate ten exit tickets. Select a bright graphic for the frontispiece of your exit ticket, and using an appropriately sized text box repeat the graphic ten times across and down the A4 sheet. On the reverse of each frontispiece enter the exit question and guillotine to create ten exit tickets yielding a bright title graphic and on the reverse a question. The aim, like the earlier 'hinge' question, is to pose a precise, narrowly focused question linked to the lesson content e.g.

What is the difference between inflation and deflation?
What was the Orthodox interpretation of the Cold War?
Solve the following equation . . .
What is the difference between civil and criminal law?
Give an example of a simile, a metaphor and hyperbole

This precision is preferable to a broad 'how far did you enjoy the lesson' type enquiry. The completed cards should be posted in a box on the way out of the classroom and can be quickly scanned once the students have left the classroom. Place the cards into three piles: correct, partially correct and incorrect. This instant poll should inform a decision to either step forward in the next lesson or to take a step back. The decision will rest on the percentage of correct answers, but clear misconceptions by the class as a whole or individuals should be addressed and corrected. You might also invite the students to add their names to the cards to facilitate placing the students into pairs or small groups at the start of the next lesson e.g. correct ticket holders with those incorrect and invite to discuss and confirm the answer.

The following exit strategies can also work well:

My learning review

Judgement	Self-assessment	Pass actions	Completed
✓	I am confident I understand . . .	I will extend my learning by . . .	
?	I have a few questions about . . .	I will seek answers by . . .	
x	I need more help with . . .	I will re-learn this by . . .	

This self-assessment table is best applied at the end of a unit rather than the end of every lesson to promote metacognition and a learning dialogue with a mentor and/or learning support staff. If you are using a big picture lesson plan as described in Chapter 4, print the table on the reverse. In place of the tick, question mark and cross you might consider using the traffic light colours of green, amber and red or even smiley faces. The significant is the action column to build self-efficacy and to drive a 'can do' spirit to either extend learning, find answers and/or gain help. Marzano identified this form of reflection as a useful prompt to metacognition and he encourages a similar questioning approach, "What are the main ideas of today's lesson? What do you feel most and least sure about? Do you have specific questions about today's lesson? With which aspects of today's class work were you successful?"[19]

- Pin up two sheets of flipchart paper on the classroom wall with the titles 'Got it' and 'Not got it.' Issue two different colours of Post-it notes and direct the students to use one colour for 'Got it' and the other colour for 'Not got it.' All write one point per Post-it note and post on the relevant flipchart paper as they leave the classroom. This generates a fast overview of learning positives and negatives to follow up on in the next lesson.
- Place three to five key learning points developed during the lesson on flipchart paper and pin up on the classroom wall. Issue the students with coloured dots in the traffic light colours of green, amber and red and apply the same prompts as specified in the previous learning review table. Invite the students to 'vote' as they leave the classroom and you will gain a very colourful overview of learning confidence to follow up on in the next lesson. Start the next lesson with the students all standing facing the display and drawn into a progress discussion and re-teach aspects as appropriate. If you want to avoid a stationery bill for coloured dots then employ a tick, a question mark or a cross instead.
- Why not a verbal exit ticket? Specify that the class must correctly answer five questions in a row before they can leave! Select a student at random and pose your first question. If correct select another student and ask question two and so on. However, when someone gives a wrong answer return to question one. You can have some fun with this by asking four straightforward factual questions and then asking a challenging question for question five and if wrong return to question one. This should produce a sense of fun (or rebellion) but once they have had enough ease the challenge sufficiently to allow your students to escape.
- An alternative version is to ask the students to line up by the classroom door. Ask the first student a question. If correct straight out the door for their refreshment break but if wrong direct the student to go to the back of the queue. This may sound cruel, but you can make it basic fact-checker questions that all should know the answers to.

Bridge questions

Our lessons should be part of a learning continuum rather than isolated events, and the key to securing this is to extend learning online between lessons. Marzano specifies 'homework and practice' as one of his nine steps of effective practice with the beneficial purpose: "to prepare students for new content or have them elaborate on content that has been introduced."[20] This is the purpose of the *bridge* i.e. a bridge to the next lesson. The intention is not to set 'homework' because of its negative connotations as a chore but to offer 'extended learning' or 'independent learning' tasks designed to explore topics to a deeper level. All will benefit. The less able students will be more likely to secure a pass after some additional research and the more able a Distinction or a Grade A. The tasks will also be more likely to be completed if they are calculated to take thirty to forty minutes to complete but over time many students may develop an independent study habit and delve deeper and further. Use a Cornell note-taking table or a 'capture and record' worksheet detailed in Chapter 8 to secure evidence of completion. The bridge task also facilitates 'flipped learning' by setting a specific research task to support a future lesson rather than simply a learning extension. In most cases factual research-based questions will work best with the answers used to inform deeper, higher-order discussion within the next lesson. The following are suggested research tasks, and most could inform an appetiser presentation, as described in Chapter 7, by a student or students in a subsequent lesson. Equally some of the appetiser tasks could be identified as bridge task. There is no rigid boundary between the two.

Biography Who was? and how significant was he or she to . . . ?	Devise a standard A4 template with space for a photograph and a series of standard subheadings to trap key information about the individual e.g. key dates, early life, career, contribution. Go for a standard one-page layout to keep it short and sharp with standard sub-headings to prevent a simple print-off or cut and paste from the internet. The aim is to prompt some investigation, reading and summarisation of the individual's career and importance. You might offer a choice of individuals to research because students often like to exercise choice and the outcome is instant classroom display. A student volunteer, with some prompting, may be willing to present the person as an appetiser at the start of the next lesson.
Vocabulary Build and test specialist vocabulary	Issue a list of specialist vocabulary linked to a topic area and invite the students to find and record definitions and examples as appropriate. Test the students during the following lesson and applying the principle of spaced practice at later random intervals. Also test for correct spellings.
Mind map Encourage visual summaries of key knowledge	Invite the students to re-read their lesson notes and to reflect on the content of the lesson and to complete a one-page mind map summary of the key points. Invite all to hold these up in the next lesson. Or apply one of the visual techniques described earlier.
Fact sheet What was the impact of . . . ?	As earlier, but in relation to key places, events, discoveries, equipment, objects, concepts – whatever fits your topic area. In land-based it might be plants or animals, in travel and tourism a holiday resort and in science a discovery, etc.

Read What are the key points made by . . . ?	Specify a reading and note-taking task from a recommended textbook or periodical article held in the library collection or an e-book to encourage the students to explore textbooks. If interest is triggered, the students may select other books to go further and deeper. For best chance of success, specify a chapter to read rather than a whole book, but again many students may elect to read the whole book or books. To check engagement pose a question to answer that draws upon the specified chapter. If interest in the subject is sufficiently aroused, some students may elect to visit a good bookstore and buy useful books to further extend their knowledge. We should encourage a book-buying habit.
Watch What are the key points made by . . . ?	As earlier, but with a direction to watch a specified DVD within the library collection or a YouTube video. Watch might also apply to a scheduled TV programme or a programme available on i-player or other form of 'catch-up' TV. Issue a worksheet with four or five pre-questions to answer while watching the video or use the Cornell note-taking system to provide evidence of engagement with the task.
Chart it What does the data reveal . . .	Most subjects have some key statistics in tables. Invite the students to convert into a pie or other chart in a presentation format of your devising with space for some summary evaluation.
Map it How well is the local area served by . . . ?	Invite the students to find some examples of whatever is being studied and map it. Health and care students might map the local health service in their area, catering students might map the origins of all the vegetables in their local supermarket, travel and tourism students might collect in brochures on a particular destination and map the resorts with arrows and resort descriptions, history students might map a battlefield, business students might map all the fast-food outlets in their local area and identify the scale of competition, etc.
Opinions What are the opinions of other people to . . . ?	To follow up on a class discussion/debate ask the students to find the opinions of five other people in relation to the issue e.g. immediate friends and family, fellow students, neighbours. How far is there a consensus on the issue? Has their personal opinion been affected? You might encourage your students to record a short Tik Tok video or similar or record a podcast.
A-Z Can you find a subject-related word for each letter of the alphabet?	Challenge your students to find a subject-related word for each letter of the alphabet. The most words should win a small prize. Mount as a list on the classroom wall and tease out definitions, descriptions, explanations, etc.
Issues What is being proposed by . . . ?	Invite the students to visit the website of a subject-related government department, charity, museum, organisation or university to examine a new report or significant research findings. This should raise awareness of a source of up-to-date information associated with their career interests.
Careers What jobs of interest can you find linked to your career plan?	Invite the students to find examples of subject-related jobs in specialist periodicals, websites or relevant supplements in the national press. Collate and display key examples. Invite the students to respond to one of the adverts and request the post description and person specification. The specification might reinforce the need for good employability skills, as well as exam passes. The application forms might support a later mock job application and interview activity.

| Chronology
What were the key steps in the development of . . . ? | List the key dates in someone's career, the steps to a discovery or invention, the development of a process or procedure, the evolution of a new organisation or a new development. A simple table to capture the key date or key step down the left-hand column with the appropriate event or development down the right-hand column. Top with a bright title sheet for instant classroom display. |

Image 5.8

The benefit of bridge tasks is not simply the value of the information collated and presented, but introducing our students to managing their time and developing the study skills associated with SRL. The straightforward nature of the tasks should ensure successful completion by all and over time will help to build high self-efficacy. The research involved may also trigger an intrinsic interest in the subject and/or suggest a possible future career pathway. As remote learning and remote working become normalised within our society, it is essential that we help students to develop self-reliance and personal confidence.

References

1 Cotton, Kathleen, *Classroom Questioning, School Improvement Research Series*, Education Northwest, May 1998, pg. 3.
2 Ibid, pg. 9–10.
3 Coe, Robert, *Inaugural Lecture Director of Centre for Evaluation and Monitoring, Improving Education, a Triumph of Hope Over Experience*, Durham University, June 2013, pg. XI, www.cem.org/attachments/publications/ImprovingEducation2013.pdf
4 Ibid, pg. X111.
5 Danielson, Charlotte, *The Framework for Teaching, Evaluation Instrument*, 2013, pg. 59, https://www.nctq.org/dmsView/2013_FfTEvalInstrument_Web_v1_2_20140825
6 Creemers, B. P. M. and Kyriakides, L., *Improving Quality in Education, Dynamic Approaches to School Improvement*, Routledge, 2012, pg. 35.
7 The Sutton Trust, *What Makes Great Teaching*, 31st October 2014, www.suttontrust.com/research-paper/great-teaching/
8 Ibid.
9 Rosenshine, Barack, Principles of instruction: Research based strategies that all teachers should know, *Journal of American Educator*, Spring 2012, pg. 14.
10 Ibid, pg. 14.
11 Black, P. and William, D., *Inside the Black Box: Raising Standards Through Classroom Assessment*, Phi Delta Kappa International, 1998, pg. 6.

12 Marzano, Robert J., *Classroom Instruction That Works*, Association for Supervision and Curriculum Development, 2001, pg. 55.

13 Wiliams, Dylan, *Embedded Formative Assessment*, Solution Tree Press, 2011, pg. 81.

14 Budd-Rowe, Mary, *Journal of Teacher Education Wait Time: Slowing Down May Be a Way of Speeding Up*, pg. 1, www.scoe.org/blog_files/Budd%20Rowe.pdf

15 Black, Paul and Wiliam, Dylan, *Assessment for Learning: Putting It into Practice*, Open University Press, 2007, pg. 33.

16 Ibid, pg. 33.

17 Peper, Richard J. and Mayer, Richard E., Generative effects of note-taking during science lectures, *Journal of Educational Psychology*, vol. 78, no. 1, 1986, pg. 34–38.

18 Mueller, Pam A. and Oppenheimer, Daniel M., The pen is mightier than the keyboard: Advantages longhand over laptop note-taking, *Psychological Science*, vol. 25, no. 6, 2014, pg. 1159–1168.

19 Marzano, Robert J., *The New Art and Science of Teaching*, Solution Tree Press, 2017, pg. 59.

20 Marzano, Robert J., *Classroom Instruction That Works*, Association for Supervision and Curriculum Development, 2001, pg. 59.

Questions to extend and deepen learning

Parents are very familiar with the regular 'why' questions asked by their three-year-old children:

- Why does the moon change shape?
- Why do frogs hop rather than run?
- Why is grass green?
- Why does it go dark?
- Why do I have to go to bed?

Curiosity is the common link between the questions. Children are fascinated by the world around them and they want answers. If the answers fail to satisfy, they will re-ask and, as all parents know, they will continue to ask 'why' until they feel they have received a satisfactory reply. As teenagers the curiosity we felt as children often returns when we explore with friends, sometimes late into the night, the 'big' questions from the realms of philosophy:

- Is life just a dream?
- Does free will exist?
- What existed before the 'Big Bang'?
- Are we all living in a glass tank on some alien's shelf?
- What is truth?
- Does God (or Gods) exist?

The late Sir Ken Robinson firmly believed that curiosity is the key to learning. If we can stimulate curiosity, we can perhaps spark a quest to know more and ultimately trigger intrinsic motivation.

DOI: 10.4324/9781003132783-8

A learning culture

Stirring curiosity and capturing interest is the first major step towards extending and deepening learning because it will produce a sense of purpose and significance, and this can translate into a positive learning culture whereby students gain the confidence to ask as well as answer questions. The 'bridge tasks' suggested in the last chapter are designed to extend knowledge beyond the immediate study goals and to promote self-regulated learning (SRL). In addition, looking to the horizon by posing 'big questions' (see Chapter 15) in relation to future social and technological developments can generate if not an intrinsic interest, at least a Google search or perhaps the motivation to take a book off the shelf and to independently pursue a topic of interest. The aim is to build the confidence of all students to ask questions and to use effective questioning techniques to bridge the gap between lower- and higher-order reasoning. The latter should step beyond targeting high exam grades to encouraging relevant original and creative thinking. Although this is largely associated with university level, much younger students are fully capable of original thinking, as illustrated by the many examples presented in Chapter 15. Higher-order thinking and reasoning can be nurtured and developed by applying the following questioning strategies:

1 Regularly acknowledging and switching between lower-order 'fact checker' questions and higher-order conceptual questions
2 Allowing sufficient wait (thinking) time
3 Asking higher-order conceptual questions of all students rather than a selected few
4 Seeking evidence for answers
5 Building dialogue – the ability to extend and contextualise answers
6 Inviting reflection and students' own questions

Those good practice considerations are reflected in Charlotte Danielson's hierarchy of questioning competencies.

Danielson's questioning competencies

Danielson's questioning competencies are part of a comprehensive framework for effective teaching and learning comprising four domains and twenty-two separate elements of professional practice. The four domains are:

- Planning and Preparation,
- Classroom Environment,

- Instruction,
- Professional Responsibilities.

Each domain is subdivided into 'elements' and elaborated across four levels of competence i.e. unsatisfactory, basic, proficient and distinguished. Danielson notes, "Questioning and discussion are the only instructional strategies specifically referred to in the Framework for Teaching, a decision that reflects their central importance to teachers' practice."[1] Danielson details the following questioning competencies:[2]

This hierarchy stretches from a base of low cognitive challenge and limited student involvement to a high cognitive challenge with full student involvement including evidence of emerging metacognitive intelligence i.e. becoming self-aware with the intellectual maturity to listen to conflicting opinions, to question one's own assumptions and to modify one's own views in response to reasoned argument.

Level One Unsatisfactory	Level Two Basic	Level Three Proficient	Level Four Distinguished
The teacher's questions are of low cognitive challenge, with single correct responses, and are asked in rapid succession. Interaction between the teacher and students is predominantly recitation style, with the teacher mediating all questions and answers; the teacher accepts all contributions without asking students to explain their reasoning. Only a few students participate in the discussion.	The teacher's questions lead students through a single path of inquiry, with answers seemingly determined in advance. Alternatively, the teacher attempts to ask some questions designed to engage students in thinking, but only a few students are involved. The teacher attempts to engage all students in the discussion, to encourage them to respond to one another and to explain their thinking, with uneven results.	While the teacher may use some low-level questions, he or she poses questions designed to promote student thinking and understanding. The teacher creates a genuine discussion among students, providing adequate time for students to respond and stepping aside when doing so is appropriate. The teacher challenges students to justify their thinking and successfully engages most students in the discussion, employing a range of strategies to ensure that most students are heard.	The teacher uses a variety or series of questions or prompts to challenge students cognitively, advance high-level thinking and discourse and promote metacognition. Students formulate many questions, initiate topics, challenge one another's thinking and make unsolicited contributions. Students themselves ensure that all voices are heard in the discussion.

Image 6.1

Lower- and higher-order debate

Factual knowledge and conceptual knowledge are two sides of the same coin. We must avoid the assumption that lower-order questions are bad and higher-order questions are good. In 2014 Marzano published the outcomes of a survey across thirty-nine research studies conducted between 1965 and 2006 and concluded "the research on higher versus lower-order questions is equivocal. There is no clear indication as to the superiority of one versus another."[3] It is a question of clarity of purpose. Questions do not have to rise from lower order to higher order within every single lesson. Danielson's distinguished level is a goal. It represents the end of a successful process of learning development not the beginning. Danielson commented,

> Not all questions must be at a high cognitive level in order for a teacher's performance to be rated at a high level; that is, when exploring a topic, a teacher might begin with a series of questions of low cognitive challenge to provide a review, or to ensure that everyone in the class is "on board.[4]

Teachers should be clear as to the purpose of their questions either to check and secure factual core knowledge or to check for the acquisition and confident extension of relevant concepts. The latter should include the correct use of specialist vocabulary, including spelling and punctuation. We perhaps all remember the embarrassment of saying hyper-bole for the first time before discovering that the correct pronunciation is hy-perb-o-le. Marzano advised, "student achievement will increase by 33 percentile points when vocabulary instruction focuses on specific words that are important to what students are learning."[5] The first page in student files should ideally be a glossary of terms to capture new vocabulary and concepts along with their definitions and remember to address accurate pronunciation as appropriate. Draw attention to a word search on Google which apart from displaying the meaning will include a clickable speaker icon to hear an accurate pronunciation of the word. Facts are the start of a learning journey, and our lessons should be peppered with regular 'fact checker' questions to help all to find their voice and to build a firm base of core knowledge. The best confidence boost any student can receive is their own self-awareness of knowing and providing correct answers to questions. Cotton advised, "When predominantly low- level questions are used, their level of difficulty should be such that most will elicit correct responses."[6] Correct answers boost self-esteem and will encourage students to engage with further and higher-level questions. This is a significant point because as Cotton's research revealed, there is a danger we may end up only selecting students we identify as more able to answer higher order questions, "Students whom teachers perceive as slow or poor learners are asked fewer higher cognitive questions than students perceived as more capable learners."[7] If this becomes a regular habit, then weaker students or those exhibiting communication apprehension (CA) will not be stretched or helped to develop their confidence, and worse, they will quickly identify the pattern of questions and/or being skipped over and, by extension, their teachers' low expectations of them. Our goal is to advance the progress of all students. It is common for many students to simply 'not get it' as they struggle to shift from concrete to conceptual reasoning. Teachers need to be alert to individual sticking points in relation to Piaget's step up from concrete to formal reasoning.

Applying Piaget

Jean Piaget (1896–1980) was a Swiss biologist who studied how children perceive the world, make sense of what they see and construct meaning. He articulated four stages of cognitive development from early childhood to adulthood:

- sensorimotor – motor zero to two years, sensing the world and permanence of objects
- Pre-operational thought two to seven years, concrete, factual responses
- Concrete operational seven to twelve years, applying logic, absorbing other points of view and exploring concepts
- Formal operational twelve and up, thinking in abstract or hypothetical terms and applying analogies

The first two stages govern the early life experiences of children as they explore and observe the world around them, and the final two stages mark the transition from concrete to abstract reasoning. The original underpinning research arose from the teaching of mathematics, but the division between lower-order and higher-order thinking and reasoning is well-established and governs the grading structures of most qualifications. Pass or fail competency-based programmes are the exception, but even here higher commercial or industrial standards exist beyond mere competency. Piaget's chronology should not be regarded as fixed. He later regretted attaching age bands to his stages, and current research confirms that cognitive development is much more fluid than the age bands would suggest. The Deans for Impact consortium of American universities concluded, "Cognitive development does not progress through a fixed sequence of age-related stages. The mastery of new concepts happens in fits and starts."[8] The American Psychological Association reached the same conclusion. The third principle of their Twenty Principles governing effective teaching states, "students' cognitive development and learning are not limited by general stages of development."[9] Essentially the shift from concrete (factual) to abstract (conceptual) reasoning takes longer for some children than others and is not firmly linked to age group. However, Piaget's core distinction between concrete and abstract reasoning has stood the test of time. Hattie ranked Piagetian programs or interventions as second in his overall rank list of 138 influences on achievement in relation to the importance of knowing and reacting to students' thinking processes. Hattie reported that "fewer than 50 per cent of (school) year 11 and 12 students are formal operational thinkers,"[10] with significant implications for progress. The Sutton Trust review of the factors underpinning great teaching commented, "As well as a strong understanding of the material being taught, teachers must also understand the ways students think about the content, be able to evaluate the thinking behind students' own methods, and identify students' common misconceptions."[11] It is at this point that the ability of a teacher to offer alternative explanations, analogies, metaphors or examples becomes significant to help bridge the learning gap for each student. In addition, it highlights the benefit of paired and group discussion to help reveal students' misconceptions. Encouraging peer dialogue and listening to responses can help to pinpoint stumbling blocks and assist all to bridge the cognitive gap from concrete to abstract thinking and reasoning. This shift in thinking is most often associated with framing questions in line with Bloom's Taxonomy, but this was not a purpose endorsed by Bloom.

Bloom's Taxonomy

The extension of Bloom's Taxonomy to questioning arose from the work of Norris Sanders from the University of Wisconsin who published *Classroom Questions: What Kinds?* in 1966. Sanders's book popularised the idea of formulating questions against Bloom's cognitive hierarchy from knowledge to evaluation to prompt teachers to extend their questions from lower to higher order. Bloom's Taxonomy was subsequently applied to framing questions in addition to objectives by most teacher training programmes. The University of Cambridge, Faculty of Education website, for instance, recommends the use of Bloom's Taxonomy to shape higher-order questions: "When you are planning higher-level questions, you will find it useful to use Bloom's taxonomy of educational objectives to help structure questions which will require higher-level thinking."[12] The leading educationalist and writer Robert J. Marzano has described Bloom's taxonomy as a "misapplied framework"[13] and states "the current practice of using Bloom's taxonomy to classify individual questions is an ineffective scheme around which to frame teacher questioning."[14] The educational blogger and author David Didau goes further by highlighting that Bloom's Taxonomy was "essentially plucked from the air" during a brainstorming session with no known research base and, more damning, "using Bloom's to design sequences of lessons is barely more useful than palmistry."[15] The primary criticisms of Bloom's Taxonomy relate to the assumption of linear cognitive development, the accuracy of pegging knowledge against the six levels of the hierarchy and finally, the observation that a high-level question doesn't necessarily result in a high-level answer and might simply trigger recall i.e. parroting a known response.

Applying the SOLO taxonomy

SOLO is an acronym for Structure of Observed Learning Outcomes and is regarded by many teachers as a superior guide to differentiation because it reflects stages of learning development rather than Bloom's focus on knowledge acquisition. It stems from the research of the educational psychologists John Biggs and Kevin Collis who published *Evaluating the Quality of Learning: The SOLO Taxonomy* in 1982. Biggs and Collis commented, "the difference essentially is that the Bloom levels are a priori ones imposed in advance by the teacher; whereas we would prefer to use levels that arise 'naturally' in the understanding of the material."[16] SOLO identifies five levels of student responses from 'pre-structural' essentially meaning 'I've no idea' through to 'extended abstract' at the higher end, but like Bloom's Taxonomy it was never designed as a guide to classroom questioning practice. The extension of the SOLO taxonomy to questioning was largely undertaken by the educationalist Pam Hook. She received Bigg's endorsement for her many SOLO-based publications and developed an app for questions based on the SOLO hierarchy:

> Using SOLO Taxonomy as a framework, this app generates questions to bring in ideas (to build surface understanding); questions to connect ideas (to develop deep understanding) and questions to extend ideas (to create conceptual understanding). Use the SOLO coded question banks within the app or create your own, either way you will learn how to ask great questions – relevant, appropriate and substantial questions.[17]

However, in practice it is not possible to divorce the process of learning from knowledge acquisition. Rather than trying to frame questions against the gradations of a generic taxonomy, the most effective and robust approach is to apply domain-specific curricular knowledge. As detailed in Chapter 4 only two levels of questions are significant: core knowledge (pass level) and advanced knowledge (high level) linked to the programme standards. This binary approach to the curriculum standards can help all students to grow in confidence by securing correct answers to core knowledge questions and from this base stepping up to answering advanced-level questions. Above this a challenge category is recommended to promote deep thinking and to raise horizons beyond the immediate curriculum goals. Kahnemann distinguished between System One and System Two thinking.[18] Imagine walking with a friend and engaging in everyday chat and your friend asks the question what is 7×7? You will answer 49 without much difficulty as you continue to walk because of the low cognitive challenge. This is System One thinking but what if your companion posed the question, multiply 247×6? It is highly probable that you would stop walking in order to focus your whole attention on calculating the answer. This is System Two thinking i.e. a question or task that prompts full concentration and deep thinking. Socrates perhaps expressed it best when he remarked, "I cannot teach anybody anything. I can only make them think."[19] Ensure your questions regularly extend into System Two to engender deep thinking and prompt dialogue.

Marzano's questioning sequence

Marzano advises similar progression within a four-stage questioning sequence by stepping from a base of domain specific concrete information to conceptual reasoning.

Image 6.2

The first step, 'details,' is orientated towards identifying and questioning the core factual knowledge in relation to a curriculum topic. The students first examine specified sources of information and build an agreed, concrete factual knowledge base. This is an approach that interlinks well with flipped learning by collating information in advance of a lesson. The second stage involves placing the information into relevant categories by identifying similar characteristics or relationships. For instance, facts and information regarding the outbreak of the First World War will involve discussion, questioning and categorisation into long term, short term and immediate causes of the war. Within a travel and tourism lesson, the facts about a holiday resort may be questioned and categorised into features of luxury hotels as against budget hotels, key attractions by region, key activities for different age groups, etc. This process of engaging with the factual information base involves identifying similarities and differences and clarifying reasons for decisions. Different levels of prior knowledge will also come into play as the facts are allocated to categories and lead to discussion, questions and beneficial exchanges between students. What may be a higher-order consideration for one student may not be for another student. Marzano's stages are based on building and consolidating curriculum information rather than a cognitive hierarchy like the Bloom or SOLO taxonomies. In practice, lower-order and higher-order reasoning and questions may arise at any stage as students engage with the curriculum information. As Marzano states, "In effect, any scheme to focus on one specific type of question for example, 'higher-order' questions to the neglect of another type for example, 'lower-order' questions is most probably doomed to failure."[20] The 'elaboration' stage focusses on a review of the decisions made and promotes an ability to justify and defend categories and conclusions and this in turn may trigger a return to checking the factual base. In relation to the First World War example, it would be important for the students to be able to defend their choices of long-term, short-term and immediate causes of the war. In terms of the travel and tourism lesson, questioning the definition and features of a luxury hotel as against a budget hotel, etc. The level of 'elaboration' expected from the students should be set against the programme standards. The final 'evidence' stage is designed to promote robust learning outcomes by discussing and questioning the students' decision making and conclusions. Marzano recommended a five-fold evidence test:

- The reliability of the sources of the information,
- The reasons for a particular conclusion,

- The identification of any possible flaws i.e. overlooked evidence, things not considered,
- The identification of any errors or mistakes,
- The consideration of different perspectives which might alter the conclusions.

Marzano's model encourages students to think carefully about the subject information and to raise questions as they occur rather than stepping through a predetermined cognitive hierarchy, "unlike previous guidance given to teachers about asking questions, our questioning sequence embraces all "levels" of questions acknowledging that each has its proper place and is very powerful when used in the right way at the right time."[21] The four stages may be completed within a single lesson in a 'quick-fire' questioning sequence to critically examine a given topic or in situations of a more detailed in-depth study spread across several lessons,

> although an entire questioning sequence can be conducted within a single class period, it is common for questioning sequences to extend across two or more class periods. This is usually the case when students work in groups or use external sources to answer questions at various phases.[22]

The reference to using external resources encompasses internet research, text, data, real objects, video and even guest speakers. Marzano does not use the term 'Socratic question and answer,' but his evidence stage reflects the Socratic method.

Socratic method

Socrates (469–399 BC) famously guided petitioners by a process of dialogue to arrive at answers to their own questions. By adopting a position of ignorance, he questioned assumptions, tested evidence and exposed contradictions. Engaging in dialogue is an approach to learning pursued by most of our leading universities including the much-admired University of Oxford tutorial system in relation to cycling through an ever-reducing sequence of question and answer to encourage deep reflection and self-questioning. Oxford's approach is described as "teaching with a Socratic spirit" and "teaching that is dialogical (wherein the student learns to question the thinking of others and to expect his or her thinking to be questioned by others)."[23] Dialectical reasoning adopts a similar approach. The difference is that whereas dialectical reasoning seeks to resolve and arrive at a conclusion between opposing beliefs or propositions, dialogical reasoning is concerned with examining and understanding different opinions and ideas without necessarily seeking a resolution. Socrates employed six main forms of questions designed to apply critical reasoning and as far as possible to separate fact from opinion or unsupported assumptions.

1 Questions for clarification	Why do you think that? What do you mean by . . .? Are you saying . . . ? Can you tell me more about what you mean? Can you give me an example?
2 Questions to probe assumptions	Why do you assume . . . ? Are there other opinions? Please explain why . . . ?
3 Questions to probe reasons and evidence	What evidence do you have? Why do you think this is true? How do you know this? Would it stand up in court?
4 Questions about viewpoints and perspectives	What alternatives are there? Can you summarise the strengths and weaknesses? Are you saying . . .? Who would benefit from this?
5 Questions about implications and consequences	How could we test this? What would happen if? Why is this important? If we do nothing what would be the result?
6 Questions about questions	Are we asking the right question? What are you trying to say? What was the point of your question? Do you see what I mean?

Image 6.3

Socratic questioning is very powerful because it helps to build metacognitive thinking e.g. *How do I know that? Why do I think that? Can I justify that statement?* Socratic questioning can promote objective reasoning by ensuring, as far as possible, that decisions and conclusions are underpinned by evidence rather than emotional attachment, confirmation bias or even guesswork. Rosenshine's 'Principles of Instruction' included the following examples of Socratic style question roots to extend and deepen dialogue:[24]

How are ? and ? alike?
What is the main idea of?
What are the strengths and weaknesses of?
In what ways is? related to?
Compare? and? with regard to?
What do you think causes?
How does? tie in with what we have learned before?
Which one is the best? and why?
What are some possible solutions for the problem of?
Do you agree or disagree with this statement?
What do you still not understand about?

Applying Socratic questioning can significantly strengthen learning because the students are drawn into questioning their own assumptions and ultimately why they hold a particular opinion. At its most basic, the questioner is assuming complete ignorance of the issue and probing deeper and deeper as to why an answer is the correct answer.

Extended study

Few programmes outside of a university education address higher reasoning. The major exceptions are the International Baccalaureate (www.ibo.org) and the Extended Project Qualification offered by most UK examination boards. The IBO 16–19 Diploma includes the Theory of Knowledge (TOK) as a core study programme for all students. The IBO website describes the Theory of Knowledge programme as follows:

> As a thoughtful and purposeful inquiry into different ways of knowing, and into different kinds of knowledge, TOK is composed almost entirely of questions.
>
> The most central of these is "How do we know?", while other questions include:
>
> ■ What counts as evidence for X?
> ■ How do we judge which is the best model of Y?
> ■ What does theory Z mean in the real world?
>
> Through discussions of these and other questions, students gain greater awareness of their personal and ideological assumptions, as well as developing an appreciation of the diversity and richness of cultural perspectives.[25]

The IBO questioning model reflects the Socratic tradition of employing inductive reasoning to probe and explore knowledge and beliefs through a question and answer dialogue. All too often cultural beliefs and religious faith limit and distort reasoning and our highest educational goal is to develop the ability to question.

The Extended Project Qualification (EPQ) is attracting growing interest and entries across the UK. From a low base of just over 5,000 entries in 2009 the entries now top 40,000 per year. It demonstrates that many of our students do actively seek stretch and challenge and relish extended study. The projects are ordinarily 5,000 words but the outcomes may also be in the form of an artefact, a presentation or the management and organisation of an event. The Assessment and Qualifications Alliance (AQA) examination board highlights the benefits of undertaking an EPQ as follows:

> By taking responsibility for the choice and design of an individual project (or an individual role in a group project) students:
>
> ■ become more critical, reflective and independent learners
> ■ develop and apply decision-making and problem-solving skills

- increase their planning, research, analysis, synthesis, evaluation and presentation skills
- learn to apply new technologies confidently
- demonstrate creativity, initiative and enterprise.[26]

The Harkness seminar method

To deepen discussion and to apply Socratic question and answer techniques, consider applying the Harkness seminar style questioning of a key topic.

The following diagram of an oval table illustrates the classic Harkness method of promoting student discussion. Edward Harkness (1874–1940) was an American heir to an oil fortune who administered a family foundation devoted to promoting education. His original and surviving concept was to seat no more than twelve students around an oval table and to engage in a seminar whereby the teacher chaired a discussion to interrogate and discuss a key concept. The oval table is reputed to promote effective discussion because the physical proximity engages all and literally removes the 'back seat' of the traditional classroom rows and the psychology of a head of table. Negative or passive behaviour is also reduced because the teacher is not the focal point. The discussion is centre stage with a focus on exploring, questioning and evaluating a key concept. This in turn raises the responsibility of all to enter the classroom having researched the topic. The underpinning information is absorbed outside the classroom, and the lesson time is devoted to discussing the key facts and different opinions supported by evidence. Again, this approach interlinks well with flipped learning. The aim is to arrive at a consensus to surface any misunderstandings and to improve critical thinking by listening to alternative opinions. The Harkness method was first adopted in 1931 by the Philips Exeter Academy in New Hampshire and is now practised in many American and English schools – although largely in the independent sector. The Sutton Trust has identified the high confidence levels of students from the independent sector as a key factor underpinning their success at university level and later dominance of leadership and professional roles. All students should be regularly involved in expressing, sustaining and justifying their personal opinions. The difficulty for most schools and colleges is that classes sizes stretch far beyond twelve students, nor do most

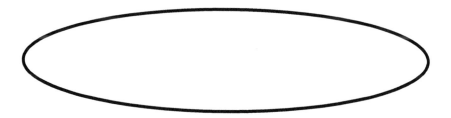

Image 6.4

classrooms have space for a large oval table. Therefore, a pragmatic solution and a fast way to experiment with the Harkness method is to re-arrange classroom desks to form a rectangle and to implement the spirit of Harkness if not the physical oval reality. Select your twelve students to engage in the seminar and invite the rest of the students to observe the dialogue and to engage in a post discussion meta-analysis of the outcomes and effectiveness of the different contributions i.e. what have we learned? What has been clarified? What questions are still outstanding? Over time all students should have an opportunity to be seated around the table.

Around the table

How do we elaborate knowledge around the table? Consider the following approaches:

- Expect advance reading/research.
- Invite all to make an initial statement of their opinion.
- Introduce Socratic questioning and permit initial 'popcorn' spontaneous responses in response rather than directing questions to individuals.
- Gather in the key positives and negatives or points for and against as appropriate.
- Give thinking time – teachers should stand back – silence encourages reflection.
- Seek further debate and arrive at a consensus.
- Summarise and confirm conclusions – check recording.
- Stretch all – suggest extension activities to further extend learning.

Clearly you need to consider the level and ability of students if this is to work well. Some will need much more structure to guide their advance research than others and more in-class support with clear step by step prompts to advance and build the discussion.

References

1 Danielson, Charlotte, *The Framework for Teaching, Evaluation Instrument*, 2013, pg. 59, https://www.nctq.org/dmsView/2013_FfTEvalInstrument_Web_v1_2_20140825
2 Ibid, pg. 62–63.
3 Marzano, Robert J. and Simms, Julia A., *Questioning Sequences in the Classroom*, Marzano Research, 2014, pg. 10.
4 Danielson, Charlotte, *The Framework for Teaching, Evaluation Instrument*, 2013, pg. 59, https://www.nctq.org/dmsView/2013_FfTEvalInstrument_Web_v1_2_20140825
5 Marzano, Robert J., *Classroom Instruction That Works*, Association for Supervision and Curriculum Development, 2001, pg. 127.

6 Cotton, Kathleen, *Classroom Questioning, School Improvement Research Series*, Education Northwest, May 1998, pg. 4.

7 Ibid, pg. 4.

8 Deans for Impact, *The Science of Learning*, Deans for Impact, 2015, pg. 3.

9 American Psychological Association, *Top Twenty Principles from Psychology for Pre K-12 Teaching and Learning*, American Psychological Association, 2015, pg. 4.

10 Hattie John, *Visible Learning for Teachers*, Routledge, 2012, pg. 44.

11 Coe, Robert, et al., *What Makes Great Teaching*, The Sutton Trust, 2014, pg. 2.

12 University of Cambridge, Faculty of Education, *Teacher Approaches: Questioning*, http://oer.educ.cam.ac.uk/wiki/Teaching_Approaches/Questioning accessed 28th October 2020.

13 Marzano, Robert J., *Questioning Sequences in the Classroom*, Marzano Research, 2014, pg. 5.

14 Ibid.

15 Didau, David, *What if Everything You Knew About Education Was Wrong?* Crown House Publishing, 2015, pg. 149–153.

16 Biggs, John B. and Collis, Kevin F., *Evaluating the Quality of Learning, the Solo Taxonomy, Structure of the Observed Learning Outcome*, Academic Press, 1982, pg. 13.

17 Hook, Pam, http://pamhook.com/solo-apps/

18 Kahemann, Daniel, *Thinking Fast and Slow*, Allen Lane, 2011.

19 Socrates, www.goodreads.com/quotes/73059

20 Marzano, Robert J. and Simms, Julia A., *Questioning Sequences in the Classroom*, Marzano Research, 2014, pg. 13.

21 Ibid, pg. 31.

22 Ibid, pg. 77.

23 Oxford University, *The Oxford Tutorial and Critical Thinking*, 2008, www.criticalthinking.org/pages/the-2nd-international-academy-on-critical-thinking-oxford-20/581

24 Rosenshine, B., Principles of instruction: Research based strategies that all teachers should know, *Journal of American Educator*, Spring 2012, pg. 14.

25 International Baccalaureate Organisation, *Theory of Knowledge*, www.ibo.org.uk

26 www.aqa.org.uk/subjects/projects/project-qualifications/EPQ-7993/why-choose

Elaboration

Dynamic direct instruction

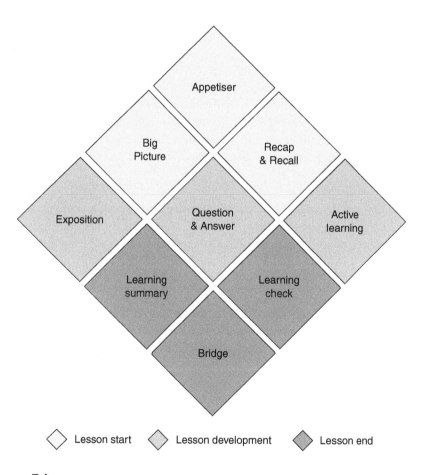

Image 7.1

DOI: 10.4324/9781003132783-10

The Diamond Lesson Plan (DLP) presents a dynamic model for direct instruction (di) that is designed to promote stimulating, imaginative and inspiring lessons. Direct instruction is often misconstrued. It is not dictation, rote learning, lecture or copying notes from the board. Direct instruction is highly starred within educational research as one of the most effective forms of teaching and learning because it combines precise explanation with time for reflection and review. This was firmly underscored in 2006 in a review of research evidence conducted by the educational psychologists – professors Clark, Kirschner and Sweller and reconfirmed in 2012:

> Decades of research clearly demonstrate that for novices (comprising virtually all students) direct, explicit instruction is more effective and more efficient than partial guidance. So, when teaching new content and skills to novices teachers are more effective when they provide explicit guidance accompanied by practice and feedback, not when they require students to discover many aspects of what they must learn.[1]

Marzano examined 580 research comparisons between direct instruction and discovery learning and arrived at the same conclusion, "Direct instruction is superior to discovery learning in most situations . . . direct instruction is essential when teachers present new content to students."[2] Equally Hattie's comprehensive surveys of the major influences on achievement (2009 and 2012) confirmed the high impact of direct instruction and summarised the major steps as follows,

> the teacher decides the learning intentions and success criteria, makes them transparent to the students, demonstrates them by modelling, evaluates if they understand what they have been told by checking for understanding, and retelling them what they have been told by tying it all together with closure.[3]

Finally, Petty was more effuse in his endorsement of direct instruction, "this is the world champion and Olympic-gold-medal-winner of teaching methods . . . if all teachers used it whenever it was appropriate, all our students would do almost two grades better in their exams."[4]

Well-planned direct instruction can communicate a passion for learning that can at least engage, if not enthuse and inspire, all students. The significant gain for students is that teachers can use their expert subject knowledge to cut through the information clutter to focus attention on the significant points. The DLP weaves together the recommended key elements of effective direct instruction and aims to stir curiosity, enthuse and ultimately inspire.

Direct Instruction (DI) or direct instruction (di)

There are two major forms of direct instruction. Direct Instruction (DI), upper-case, is primarily associated with 'scripted' or programmed learning developed by Siegfried Engelmann in the 1960s, whereas direct instruction (di) lowercase is associated with a recommended sequence of teacher instruction primarily arising from 'teacher effectiveness' research in the 1970s. DI emerged from the DISTAR research programme (Direct Instruction Systems in Arithmetic and Reading) as a step-by-step sequence of teaching arithmetic and reading using mastery learning principles. DISTAR was tested as one of twenty-two models of instruction in the largest ever educational research programme in the United States entitled, *Project Follow Through* (1967–1997). DISTAR, later abbreviated to DI, consistently produced the highest learning outcomes. Kim and Axelrod noted, "The students in the Direct Instruction programs improved, on average, from about the 20th percentile to the 41st percentile in reading scores alone."[5] More recently in January 2018 a review of the impact of DI arising from 328 separate research studies conducted between 1966 and 2016 demonstrated that DI resulted in statistically significant performance gains.[6] Engelmann established the National Institute for Direct Instruction (nifdi.org) in 1997 to extend and promote DI with common 'scripts' for teachers to follow to ensure consistency of standards between different teachers and different schools. The scripts and linked resources freed teachers from lesson preparation in favour of allocating more time for monitoring and correcting and coaching students' performance. Those advantages were outweighed for many by the lack of choice over topic content, selected resources and the specified teaching and learning methods. However, the principles underpinning DI are increasingly being applied in the development of online personalised learning programmes (PLPs), with students following standardised learning pathways. DI in the form of online 'instructional design' may well become a standard component of future learning as detailed in Chapter 16.

The more common usage of the term direct instruction (di) applying the lowercase abbreviation relates to the outcomes of 'teacher effectiveness' observational research programmes. In a succession of overlapping research studies in the 1970s and early 1980s observers catalogued and isolated the key instructional steps common to teachers whose students consistently gained high examination pass rates. Rosenshine and Stevens summarised and confirmed the major steps as follows:[7]

- Begin a lesson with a short statement of goals.
- Present new material in small steps, providing for student practice after each step.
- Give clear and detailed instructions and explanations.
- Provide a high level of active practice for all students.
- Ask a large number of questions, check for student understanding, and obtain response from all students.

- Guide students during initial practice.
- Provide systematic feedback and corrections.
- Provide explicit instruction and practice for seatwork exercises and monitor students during seatwork.

These steps are integral to the DLP.

Instructional guidance

Guidelines for effective instruction have a long history dating back to the 'father' of modern-day pedagogy, Johann Herbart (1776–1841). Herbart's five principles of effective instruction first published in 1806, as presented in Chapter 1, detailed a sequence of instruction that dominated lesson planning into the early 20th century. In 1910 the author Fennell produced a volume of lesson plans based on the Herbartian method and praised the Herbartian steps as "lucid and concise and must infallibly prove extremely helpful to new teachers."[8]

In the interwar period Henry C. Morrison's five instructional steps allied to mastery learning principles also attracted many adherents. The Morrison Method identified a sequence of five interlocking steps: 1) pre-test to gauge prior learning, 2) teaching the new content, 3) testing the result of instruction, 4) changing the instruction procedure, as necessary and 5) teaching and testing again until the unit has been completely mastered by the students. His principles still find expression today and particularly in recommendations for adaptive teaching. In 1962 Glaser (1921–2012) introduced four widely adopted instructional steps as the core of effective teacher practice:

1 Instructional objectives (sharing the learning intentions)
2 Entering behaviour (establishing and building upon prior learning)
3 Instructional procedure (varied range of teaching and learning strategies)
4 Evaluation (gaining feedback and positive checks on progress).

Over a decade later in 1974 Robert M Gagne (1916–2002) detailed a set of more precise sub-steps designed to guide the interactions between teachers and students with a focus on learning outcomes:[9]

1 Gain attention.
2 Inform the learner of the objective.
3 Stimulate the recall of prerequisite learning.
4 Present stimulus material.
5 Provide learning guidance.
6 Elicit the performance.

7   Provide feedback about performance correctness.
8   Assess the performance.
9   Enhance information retention and transfer.

Gagne, writing well before the popularisation of neuroscience, identified the limitations of working memory and the importance of regular retrieval practice to strengthen and imprint new knowledge into long-term memory. His instructional steps specified the value of an "attention grabbing" opening, the clarity of lesson objectives, the balance between presenting and assimilating new knowledge and finally a plenary with a focus on checking learning retention over time.

Direct instruction models tend to have a marmite quality in relation to repelling and attracting teachers and academics in fairly equal measure. Whereas many teachers gain confidence from a recommended sequence of instruction, others see regimentation, the suppression of individual teacher creativity and limits on student participation. At its most basic critics question whether the 'art' of teaching can be reduced to a single good practice checklist. Donald Clark in a 2006 blog-post dismissed Gagne's nine steps as "an instructional ladder that leads straight to Dullsville."[10] However, there are few professions or businesses that operate without any consensus on good practice systems or procedures. It would also be unusual if after 200 years of compulsory education no consensus had arisen as to the core elements of an effective lesson. In 1982 Dr Madeline Hunter published 'Instructional Theory into Practice' (ITIP) summarising the core good practice elements arising from lesson observations.

Hunter's lesson plan

Madeline Hunter (1916–1994) spent a major part of her career as a head teacher before finishing her career as a professor of education in the University of California Los Angeles (UCLA). Hunter wrote numerous articles and was the author of twelve books on different aspects of effective teaching practice, but she is best known for Hunter's lesson plan.

Hunter never specified a fixed-order lesson plan but the seven steps, or eight or nine if the sub-steps included within 'input' are counted, became the popular interpretation of her ITIP guidelines. The widespread adoption of her model demonstrated that teachers welcomed practical guidance, but the model was criticised by many academics as a formulaic approach to teaching and learning that de-professionalised teachers. In 1987, Slavin complained of the 'Hunterization of America's schools.' The merits of Hunter's lesson plan remained a major issue of educational debate as late as 2000 marked by the publication by Andrew P. Johnson of an article entitled, 'It's Time for Madeline Hunter to Go: A New Look at Lesson Plan Design.[11] Johnson was assistant professor of curriculum and

Hunter's lesson plan

Aspect	Actions
1 Objectives	To enter the lesson with clear behavioural objectives closely specifying the desired learning outcomes
2 Standards of performance	To share the success criteria, to explain the lesson plan in relation to teacher and student actions/roles and to highlight the minimum standard all should achieve by the end of the lesson.
3 Anticipatory set	Raising interest and motivation with a 'hook' to capture attention in relation to the lesson content. This might involve a video clip, newspaper article, reference to published research, short discussion, opinion poll, quiz etc.
4 Input	Introducing and presenting new knowledge in short steps, modelling concepts and procedures and regularly pausing and checking understanding before moving forward.
5 Guided practice	Setting relevant tasks to practice and consolidate new knowledge while circulating and closely monitoring progress and answering questions.
6 Closure	Reviewing and confirming the major points developed during the lesson and gaining feedback.
7 Independent practice	Setting tasks for completion beyond the lesson to provide further practice to reinforce the new knowledge.

Image 7.2

instruction at Makato University in Minnesota, and his 'new look' lesson plan specified four steps:

1 Objectives – a clear statement of what the students should know and understand.
2 Introduction – an overview of the content designed to arouse curiosity and interest.
3 Input and activities – a precise step-by-step listing and presentation of new knowledge supported by relevant practical activities to explore and deepen understanding.
4 Closure – a short review of the lesson content.

Johnson's four steps represent a truncation rather than a radical departure from Hunter's lesson plan and echo Glaser's much earlier four-part lesson plan. Hunter responded to her critics by emphasising that individual steps could be omitted, extended or re-ordered to reflect different learning intentions and that teachers should use the ITIP as a guide to practice rather than a fixed prescription. The same considerations apply to the DLP.

Principles of Instruction

In 2010 Barak Rosenshine updated and extended the original 'teacher effectiveness' research with relevant findings from neuroscience and cognitive support research. Rosenshine detailed seventeen principles of effective teacher-led instruction as follows:[12]

1 Begin a lesson with a short review of previous learning.
2 Present new material in small steps with student practice after each step.
3 Limit the amount of material students receive at one time.
4 Give clear and detailed instructions and explanations.
5 Ask a large number of questions and check for understanding.
6 Provide a high level of active practice for all students.
7 Guide students as they begin to practice.
8 Think aloud and model steps.
9 Provide models of worked-out problems.
10 Ask students to have explained what they have learned.
11 Gain the responses of all students.
12 Provide systematic feedback and corrections.
13 Use more time to provide explanations.
14 Provide many examples.
15 Reteach material when necessary.
16 Prepare students for independent practice.
17 Monitor students when they begin independent practice.

Rosenshine's principles emphasise that learning advances in small steps involving rigorous checks on progress via extensive question and answer, close monitoring of active practice, systematic feedback, coaching, and independent practice. Rosenshine's principles place a major emphasis upon teachers employing mastery learning techniques to check and secure understanding before moving forward. This step-by-step approach was endorsed by Clark, Kirschner and Sweller, "controlled experiments almost uniformly indicate that when dealing with novel information students should be explicitly shown what to do and how to do it."[13] The starting point is to build and sustain a positive learning culture by displaying the key attributes of great teachers, enthusiasm, passion and inspiration as elaborated in Chapter 3. Those attributes are not 'charisma' but involve close attention to building and sustaining high expectations and warm, caring relationships.

Greet and welcome

It is often not possible to be in the classroom before the students arrive but whenever possible teachers should be first into the classroom to greet and welcome the students as they enter. Offer some positive comments, ask how their day is going, what's happening in their part-time job, how pleased you were by something. A warm welcome that recognises and shows an interest in each person will quickly build a positive rapport and perhaps lift low moods and renew the learning partnership. The trend towards individual handshakes, introduced by some teachers, is unnecessary and perhaps leans more towards teacher control and dominance rather than welcome. As students enter the classroom scan faces for signs of any unhappiness or potential problems and provide, as necessary, a few quick encouraging words and offer to discuss any issues at the end of the lesson. The simple acknowledgement that someone is troubled is often sufficient to calm a stressful situation and to prevent the continuation of an argument or problem into the classroom. Hattie identified an effect size of 0.72 for positive, teacher–student relationships significantly above the 0.40 threshold for positive influences on achievement. Developing a positive rapport is a significant motivator. Avoid sharing your own frustrations or problems with the students and develop the capacity to leave personal and professional problems in the corridor or the staffroom and adopt an upbeat presence with positive body language and an enthusiastic tone.

Start on time

Lessons should start exactly on time to condition students to arrive on time. Too many teachers wait for latecomers because they feel they will need to repeat and explain the lesson aims and content for the inevitable (and often the same regular) latecomers. Essentially the teacher has become conditioned by the behaviour of some of the students not to start on time and this can quickly become part of a class culture. Timetables often do not help because whereas one lesson may end at 11 a.m. the next may start at 11 a.m. Ideally, 'transfer time' should be built into the timetable, but otherwise it is better for a lesson to end early than for a lesson to start late. Act on lateness by having a reputation for always starting on time and this will prompt students to attend on time. The appetiser forms part of this strategy because it precedes the sharing of the learning intentions and by the time it is concluded all students should be present. Nor is it just a buffer against lateness. The latecomers will have missed a fun or innovative item of interest and over time this might nudge all students to arrive on time. If lateness remains a significant issue, then place some A5 late slips by the classroom door and when a late student enters point to the late slips. The late slip should have space to record name, date, lesson, number of minutes late and the reason for being late. The consistent application of this approach will soon encourage most to attend on time and for those who do not you will soon have a stack of late slips to discuss with them on a one to one and/or with their mentor. If there are persistent offenders reinforce the importance of arriving on time by ending the lesson a few minutes early and holding the latecomers back to read and discuss their late slips. Do this every time and they will soon conclude that it is easier to arrive on time rather than always being the last to join the refectory queue. It also has the advantage that those who were present on time see clear sanctions for those who do not make a similar effort. However, remember that many students will have a valid reason for being late – it is not always a discipline issue. You may end up giving sympathy for some personal emergency or problem.

Applying the Diamond Lesson Plan

The DLP weaves Rosenshine's principles of direct instruction into a step-by-step sequence of rich, active participation. This is teaching at its most effective when a stimulating presentation coupled with varied resources and tasks is designed and calculated to raise interest levels, deepen knowledge, provoke questions enlist peer collaboration and promote learning beyond the classroom. Note that the individual steps of the DLP model may be stretched across several lessons rather than the confines of a single lesson or as a recommended sequence for online instructional design. It also offers a dynamic structure to enhance formal lectures within Higher Education. The DLP is not a fixed formula, but rather a spur to creativity.

Appetiser	***Open your lesson with a bright, upbeat four- to five-minute 'hook' to capture attention and to stir enthusiasm and interest.*** The terms starter, energiser or icebreaker activities are more common but 'appetiser' is more in tune with Hunter's 'anticipatory set' involving a positive feel-good 'hook' to capture attention. Introductions of this type are often criticised as a distraction, committing teachers to additional preparation and sailing too close to edutainment. However, our purpose is to develop and extend knowledge of the topic by drawing attention to relevant 'in the news' developments, newly published research, a journal article, a key book, a TV documentary, a video on YouTube, etc. The aim is not only to win engagement but to stir curiosity in relation to the topic, the subject or vocation and future careers with the goal of triggering an intrinsic interest in mastering the subject skills and/or knowledge. It should be kept short and sharp. Over time students should be expected to take the lead in researching and regularly presenting the appetisers. This will offer students a regular lead role in the lesson, provide opportunities to practise and develop their speaking and presentation skills and encourage open-ended research involving higher-order analysis and evaluation. Appetisers can be used not only to open lessons but between episodes to re-energise students if attention is judged to be on the wane. A wide range of appetiser suggestions are described and presented at the end of this chapter.
Big Picture	***Share the learning intentions and success criteria with a student-friendly 'big picture' lesson introduction.*** The reading aloud of lesson objectives in the manner of "by the end of the lesson you will be able to . . ." is a highly mechanistic and ineffective means of engaging students. All too often it sounds and feels rushed and can seem to be more about fulfilling a bureaucratic 'requirement' rather than a genuine sharing of the learning intentions. The replacement of formal objectives with the prompt "I would like you to be able to answer . . ." followed by some graduated pre-questions is a more direct and effective way of communicating the learning intentions as described in Chapter 4. Questions remove the barrier of formal language and provide a direct prompt to in-lesson assessment. In survey after survey, our students describe great teachers as enthusiastic, passionate and inspiring. Those qualities should be to the fore in the lesson introduction with time invested to describe the planned lesson in an upbeat, enthusiastic manner. The 'big picture' introduction relates to being expansive

(Continued)

	i.e. explaining the importance of the topic, how it links to previous learning, how it might link to the workplace, the expectations of examiners, the opportunities to build employability skills and the knowledge to be gained. Care should also be taken to apply Ausubel's primary rule to check and ascertain prior learning. The overall purpose is to generate interest and commitment by 'selling' the lesson i.e. selling the benefits of engagement. What will the students gain and know that they didn't know when they entered the room? Finally, as an aid to concentration and note-taking employ bright graphics as the centrepiece of a student facing 'big picture' lesson plan as also described in Chapter 4.
Recap & Recall	***Check and confirm the progress of students by engaging in 'all response' recap and recall assessment activities.*** Engagement, although highly welcome, is not learning. It is participation. Our goal over time is to elicit evidence of learning and therefore recap and recall should form a regular feature of our lessons. Recap is a summary of the previous lesson, both as a reminder and to carry forward and test understanding of key concepts and vocabulary. Recall is of greater importance because it introduces a firm check on learning retention by regularly employing Wiliam's 'all response' questioning strategies. The recall questions should involve 'spaced practice' i.e. returning to topics studied weeks or months before rather than the immediate past topic. Teachers should react to evidence of poor recall and misunderstanding and be prepared to re-teach as necessary. Each lesson is a link in a learning chain and a broken link should not be ignored. The application of recap and recall and a range of appropriate strategies are described in Chapter 5.
Exposition	***Capture and hold attention with a clear step-by-step enthusiastic presentation of new knowledge.*** Most lessons will involve some form of teacher presentation or exposition to introduce, explain, model and elaborate new knowledge. They key is to chunk the new knowledge into three or four points with respect to cognitive load theory and the limitations of working memory. This is preferable to an extended monologue with largely passive students recording notes. Silent note-taking is rarely a reliable indicator of interest in the topic let alone understanding. Each key point should be supported by appropriate PowerPoint or equivalent slides to take advantage of dual coding and as an aid to concentration. It has become popular to deride the use of PowerPoint with the dismissive phrase 'death by PowerPoint' but it is the presenter and not the medium at fault. Too many presenters fill slide after slide with dense text bullet points and even worse read them aloud. The result is cognitive overload because we cannot read and listen well at the same time. Text should be kept to a minimum and PowerPoint should be used to reinforce and clarify the key points by displaying relevant photographs, diagrams, tables, quotations, statistics, apps, websites or video clips. Finally, acknowledge all those student surveys and consciously project enthusiasm, passion and inspiration rather than falling into flat, dull and boring. Contrary to folklore the former qualities are not genetic. Great teachers consciously switch them on and all teachers can and should practise and develop warm, upbeat, motivational presentational skills.

Question & Answer	***Check for attention and understanding by engaging all students in question and answer and developing a learning dialogue.*** Question and answer is deceptively straightforward but full of pitfalls for the unwary teacher. Consider entering the lesson with a list of relevant questions to test the expected learning outcomes from basic factual knowledge to more demanding conceptual awareness. This is preferable to relying upon the hit and miss of generating appropriate questions spontaneously during the lesson. Chapter 4 highlights how questions can form the basis of lesson planning with the use of 'big picture' lesson plans to punctuate the lesson with regular checks on understanding. The key is to draw all students into full participation via Wiliam's 'all response,' 'PPPB' and 'hinge' questioning techniques and to develop their confidence to ask as well as answer questions. Chapter 5 details a range of questioning strategies and stimulating methods of random student selection designed to gain full participation and to help students to extend and defend their answers within an overall learning dialogue.
Active learning	***Engage all in regular individual, paired and group guided practice to reflect upon and consolidate new knowledge and to provide opportunities to practise and develop employability and life skills.*** Few students immediately grasp a new concept or perhaps mishear or misunderstand an aspect of new information. Granting reflection time as short as three to five minutes individually or in pairs, can reveal misconceptions and give rise to questions that otherwise might not be asked. The aim is to promote thinking about the new information rather than simply receiving and recording it. Without discussion involving questioning and testing opinions many students might fail to make connections and to step from shallow to deeper understanding. Employ a variety of timers to maintain a brisk pace and preferably visual rather than a pedestrian countdown clock. In longer lessons or as a planned feature of a lesson offer time for a more extensive group review of new knowledge to promote deep rather than surface understanding. While the students are working circulate, monitor progress and pick-up issues for correction or further whole class elaboration. Continually read the body language, probe and encourage questions. Take the opportunity for one to one and small group coaching in response to any observed difficulties. To work well groups need to be kept small (three to four is optimum) have a clear task focus and conclude with an answer or relevant end 'product'. Heterogeneous is the guiding principle to foster a classroom culture of peer support and crossover. Chapter 8 presents full guidance on all aspects of planning and managing collaborative learning tasks.
Learning summary	***Summarise the major learning points to ensure accuracy of recording and to encourage good note-taking habits.*** Control the end of the lesson by reserving time to summarise the major learning points introduced during the lesson as detailed in Chapter 5. Return to the lesson objectives or preferably pre- questions and invite the students to summarise the key points. Reinforce the importance of good note-taking – memory is weak – and seek assurances of accurate recording of key points. As necessary direct the recording of a summary paragraph.

(Continued)

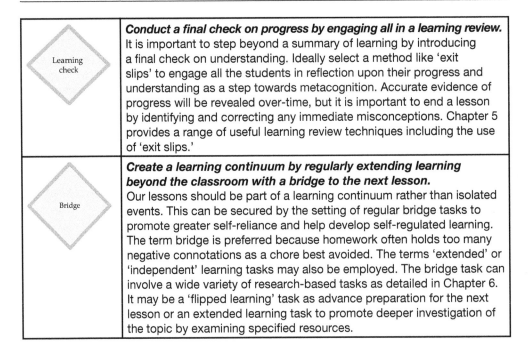

Image 7.3

The DLP seeks to rebalance the conventional direct recitation (CDR) model of teaching that has dominated our classrooms since the earliest days of compulsory education by focussing on the response rather than the recitation. CDR represents the conventional view of teaching. The teacher presents information (direct recitation), poses questions and seeks responses. Most teachers believe that they strike a balance between recitation and responses/dialogue in their classrooms, but observation studies reveal that teacher talk dominates and that responses only arise from a small minority of the students with most remaining silent. One of the significant and widely quoted observational studies was conducted by Goodlad (1994) in the United States. He concluded that 75% of lesson time was dominated by teacher presentation and that questions and answers and opportunities for students to gain feedback were largely tokenistic. Hattie similarly commented, "teachers talk between 70 and 80 per cent of class time on average . . . there needs to be less teacher-dominated talk and more student talking and involvement."[14] In essence, too many lessons are a process of listen, copy and repeat. The DLP seeks to avoid the trap of overtalking by specifying 'teacher exposition' as one element within a lesson with the other elements calculated to draw the students into full, purposeful participation. Once the DLP model is absorbed the individual diamond elements will merge and flow as a seamless whole. The DLP is a guide rather than a fixed model, and the sequence may be altered to suit different learning intentions. Teaching should never be static or predictable. In practice 'active learning' might be shifted from sixth position to first position and perhaps as the pupils or students enter the classroom, they might be directed into pairs or groups to engage in discussion. This might be followed by the 'big picture' to explain the purpose and point of the activity and how it links to the rest of the lesson and what the students might be expected to learn. An appetiser may be applied at the start of a new unit rather than every single lesson or pop-up during a lesson at a transition point to re-energise. A lesson might be planned with a major exposition and a minor active learning component or vice versa to fulfil different learning intentions. The DLP may also be stretched over time and applied across the development of a unit as a whole rather than each individual lesson. Whether the DLP is applied to a single lesson or across the span of a unit the key is to share and make explicit the learning intentions by posing pre-questions, offering precise feedback and providing coaching support to assist all students to arrive at answers. The first goal as introduced above is to open the lesson with an appetiser to capture and hold attention.

Appetisers

The purpose is to raise motivation and over time to seek to stimulate an intrinsic interest in the subject and related career pathways. Aim for a four- to five-minute burst of information to grab attention, arouse interest, spark questions and overall to generate a 'feel good' factor to immediately settle the students into the lesson. Marzano describes appetisers of this type as 'informational hooks' and commented, "The teacher uses activities to stimulate interest in the lesson's content. These activities might include anecdotes, video clips, audio clips, newspaper headlines, and other short attention-grabbing media to spark students' attention."[15] The majority of the following appetiser suggestions are subject linked 'informational hooks' as described by Marzano but the goal is also wider personal development by seeking to raise horizons and address active citizenship. Consider spotlighting news items in the form of 'in the news . . . or 'trending on social media . . .' to raise awareness of issues related to equality, diversity, sports, lifestyle, citizenship, health and diet. The following suggestions cover a wide range of possibilities:

- **Image of the month or week** – Select an arresting visual of a place, event, object, person, painting, new product, etc., linked to your subject. Project the image via PowerPoint for maximum visual impact. Multiple images for most topics can be easily sourced on Google, but be alert to any copyright restrictions. Remember to select 'images' as the search field on Google and to select the most appropriate image to display. You might also select images to highlight cultural diversity, role models or to link into current affairs, relevant anniversaries, etc.
- **Person of the month or week** – It is common for students not to know what a key person they are studying actually looks like or to know any general biographical information about their background. Introduce engineer, poet,

hairdresser, chef, hairdresser or scientist of the week or month, etc., as relevant to your subject. Issue a list of key subject related famous people and invite a student volunteer to select a person of interest to research. Create standard pro-forma on one side of A4 for a mini biography with space for a photograph and some standard sub-headings like key life chronology, career development and major achievements. The student or students can present their famous person on PowerPoint, issue the mini biography to their classmates and over time post a display of famous subject related people around the classroom wall and online with links for further information. This will ease the students into developing the skills of independent research and confident presentation – vital future employability skills.

- **Website of the month or week** – Highlight a useful website linked to the subject area or of wider study benefit. Invite students to submit websites they would recommend to others for study help or subject information. The issue of the reliability of websites can be discussed and pointers given on how to check the source of a website to ensure the use of authoritative and respected sources. Wikipedia can be recommended for a swift overview but always with the rider to question and to crosscheck the information with other sources. Wikipedia articles can be posted or edited by non-experts who may introduce their own prejudice or personal 'spin' to a topic. The presentation of useful websites can also be used to raise the issue of plagiarism with guidance on how to research and to use 'own words' rather than the temptation to 'cut and paste' Some students do not appreciate that they are doing anything wrong when they 'cut and paste' and need to be supported on how to quote from a source rather than copying from a source. Warn your students that most universities use Turnitin software from Northumbria Learning which scans the web for text matches with students' work.

- **App of the month or week** – As noted earlier, identify and recommend useful apps and give a quick overview and demonstration.

- **Book of the month or week** – Select a useful book from the library stock to highlight and encourage a general independent research and reading habit. Also identify useful e-books and aim to build a virtual library of downloadable books for ease of access. The days of short-term loan and waiting for a key book to reappear on a library shelf are fast disappearing. As noted earlier, invite students to be involved and to present any books they have found personally useful. Extend this approach into looking out for new publications and encourage a book buying habit with regular prompts on useful books, dictionaries, study aids, revision aids, etc. Highlight how the detail provided by a book can substantially deepen and extend subject knowledge beyond what can be covered in the classroom. Ensure that parental newsletters/social media contain references to the purchase of useful books and study aids to raise the awareness on how parents and guardians can help support their children. Clearly sensitivity applies and in cases of genuine hardship ensure discreet access to college or school hardship funds.

- **TED talk of the month or week** – Technology, Entertainment and Design (TED) Talks started in 1984 under the banner 'ideas worth sharing.' TED (www.ted.com) has since expanded worldwide and is an outlet for the most up-to-date research and new ideas across all disciplines. TED Talks are famously restricted to eighteen minutes. This is beyond the time allocation for an appetiser but rather than show a whole video give the students a taster. Many may choose to follow up and watch the whole video in their own time and perhaps browse further.

- **Museum/art gallery of the month or week** – There are museums with collections linked to most subject areas and of course art galleries. The website museums.co.uk lists 1722 museums in the UK with, in many cases, access to their collections online.

- **Charity of the month or week** – It is possible to overlook charities but many of them fund and promote up-to-date research in the relevant field. Highlight any useful resources. If there is sufficient interest the students might be encouraged to mount an appropriate information display in the college or school or undertake some related fundraising. Sometimes, as adults, we can have a jaundiced view of some events or groan that a certain national day has come around again but for our students it may be only their first or second exposure and their involvement can be very stimulating, and significantly raise their horizons and awareness of wider issues.

- **Employer of the month or week** – Reference to future employment opportunities is a good motivator. Highlight the major employers linked to the relevant subject area, the types of jobs on offer, qualifications expected and possible future salaries. Invite students to research and present a particular employer i.e. when the company was founded, size, turnover, major markets and products. The same applies to individual entrepreneurs who have exploited an invention, discovery or personal skill to found, a new business. Seek photographs and brief biographical details of suitable role models to inspire your students. Perhaps mark the position of major employers on a map of the UK to raise personal horizons beyond the immediate local area. Many large companies will also have public relations departments and may offer free information packs for useful classroom display and may also provide a speaker to visit your class. Alternatively, you might be able to arrange a visit to the employer's premises to encourage and motivate your students. All of this can again make useful research tasks for your students to research and present.

- **University of the month/week** – As noted earlier, but related to programmes whereby university is the expected next destination for most of the students. Highlight when the university was founded, major courses, pinpoint the location, identify past students who have attended, etc. Seek to raise ambition and promote applications to Oxford or Cambridge or a major Russell Group university.

- **Study tip of the month/week** – Some students are disorganised in their approach to study and boys in general are reputed to be poor at maintaining their files and adopting systematic approaches to personal study and revision. Invite students to submit their study tips and how they revise and learn. Confirm good practice and encourage all to support one another and over time aim build a learning and study culture. Girls will often enter into cooperative 'study buddy' and revision support relationships but boys often need encouragement to see the benefits of cooperative study and especially in the run-up to examinations. Make reference to some of the popular Studytubers as identified in Chapter 8 and their study and revision methods.

- **Quote of the month/week** – Who said it and context; can be subject related or of wider interest. Websites like www.quotationspage.com and www. quoteworld.org should supply all your needs. Adopt the same approach for the following and illustrate with any relevant photographs from Google. The approach is essentially Who, What, Where, When and How as appropriate.

- **Key statistic**
- **Key date**
- **Key discovery**
- **Key invention**
- **Key concept/subject vocabulary** plus spelling test!
- **Key event**
- **Key hypothesis**

- **Mini poll of the month or week** – Introduce an instant opinion poll. Try some random questions like, Could we survive without electricity? What was the world's greatest invention? Does it matter if tigers become extinct? Do teenagers need more sleep than adults? Is our quality of life better than it was 200 years ago? How do we know life is not a dream? Is it important to be able to cook when you can even buy mashed potato in the supermarket? Should we protect whales? Would it matter if flies became extinct? The ability to hold and to express opinions is an important life skill plus developing the tolerance of hearing and accepting contrary opinions. Give two minutes thinking time and vote by standing on the 'yes' or 'no' sides of the classroom or project an electronic poll using one of the many apps listed in Chapter 5. Give a further two minutes for each group to compare arguments and to list their three top reasons for yes or no. Offer a further opportunity to vote and to physically change sides or repoll. Declare the winning vote and keep a record of the outcomes of your mini polls on the classroom notice board and perhaps debate issues current in the media.

- **Subject specific** – Apply your own creativity to introduce subject specific appetisers. Perhaps in engineering impressive bridge of the week, construction building of the week, motor vehicle car of the week, catering recipe of the week, sport quirky sport of the week, English poem of the week, maths problem of the week, travel and tourism resort of the week, etc.

- **In the news . . .** Sky News and BBC News regularly feature 'in the news . . .' and select a range of newspaper articles for comment either quirky stories or something of greater significance. Consider the age group, course level and social backgrounds of your students and spotlight a news items of potential interest. Consider aspects of wider citizenship, sports events, diet, health, diversity, lifestyle, charitable events, etc., and encourage our students to hold opinions and to think about significant issues and often from the viewpoint of others. Fun items should also not be ignored because like the thunks detailed in Chapter 5 they can provoke comment and help all to find their voice and to be confident in expressing their opinions. It is through micro-steps like these that we start to build confidence encourage students to speak in front of the class.

- **Music** – Capture attention with a short burst of music that is relevant to the topic or perhaps some reputed 'brain' music to aid concentration. Select music that is associated with the topic, perhaps relevant period music to accompany a novel in English literature, atmospheric music to accompany a poem, music from the relevant region or country in travel and tourism or in languages, Beatles for 1960s Britain, Wagner for Nazi Germany, a relevant national anthem, a sporting theme tune, etc. There are many legal websites for finding music to play. The major ones are iTunes for purchase and download and spotify.com but YouTube also offers a wide choice. Occasionally introduce relaxing and soothing music coupled with eyes closed for a peaceful short burst of meditation. Any music by Mozart or baroque in general is reputed to stimulate the brain and promote relaxation. The website www.thetrainingshop.co.uk sells compilations of suitable reflective and energising music. Offer information about the music and composer to help extend general knowledge and to expose students to a wider musical range. This could be extended into *music of the week or month* by inviting students to submit a favourite track plus why they enjoy it. This can also lead to cultural diversity in the selection of music and or types of music soul, jazz, rock, rap, bhangra, etc. Give praise for choices of music and avoid sarcasm to build motivation, rapport and confidence over time. You should also be aware of the need to be covered by a performance rights licence because under copyright law your class is an audience. Most schools and colleges hold site licences, but if in doubt confirm with the head librarian who will be able to check.
- **Flashmob of the week** – A variation on music of the week is to invite suggestions for a favourite flashmob from YouTube. Invite the relevant student to introduce the flashmob and to say why it is a favourite. The underpinning goal of this and many other appetisers is to get the students to talk and to experience a minute or two in the spotlight. However, be wary. Some videos and song lyrics are less than wholesome, and you may have to veto a particular choice and steer towards something more neutral.
- **Digital skills** – The effective use of Microsoft Office (Word, Excel, PowerPoint and Publisher) and wider digital skills like maintaining a blog, creating a podcast, editing photographs and video, searching the internet, uploading documents to the Virtual Learning Environment, posting messages

on a forum, etc., are important not just for study and presentations but also as future employability skills. Our students are all at different stage of IT skills development. Invite student volunteers to demonstrate various applications from how to shoot a video, animate a slide in PowerPoint or Keynote, import photographs, convert data into a chart, manipulate tables, design a document, use shortcuts in Word, etc. This approach permits students to demonstrate their digital skills and present a 'how to' approach of benefit to all.

- **Brain teaser challenge** – This is essentially fun, but a good puzzle can intrigue and promote deep thinking. Brainteaser apps and games have expanded over the past five years with many claims for high learning impact. However, to put it into perspective, experts dismiss most of the claims and reserve the highest ratings for a daily crossword or Sudoku puzzle. Try www.brainbashers.com for a wide range of visual, number and word puzzles.

Plan regular appetisers to start your lessons and also consider introducing an appetiser mid-lesson to offer a pause between learning episodes and if need be as a re-energiser if attention is faltering. The DLP as described should be selected as regular strategy and particularly to introduce the key learning issues associated with a new unit of study before allocating time for peer dialogue and deeper online research and investigation.

References

1 Kirschner, P. A., Sweller, J. and Clark, R. E., Why minimal guidance during instruction does not work: An analysis of the failure of constructivist, discovery, problem-based, experiential, and inquiry-based teaching, *Educational Psychologist*, vol. 41, no. 2, 2006, pg. 6, 75–86, Copyright ©, Lawrence Erlbaum Associates, Inc.

2 Marzano, R. J., *The New Art and Science of Teaching*, Solution Tree Press, 2017, pg. 29.

3 Hattie, J., *Visible Learning, a Synthesis of Over 800 Meta-Analyses Relating to Achievement*, Routledge, 2009, pg. 206.

4 Petty, G., *Evidence-Based Teaching*, Nelson Thornes, 2006, pg. 101.

5 Kim, T. and Axelrod, S., Direct instruction: An educators' guide and a plea for action, *The Behavior Analyst Today*, vol. 6, no. 2, 2005, pg. 112, http://psycnet.apa.org/fulltext/2014-44024-004.pdf

6 Stockard, W. and Coughlin, Cristy, *The Effectiveness of Direct Instruction Curricula: A Meta-Analyse of a Half-Century of Research*, 7th January 2018, http://journals.sagepub.com/doi/abs/10.3102/0034654317751919

7 Rosenshine, B., *Five Meanings of Direct Instruction*, Centre on Innovation and Improvement, 2008, pg. 2, www.centerii.org

8 Fennell, M., *Notes of Lessons on the Harbartian Method*, Longmans Green and Co., 1910, pg. VII, https://archive.org/details/notesoflessonson00fennrich

9 Gagne, R. M., et al., *Principles of Instructional Design*, 4th edition, Harcourt Brace Jovanovich College, 1992, pg. 190.

10 Clark, D., https://donaldclarkplanb.blogspot.com/2006/09/gagnes-nine-dull-commandments.html

11 Johnson, A. P., It's time for madeline hunter to go: A new look at lesson plan design, *Action in Teacher Education*, vol. 22, no. 1, 2000, pg. 72–78, http://doi.org/10.1080/01626620.2000.10462994

12 Rosenshine, B., Principles of instruction: Research-based strategies that all teachers should know, *Journal of American Educator*, Spring 2012, pg. 7.

13 Kirschner, P. A., Sweller, J. and Clark, R. E., Why minimal guidance during instruction does not work: An analysis of the failure of constructivist, discovery, problem-based, experiential, and inquiry-based teaching, *Educational Psychology*, 2006, pg. 79, www.cogtech.usc.edu/publications/kirschner_Sweller_Clark.pdf

14 Hattie, John, *Visible Learning for Teachers*, Routledge, 2012, pg. 80–81.

15 Marzano, R. J., *The New Art and Science of Teaching and Learning*, Solution Tree Press, 2017, pg. 54.

Collaborative learning

Collaborative learning or cooperative learning in the form of paired and group working can significantly consolidate, deepen and extend new knowledge. The act of elaborating new information by explaining and discussing key learning points in detail with peers as well as teachers can reveal misconceptions and through the process of retrieval and articulation strengthen the retention of new information within long term memory. Johnson and Johnson (1999) reported, "working together to achieve a common goal produces higher achievement and greater productivity than working alone. This conclusion is confirmed by so much research that it stands as one of the strongest principles of social and organizational psychology."[1] The influential UK Education Endowment Foundation (EEF) 'Teachers' Toolkit' scored collaborative learning as significant at all levels:

> Over 40 years a number of systematic reviews and meta-analyses have provided consistent evidence about the benefits of collaborative learning. . . . Collaborative learning appears to work well for all ages if activities are suitably structured for learners' capabilities and positive evidence has been found across the curriculum.[2]

The promotion of collaborative learning can also generate a positive learning culture of mutual instruction by reviving the principles of the bygone Monitorial system as detailed in Chapter 1. The Monitorial system developed by Andrew Bell to overcome shortages of teachers was so successful that it dominated education provision for fifty years (1790–1840). Today the benefits of collaborative working are being firmly renewed as students not only enter supportive relationships with their immediate peers but seek and find support online, and this can be facilitated in safe, managed social media hubs. Collaborative learning nurtures personal confidence, encourages social cohesion and builds wider interpersonal and intrapersonal skills through the process of listening to other opinions, absorbing alternative ideas, respecting different perspectives and crucially sustaining and justifying own beliefs. Johnson and Johnson (1999) identified significant psychological benefits

DOI: 10.4324/9781003132783-11

arising from those experiences as students support and help each other to learn in the context of a common learning journey:

> Working cooperatively with peers, and valuing cooperation, results in greater psychological health, higher self-esteem, and greater social competencies than does competing with peers or working independently. . . . Students learn how to communicate effectively, provide leadership, help the group make good decisions, build trust, repair hurt feelings, and understand other's perspectives.[3]

Hattie equally emphasised the benefits arising from a sense of belonging and acceptance, "peers can influence learning by helping, tutoring, providing friendship, giving feedback and making class and school a place to which students want to come each day."[4] Those social skills matter. The Sutton Trust report 'Life Lessons' published in 2017 detailed how students from the independent schools sector dominate our elite universities and leadership positions within public services, industry and business because of their noticeably higher levels of personal confidence and cultural capital:

> private school pupils tend to have higher scores across a range of 'soft skills' . . . the increased 'locus of control' and aspirations associated with these schools form a component of the private school earnings premium, contributing to a long term advantage in the labour market, measures, including 'toughness', commitment and openness to challenge.[5]

An earlier and separate report commissioned by the UK government revealed the scale of the dominance of the professions by those from an independent school background.

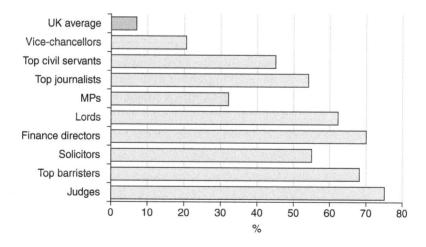

Figure 8.1 Percentage in professional occupations with a public school education[6]

The UK average for people with an independent school education is 7%, but as indicated earlier, as many as 75% of judges are publicly educated. The most recent data published in 2019 by the Sutton Trust reveals that 39% of 'leaders' across the professions, public services, sports, media and business attended an independent school. The data should not be used to prompt resentment of the successful progression of privately educated students, but rather focus attention on developing similar opportunity-rich curricula to help all students to practise and refine their 'soft' skills and improve their personal confidence. Collaboration is key in this regard because regular paired and group working opportunities build confidence in expressing and sustaining personal opinions. Collaboration also improves attainment by providing opportunities for knowledge and/or opinions to be tested, modified, corrected or extended through discussion and thereby avoiding students carrying forward misconceptions into the exam room. The annual publication of exam howlers by examination boards reveals a catalogue of misapplied and misunderstood knowledge.

Applying cognitive load theory

Professor Paul Kirschner has qualified these affirmations by considering the implications of cognitive load theory (CLT) in relation to planning and implementing effective collaborative learning. He identified and weighed the impact of the high 'cognitive load' associated with interacting with other group members in comparison to individuals completing a task alone:

> In cognitive load theory, communicating and coordinating costs due to collaboration are associated with the specific extra acts that a learner has to carry out when studying, namely communicating with other learners, and coordinating both their own learning and the learning of other team member.[7]

Kirschner concluded that it was the nature of the task and the learning goals that made the difference. Too straightforward a task, and the 'interaction cost' involved in collaboration might be too high in relation to the learning gain, whereas setting more complex tasks involving group members taking responsibility for researching and presenting different elements transcended the 'transaction cost' by permitting greater in-depth coverage of the topic. Kirschner concluded,

> Effective collaboration occurs when a task is complex enough to justify the extra time and effort involved in the necessary transactional activities. If a task is not complex enough, unnecessary transactional activities will cause extraneous cognitive load and will, thus be detrimental to learning.[8]

At its most basic the knowledge processing capacity of a group trumps the limited capacity of an individual's working memory. In addition, the differing levels of prior knowledge across a heterogeneous rather than a homogeneous group can raise the knowledge of the group as a whole. As Slavin commented, "Students will learn from one another because in their discussions of the content, cognitive conflicts will arise, inadequate reasoning will be exposed, disequilibration will occur, and higher-quality understandings will emerge."[9] A warning against employing homogeneous groups was raised as early as 1546 by the writer John Heywood, "Some heades haue taken two headis better then one: But ten heads without wit, I wene as good none."[10] As we move deeper into a blended learning era, collaborative learning raises many benefits for mutual student support in the form of study groups as differential rates of progress emerge.

Study groups

Study groups should be introduced as a norm within the first few lessons of a new programme to help the students to bond, avoid isolated students and inhibit the emergence of potentially divisive sub-groups. It is a common observation that some students gravitate to the back row and some to the front rows of our classrooms with noticeable differences in behaviour and participation. Placing our students into study groups can bridge those divides before they become established and influence the class dynamic. Johnson and Johnson commented,

> Cooperative learning promotes the development of caring and committed relationships for every student. Even when individuals initially dislike each other or are obviously different from each other. . . . Cooperative groups help students establish and maintain friendships with peers. As relationships become more positive, there are corresponding improvements in productivity, morale, feelings of personal commitment and responsibility to do the assigned work.[11]

Ideally, our students should be placed into small heterogeneous rather than homogeneous groups with considerations ranging beyond ability to mix socio-economic, gender, ethnic and personality differences. The optimum number for productive engagement is, surprisingly, just three students and at the most four i.e. 'quad groups.' Larger groups provide 'hiding space' permitting some students to fade into the background either by choice or because other more able or more vocal students dominate. Study groups can be identified as 'home groups' or 'base groups,' although 'study buddy' is often the preferred term with younger students to emphasise the central aim of building supportive friendships. You might also consider nominating 'teams' rather than groups, thereby introducing a suggestion of healthy competition and allowing your students to select their own unique team names. Once formed the students can quickly move into their groups or teams with minimal disruption to the flow of the lesson. Equally pairs can become quads by doubling up and doubling again to create teams of eight. Teams should undertake tasks that involve turn turn-taking or identified sub-roles as detailed later to avoid passengers within the larger group membership. As blended learning becomes the norm, ensure the continuation of peer support online so that students are not isolated at home but have the support of their study group just a click away. Most learning management systems (LMSs) offer an array of collaborative learning channels; otherwise, create invitation-only groups on WhatsApp or similar social media. Students are keen to learn from each other as highlighted by the rise of Studytubers on YouTube. Studytubers are students who not only share their study methods but also document their morning and evening study routines and their planning and completion of assignments and approaches to exam revision. Ruby Granger has attracted over 11 million views followed by Jade Bowler with over 6 million and Eve Bennett with 5 million views. Blair Fiander also hit the headlines in December 2020 by attracting 7.4 million students to join her study sessions on Tik Tok. Her initiative to connect students has expanded into mutual support chatrooms for different age groups and curricula. The concept of study groups and peer-to-peer support can also involve entry into managed peer support networks as promoted by https://ambi.network. Within our classrooms, wider student interactions beyond the immediate study group are also significant so that the bonding process extends to the whole class. This can be achieved by regular random pair and group selection techniques as described later. Ultimately, rather than a classroom with a single teacher, we can encourage our more able students to undertake coaching roles and build a learning culture of mutual support in the spirit of the Monitorial system.

More knowledgeable other

The positive benefits of encouraging wider learning support were emphasised by Lev Vygotsky (1896–1934). He believed that learning was developed and heightened through social interaction and discussion with others and especially a 'more knowledgeable other' (MKO). The MKOs were not just teachers but parents, siblings, friends and peers. Vygotsky believed that there was a limit to what each student could achieve unaided and careful monitoring of progress was necessary to pinpoint each student's 'zone of proximal development' (ZPD) i.e. the optimum time for intervention by a MKO to offer support and help resolve a learning difficulty. Many of us will remember thanking a big brother or sister or friend for providing an explanation that bridged a personal learning difficulty, and this informal support can be enhanced by membership of a study group. Wiliam introduced the abbreviation C3B4ME, meaning that students should 'see three before me'[12] to encourage students to seek answers from a MKO before asking their teacher. Perhaps the most celebrated example was Sal Khan, the hedge fund analyst, who responded to his cousin Nadia's difficulties in managing her maths homework by posting videos on YouTube to help her. It was the starting point of the Khan Academy and the development of the world's most extensive online learning platform. It serves as a reminder that today the internet is more often than not the 'go to' MKO for our students and underlines the importance of curating recommended online resources for our students to access.

Ensure a challenge

Collaborative learning should not be confused with discovery learning, nor should it be primarily directed towards social and life skills outcomes. The primary purpose of collaborative learning should be to test, deepen and extend core subject knowledge. This should involve Kahemann's System Two thinking by introducing challenging tasks that prompt deep rather than superficial thinking as described in Chapter 6. Consequently, teachers should apply their curricular knowledge to design tasks that fully challenge rather than simply engage students. Danielson commented, "Virtually all students are intellectually engaged in challenging content through well-designed learning tasks and activities that require complex thinking by students."[13] In this context care must be taken not to treat collaborative learning as a bolt-on extra within a lesson, but rather as an integral part of fulfilling the overall learning goals. This was a point emphasised by Marzano: "Students should be engaged in activities that help them analyse and process new information in ways that facilitate their understanding."[14] Our students are very alert to pedestrian tasks that carry no apparent knowledge deficit or penalty for non-completion. The setting of inconsequential tasks is counterproductive because once detected many students will simply sit back and mark time until teacher-led direct instruction is resumed. Collaborative learning tasks should be designed to test and deepen understanding of a major aspect of new knowledge through application and/or study of a range of identified resources. The associated benefit is that students are much more likely to reveal misunderstandings in the close and supportive confines of a pair or a small group discussion than the wider classroom. In addition, teachers, released from their normal position at the front of the classroom become much more accessible. By circulating around the classroom teachers gain the opportunity for micro-encounters and to warmly reinforce positive behaviours, praise evidence of progress and equally intervene quickly with any students observed to be slipping off task. Less confident students also gain the opportunity to informally raise a question with their teacher without having to speak-up in front of the whole class and can gain valuable one to one coaching support. The encounter(s) also provide valuable feedback for the teacher because a student may raise an undetected misunderstanding. Those rich teacher–student interactions were identified by Creemers and Kyriakides as a major part of one of their eight elements of dynamic teaching and learning:

> Effective teachers also use seatwork or small group tasks since they provide needed practice and application opportunities. The effectiveness of seatwork assignments is enhanced when the teacher explains the work that students are expected to do and once the students are released to work independently the teacher circulates to monitor progress and provide help and feedback.[15]

Developing the 4Cs

Knowledge is the focus, but confident and competent employability skills, as detailed in Chapter 12, are also vital future requirements. The Partnership 21 research group defined the core employability skills valued by industry and business as the 4Cs:

- Collaboration
- Communication
- Critical thinking
- Creativity

A rich mix of paired and group tasks involving researching, questioning, discussing evaluating and presenting new knowledge can offer multiple opportunities to develop the 4Cs. Knowledge leads, and as E.D. Hirsch has indicated skills will follow, "Skill objectives are most effectively targeted when they are anchored to the content in the context of a domain of knowledge."[16] Hirsch's Core Knowledge Foundation is often misrepresented as eschewing collaborative learning. However, there are many examples of Core Knowledge schools like the Liberty Common Elementary School being awarded 'School of Distinction' status for the quality of their group learning practice:

> high expectations are evident in the phrasing teachers used. Several were observed encouraging students to "think like a scientist . . . historian . . . or detective" as they approach their work. Teachers used a mix of direct and inquiry-based instruction that ensured that students had the support they needed when tackling new knowledge and skills, and also provided time for independent and small group work.[17]

Likewise the Grayhawk Elementary School, also a 'School of Distinction,' published the following example of a project to help improve writing skills:

> Sixth graders, for example, participated in a simulation of Ellis Island to help students better understand the concepts and experiences they had been discussing in their Immigration domain. Students came dressed as immigrants bearing passports from their countries of origin. . . . By making real the historical experience of immigration for students, teachers paved the way for a deeper understanding of the time period and of immigration today. Experiential and factual knowledge was then manifested in students' vocabulary-, content-, and emotionally-rich written responses to the activity.[18]

Group and exploratory learning experiences of this type are often helpful to practise and apply knowledge specific vocabulary, promote questions and connect new knowledge with what is already known.

Dialogic classrooms

Altering the classroom layout to physically reflect learning intentions presents students with an immediate visual stimulus. It also reinforces classrooms as places for dialogue and evaluation as we increasingly adopt a flipped learning pedagogy. Ideally, classrooms should be furnished with individual desks to allow for easy movement and re-arrangement. However, all too often desks are fixed or much too heavy to move easily, and teachers must make the best use of the limited space and the available furniture. Lesson observers should report any limitations placed on learning activities by either the furniture or the classroom space, and relevant managers should seek improvements. The major configurations to facilitate dialogue are as follows:

- Pairs – desks spaced in pairs to facilitate think, pair and share
- Quads – desks grouped in fours to facilitate opinion sharing or small group tasks
- Teams – desks grouped in blocks of eight to facilitate a competitive quiz or other Q&A activity or jigsaw task with sub-roles
- Straight rows theatre style to watch a video or attend to a whole class presentation
- Two facing straight rows to stage a debate
- One large central block for a whole group seminar e.g. Harkness method
- A single 'hot' seat in the centre of the room (preferably a swivel chair) and the rest of the chairs in a circle ready to question the student in the hot seat – (or the teacher) on a prepared topic
- A horseshoe arrangement to encourage discussion
- A circle without desks to encourage sharing of opinions

These examples illustrate how the physical repositioning of classroom furniture can facilitate and change the class dynamic. Rather than facing the front with an expectation of teacher presentation and listening, the layout cues an expectation for dialogue and interaction. In addition, if furniture is never rearranged there is a danger that students will sit in the same seat, beside the same person every lesson and fall into a 'comfort zone'. However, sensitivity does apply in relation to knowing your students. Routine is important for some students, and in those circumstances 'comfort zones' are not a negative but a positive. Otherwise, the re-arrangement of furniture is recommended to immediately raise interest levels by 'removing' each student's normal seat and spotlighting the learning activity.

Random student selections

Selecting students at random should be a regular strategy for placing students into pairs and groups. It will capture attention, introduce a sense of fun and help to cement class relations as one single team engaged on a common learning journey.

Random pairings

The fastest technique for placing students into random pairs is to ask the students to turn their chairs around and to work with the person seated in the row behind. Clearly this technique relates to a classroom set out in rows, but it can also work well in a lecture theatre. Within a horseshoe setting you might invite those on the left-hand side to take their chairs and to sit and face the person opposite on the right-hand side of the classroom. However, to ensure fully random pairs and to introduce a sense of fun and movement consider using randomly distributed Post-it notes (one for each student) and ask the students to circulate to find their partners. There are a variety of pair possibilities as follows.

Fun – Opt for naturally occurring pairs like fish and chips, bangers and mash, Ben and Holly, Wallace and Gromit, Fiona and Shrek, Tom and Jerry, Mork and Mindy, Ant and Dec, Sooty and Sweep, Peppa and George, Scooby Doo and Shaggy, Sonny and Cher, Holmes and Watson, etc. You can also theme your pairs at different points of the year. For instance, at Christmas time opt for Santa Claus, mistletoe, snowman, sleigh bells, Christmas Tree, etc. Or for Valentine's Day select romantic pairs like Gavin and Stacey, Romeo and Juliet, Napoleon and Josephine, Elton and David, Posh and Becks, William and Kate, etc. You can similarly use your imagination to generate themed pairs for Easter and summertime.

They say opposites attract – Hot or cold, Ying or Yang, little or large, stop or go, top or bottom, upstairs or downstairs, right or wrong, fire or ice, sink or float, etc.

Curriculum pairs – In English select characters like Romeo and Juliet, Cathy and Heathcliff or names of poets and the opening line from one of their poems or the name of an author and the title of their novel. In maths, try simply arithmetic e.g. $7 \times 7 = 49$ or raise the bar with a more demanding formula and matching answers. Within motor vehicle select Ford and Mondeo, Rolls and Royce, Vauxhall and Astra, etc. In catering try matching celebrity chefs with the names of their restaurants or just first names and surnames or a list of ingredients and a dish, etc. In art, the name of an artist and their style of art like Picasso and Cubism, etc. You might also consider uses pictures instead of words and matching an artist with one of their paintings. In travel and tourism match the name of a city or place with a famous attraction or consider the use of pictures. In hairdressing the surnames and first names of famous hairdressers like Nicky Clarke or matching the hairdresser with the name of their salon or with a celebrity client i.e. Who cuts the queen's hair? Who cuts David Beckham's hair? In politics the names of British prime ministers or match against dates in office. In economics select the names of economists or match relevant names with economic theories. Overall apply your curriculum knowledge to introduce relevant pairs.

Snap cards – All of these examples require the advance preparation of individual Post-it notes but for speed simply distribute snap cards at random.

To ensure no one is left out you will need an accurate count of the students present. In the case of odd numbers you can opt for one group of three. To match up three students try *Fish & Chips* and on a further Post-it note write *Mushy Peas* and see if they work it out. They generally do. Use your creativity to arrive at similar trios e.g. Bill, Ben and Little Weed, although that might be lost on current generations.

Jazzing up group selections

Counting off 1, 2, 3, etc., is perhaps the most immediate and well-known method of randomly placing students into groups but consider jazzing up the ordinary with one or more of the following techniques.

Colours

Assuming four groups, label four tables orange, red, green and purple by placing coloured cards on stationary stands in the centre of each table. Buy a bag of Starburst sweets and drop into a container the number of sweets of each colour to match the number of students for each group. Invite each student to dip their hand into the container and to select a sweet at random. A purple sweet indicates joining the purple table, an orange sweet the orange table, etc. Other brands of sweets will also work well but select wrapped sweets for good hygiene. If you would like to avoid sweets, then in advance of the lesson place appropriate coloured dots on the top-right-hand corner of the students' worksheets. When it is time for the group task, invite the students to move to the relevant table according to the colour of their dot.

Jigsaw

Place a relevant photograph on each tabletop linked to your subject. It might be chefs, poets, business leaders, hairdressers or photographs of cars in motor vehicle, or a holiday destination in travel and tourism, etc. Cut up another copy of each photograph into pieces according to the number of students planned for each group. Jumble all the pieces in a container and invite the students to select a piece at random. The students should move from table to table to find a match and assemble their 'jigsaw.' Once all are seated, expect the students to tell you something about the person, place, or event to tease out wider knowledge.

Restaurants

Place the titles of different restaurants on the tabletops like Italian, Greek, Indian, etc. You could also ask restaurants for a copy of their menus or print them off from the internet and build up a collection. On individual slips of paper record dishes corresponding to the different restaurants and drop into a container. Invite each student to select a dish at random. Pizza? Sit at the Italian table. Korma? Sit at the Indian table, etc. Reflect students' backgrounds. If you have students from Poland, then ensure you include a Polish restaurant in the mix of restaurant choices, etc. Some food choices may well be a mystery to other students, but this creates an immediate talking point and contributes to wider cultural awareness.

Music scene

Place the names or photographs of popular bands on the tabletops and remember not to show your age by selecting the Beatles or the Rolling Stones or the Spice Girls, etc. Instead reflect the music scene of the students. Invite your students to select a name from a container at random. If Perrie Edwards, sit at the Little Mix table; Ally Brooke, sit at the Fifth Harmony table; or James McVey, sit at the Vamps table; etc. You could achieve the same thing with football teams and similar themes.

Holidays

Label your tables with favourite holiday destinations like Paris, Rome, Berlin, etc. Select a famous tourist attraction from a container, and if the Brandenburg Gate, sit at the Berlin table; the Eiffel Tower, sit at the Paris table; and the Spanish Steps, sit at the Rome table, etc. To make this harder, rather than the names of attractions issue photographs of popular tourist sites, including some more obscure tourist attractions.

Films/TV shows

Place the titles of popular films or TV shows on the tabletops and then invite your students to select a name. Captain Kirk sits at the Star Trek table, Sam Neill sits at the Jurassic Park table or Cher sits at the Mama Mia table, etc. Or you could use well-known quotations to be matched with a character or a particular film.

Events/people

Name your tables after historical events like Battle of Hastings, Great Fire of London or Tolpuddle Martyrs, etc. Select a fact, date or event at random and if 1066 sit at the Battle of Hastings table, or George Loveless sit at the Tolpuddle Martyrs table, or Pudding Lane sit at the Great Fire of London table, etc. As a variation the events can be themed in terms of relevant subject developments e.g. inventions in engineering, scientific discoveries, theories in psychology, characters in a novel.

Birth date

Invite all the students to line up along one side of the classroom in order of their birth dates from January to December and then walk along and sub-divide the students into the number of groups required e.g. January to March is Group A.

Flags

Place a national flag on each tabletop (print these off from the internet) and invite the students to select at random the name of a country. The students move to the relevant table. You can make this harder with obscure flags, and remember to select flags that might reflect the backgrounds of some your students. You can vary this with matching the photographs of prime ministers or presidents with countries or matching capital cities with countries, etc.

These strategies are not just for fun but will create heterogeneous student pairs and groups. Mixed ability, rather than students of the same or similar ability, working together generates higher learning outcomes. In addition, nominating and placing students into teaching roles within a pair, group or front of class will activate the Protégé Effect. Nestojko (2014) identified a 12% gain in performance for students who were asked to teach or coach other students because the 'spotlight' prompted more thorough preparation and careful checking of information.[19] The effect persists even if the student does not undertake a teaching role because of the advance preparation. When applied it is recommended to introduce within the 'shelter' of pairs and groups to build confidence before more formal front-of-class presentations. Slavin has highlighted that the more able students deepen their knowledge through the process of explaining a key concept or process and the 'receiver(s)' gains from a one-to-one explanation:

> Students who gained the most from cooperative activities were those who provided elaborated explanations to others. In this research as well as in Dansereau's, students who received elaborated explanations learned more than those who worked alone, but not as much as those who served as explainers.[20]

The act of explaining an answer might also prompt the 'explainer' to check the accuracy of their explanation with the teacher and further confirm and consolidate their personal understanding. Less able students also gain by raising a question or difficulty within the 'shelter' of the pair or group and often find that the less formal language of a fellow student succeeds in clarifying and resolving their learning difficulty. Wiliam reported evidence that students will often pretend to understand a teacher's explanation, even when they don't because of social embarrassment but they are happy to press a peer until their misunderstanding is resolved:

> Hardly ever would a student interrupt a teacher for clarification or to ask the teacher to go over something a second time. And yet, when working with peers, a student would ask the peer to slow down or to go over something again and again until it was understood.[21]

Reserve homogenous pairs or groups to address differentiated learning tasks designed to grant extra support or to introduce a challenge.

Paired collaboration

A paired discussion or task is highly effective because it permits individual students to compare their thinking and to bounce their ideas off someone else. Confidence is significantly boosted when a peer confirms the same answer or shares the same explanation. A paired discussion may be as brief as two to five minutes to punctuate teacher exposition or involve a longer time allocation to permit deeper reflection. Working beyond the classroom should also be encouraged with the students expected to meet and conclude discussions or tasks outside of the lesson either physically or online. All LMS offers collaboration tools to support remote joint or group working on an assignment or task otherwise Padlet is a popular option or Google Hangouts. Consider the following applications of paired working:

- Two-minute pair reflection – Invite students to discuss with an immediate neighbour a key point for two minutes to surface any misunderstandings and as a prompt for any questions. Students are much more likely to express a difficulty or to raise a question if their partner shares the same uncertainty. Use a bright, visual countdown timer to add pace.
- Five-minute pair discussion – Seek more substantial feedback by moving the students into random pairs to engage in 'think, pair and share'. Pose a key question and time one minute for individual thinking followed by four minutes for a paired discussion. Gain feedback by inviting the pairs to share any opinions, conclusions or questions with the whole class. The timings are brief but are designed to gain feedback without too much loss of pace and may be used with a 'hinge' question as discussed in Chapter 5 to inform progress.
- Extended discussion – As noted earlier but with a greater time allowance to permit a more in-depth exchange of opinions on a particular issue. This might involve doubling up to form quads to share opinions and build a consensus. Scaffold the discussion with a set of structured sub-questions to avoid the discussion stalling and to funnel the discussion towards a clear consensus.
- Task completion – The completion of a specified task designed to extend, test or consolidate understanding e.g.:

  Reacting to and answering specified questions linked to:
  - a YouTube, Ted Talk or other video
  - a chapter in a textbook
  - a journal article
  - a podcast
  - a website or blog commentary

Alternatively allocate time for each pair to engage with a task involving a specified outcome and often involving digital tools or digital presentation:

- Completing gapped handouts – Not spot the missing word, but rather gaps to be filled with a paragraph explanation of a concept, event, discovery, etc.
- Completing a multiple choice test/quiz paper
- Answering a questionnaire
- Taking turns to demonstrate a practical skill
- Preparing an oral presentation
- Hotseat(s) activity – prepare to answer questions on a specified topic
- Creating a poster/infographic/visual summary of key learning

As noted earlier but in electronic form using Padlet or Glogster or Canva

Creating a spider diagram summary of learning

Answering a past exam question

Creating a PowerPoint, Keynote or Prezi presentation to explain a key point

Brainstorm ideas and create a mind map

Create a timeline

Create a photo slideshow

Rank and sort information

Record a podcast

Record a video

Tabulate and explain data or display in an appropriate chart or pictogram

Clearly many of those tasks could also be set as individual tasks, but working in pairs provides many additional advantages in relation to building confidence, skills and joint discussion and confirmation of key knowledge. Essentially, what one person finds difficult another may understand, and what one person thinks is the answer another may correct. Our most successful students have always pooled their knowledge and supported one another.

Good planning is essential to ensure that these tasks involve both challenge and depth of knowledge. All too often activities like designing a poster or mounting a display have been criticised as shallow endeavours but commercially produced posters and displays as employed by our leading museums or organisations offer a stimulating summary of information involving photographs, text, statistics, charts, personal profiles, timelines, diagrams, etc. The outcome is only shallow if it is permitted to be. Take a look at the depth and quality of the collaborative learning 'expeditions' at the XP School Doncaster (www.xpschool.org) or School21 (www.school21.org.uk) in East London. Both schools apply the principles of expeditionary learning (EL) founded by Ron Berger following an initiative between Harvard School of Education and Outward Bound, USA to create highly interactive, challenging learning investigations or expeditions.

Group tasks

Well-designed group tasks have clear goals to ensure that the task is completed with well-defined and presented outcomes that carry forward curricular knowledge. Vague goals and inconsequential outcomes are the enemies of group work because there is a danger of encouraging drift and reducing participation. Consequently, the task should involve a sequence of precise steps or sub-tasks to be followed or precise questions to be answered supported by relevant resources as necessary. This high level of scaffolding is essential because students are often uncertain how to collaborate and may simply wait for one of their number to interpret the task and take the lead. Group tasks will most often require a longer allocation of time in comparison to paired tasks to give time for interactions between the group members. Ideally form quad groups i.e. a limit of four members to promote effective interactions. Larger groups or teams may be formed to undertake more in-depth multi-outcome research tasks or projects as indicated:

- Single outcome task – Form quad groups and specify a single key question to be answered within the allocated timescale by reference to identified resources. The task should be demanding and encourage higher-level thinking and reasoning involving comparisons, analysis, critical thinking and decision making, etc.
- Multiple outcome task – Form teams or large groups and allocate a whole lesson or more to a major investigation of a key aspect of new knowledge or introduce a 'big question or 'big idea' as discussed in Chapter 15. As possible adopt an interdisciplinary approach so that knowledge from different disciplines is applied to a particular question or contributes to the development of a given theme. Scaffold the task so that the group works through a series of sub-steps often involving roles for the different group members by applying jigsaw learning approaches. As before, the task could extend beyond the lesson, as necessary, with the students directed to meet physically and/or online to complete the task.

Sub-roles

The introduction of individual sub-roles with responsibility for a single element of the overall task can prompt effective participation and play to different skills and abilities e.g. presenter, designer, researcher, writer, data cruncher. Not all students are confident presenters. Communication apprehension may apply, but confidence can be built over time by applying the support measures identified in Chapter 5. Initially offer students a choice of role but over time ensure that roles are rotated and that appropriate support is extended to model and help students to develop the skill set associated with each role. The following group roles might be considered and allocated. All will help to promote the Protégé Effect as described earlier because the outcomes are public i.e. presented and shared with others.

- Leader – Chairs the discussion/task and ensures all have a say, relevant information is collated and that the question is answered or task completed to a high standard within the time limit.
- Visualiser(s) – Produce any specified visual outcomes for the discussion i.e. spider diagrams, posters, PowerPoint, display, video.
- Statistician(s) – Produce any tables, charts, diagrams required.
- Researcher(s) – Find out additional information as required from textbooks, video, library, newspapers, internet, etc.
- Interviewer(s) – Plan questions and conducts any necessary interviews/surveys of opinion etc

- Writer(s) – Draw together all the information from the different sources to produce an overview summary of findings or booklet or report format.
- Presenter(s) – Deliver any oral overview presentation of all findings/outcomes. This is perhaps the most demanding role, but a key aim over time is to coach the skills of confident public speaking.

Prepare a 'job card' describing each role on A5 card and laminate for durability. Provide an upbeat description of the role and bullet point the employability skills and personal competences they will have the opportunity to develop. Skills can and should be modelled and coached e.g. how to write a report, give a presentation, produce a chart, design PowerPoints or similar slides. Invite students to share their skills e.g. a student who can confidently use Excel can demonstrate and help a peer who is new to Excel.

Presentation of outcomes

The following methods of presentation carry forward some of the suggestions for paired tasks. As previously highlighted, it is about ensuring challenge and depth of knowledge and offering opportunities to build the 4Cs of employability.

- PowerPoint or equivalent, Sway, Prezi, etc., but model the expected structure, layout and good practice in relation to highly visual rather than text-laden slides and perhaps specify a fixed number of slides.
- Flipchart – design colourful spider diagrams or mind maps.
- Posters – condense a whole key topic onto one side of flipchart paper or a display board.
- An electronic billboard or poster using Padlet or Glogster or Canva.
- Pyramid ranking – use Post-it notes or A4 pages on the wall for each separate point of a rank order pyramid.
- Chart it – use Excel or similar to analysis data and present data in an eye-catching infographic format along with related analysis.
- Washing line – physically stretch across the room and peg the steps of a sequence or a process or chronology in the correct order.
- Class blog – invite students to record and build key topic information arising from the group task along with links to online resources.
- Podcast – record a discussion/roleplay/interview or explanation of a topic.
- TV news – shoot video of a mock news bulletin on a key topic.
- Advert – design an advert story board to 'sell' a new theory, product, etc.
- Cartoon strip – as noted earlier, but present as a cartoon strip storyboard.
- Video – create a video on an aspect of key knowledge involving integrating relevant photographs, statistics, images, etc. Place on the school or college LMS.

- Photo slide show – create a photo slide show on PowerPoint or equivalent with captions or a voice over to explain a key topic.
- Learning wall – build topic information across one wall of the classroom or corridor or translate into an exhibition or free-standing display for wider viewing in the school or college foyer or other prominent location e.g. local shopping centre.
- e-book – use bookcreator.com to design and publish a professionally presented booklet/report on a key topic.

A substantial group task might involve more than one of these methods of presentation and link to individual sub-roles and the application of a variety of digital tools and apps to support and generate high-quality outcomes.

Visual learning

Presenting learning outcomes on flipchart paper still has benefits within the digital age for its immediacy and impact, but without clear guidance the results can be underwhelming. Flipchart outcomes are often very poorly presented with insufficient consideration of layout and content. A blank sheet of flipchart paper is a spatial challenge for most students and can generate uncertainty of what and how to present the information. The adoption of a Microsoft SmartArt template can improve confidence by clarifying expectations. Hattie refers to graphic organisers and Marzano to 'non-linguistic representations,' but perhaps visual learning is more descriptive. The intention is to introduce a bright, eye-catching template to capture the outcomes of a group task. Marzano notes that teachers primarily operate in a linguistic mode i.e. speech and text whereas cognitive research recommends 'dual coding' i.e. the application of high impact visual representations to strengthen memory: "when teachers help students in this kind of work, however, the effects on achievement are strong. It has even been shown that explicitly engaging students in the creation of non-linguistic representation stimulates and increases activity in the brain."[22] The following templates, wherever possible, draw upon standard 'Shapes' and 'SmartArt' available in Microsoft Word and PowerPoint. You can adopt and adapt the relevant templates. Share the selected template with the students on A4 paper or A3, if preferred, to aid planning and to capture a personal record of the presentation for their own files. Although many may take the shortcut of a photograph. The visual template should be reproduced on a sheet of flipchart paper to capture the final learning outcomes and for display in the classroom. Alternatively, many of the templates can be reproduced and converted into interactive learning activities using PowerPoint to engage a whole class in discussion, completion and display. The templates may also be attached to independent online study as 'record and capture' worksheets (see Chapter 9) to ensure students step beyond passive viewing of a video or reading of an e-book, etc., and fully engage with the resource. Consider the following twenty-one visual templates, and use your own creativity to generate more.

21 visual learning group tasks

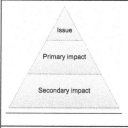	**1 Impact pyramid** Issue your class with a case study of a new theory, new product in the market, new development, new road, new airport, new law, rise in unemployment, increase in population, increase in global temperature, discovery of a major new oil field, etc. We can also introduce the 'What if' question in terms of what if this change occurred? There are changes and developments within all subject areas, and we can encourage higher-order thinking by inviting completion of the Impact pyramid.
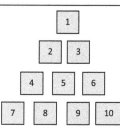	**2 Rank order pyramid** Identify a top set of reasons, theories, explanations, factors, etc., and invite the students to place into a rank order of importance, difficulty, logic, relevance, impact, change i.e. whatever is most applicable to the issue under discussion. The group can build the pyramid from A5 paper or sticky notes during the discussion phase for ease of re-ordering, but when ready use A5 coloured card or large coloured sticky notes to mount onto the flipchart paper.
Concept	Definition	
---	---	---

Concept	Definition	**3 Match**
		Issue a worksheet with two columns of key concepts and definitions and list as many as you wish. Mismatch the order of the concepts and the definitions and invite the students in pairs or small groups to correctly match up by drawing lines between. Alternatively print onto card and cut out to make a set of cards for the students to sort into matches on their desktop. In maths, it can be questions and answers, etc. Attach a timer to add pace. This can also be placed onto a Smartboard for students to drag and drop. Individual students should select a concept and matching definition to elaborate to the rest of the class.

	**4 Poster** Invite students to research a topic in more depth by creating a poster composed of at least four sections. The title goes across the top. The first square should be an image that illustrates the topic theme e.g. a person, place or object. The second square is a text box with some descriptive overview text. The third square has some relevant data or statistics linked to the topic and presented as a chart or a table. The fourth square recommends key websites, books or periodicals for further information on the topic. Perhaps in groups of four one student can take charge of a section each. You might also generate an electronic copy and place onto your LMS with relevant parts clickable to further information, short video clips, websites, etc.

(Continued)

	**5 Similarities and differences** Discuss and compare and contrast two theories, developments, products, leaders, events, etc. List similarities in the centre circle and significant differences in the outer circles e.g. comparison of two cars in motor vehicle, two laptops, two holiday destinations, two leaders, two economic policies, two pathogens, etc. Marzano identifies this as one of the most significant activities for promoting higher-order thinking.
Problem/ Issue / **Solution/ Strategy** 1. 2. 3. 4.	**6 Problems and solutions** Present relevant problems or issues into the left-hand column and alongside invite groups to discuss and arrive at the recommended solution or strategy. This grid has four rows for four groups. Adjust according to the number of problems or issues for discussion. Each group is given time for discussion and research before presenting their solution to the whole class for wider discussion. The topics do not have to be separate topics, but might be sub-topics related to an over-arching lesson theme.
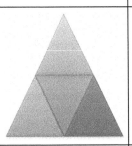	**7 Triangular connections** Place the title of a topic, issue, event, person, place, etc., into the centre triangle. Place a mix of three related facts, formula, statistics, quotations, people, objects, etc., into the outer triangles. Print on card and cut out. Devise at least three sets and jumble all the pieces into an envelope. Issue an envelope to each pair or small group and invite to sort. Add a timer for pace and perhaps a small prize for first to finish and then invite connections, elaboration and explanations to confirm key learning.
	**8 Blue sky thinking** Place the topic into the large cloud and radiating outwards identify key sub-topics and sub-sub-topics. This is essentially a mind mapping task along the lines of "tell me all you know about . . . ?" The first set of sub-topics might be placed into different colours and a smaller set of clouds linked to each sub-topic. Extend as far as possible across the flipchart paper as a summary of a key topic or issue i.e. lots of linked facts and information. You might also place the large cloud in the centre of the page and below the sub-topics as falling raindrops if preferred. A whole class presentation of topic information in this format can make an attractive wall display. Alternatively invest in the giant starburst sticky notes from stationery shops. Use a giant one for the main topic heading and then different coloured standard (or fancier shaped) sticky notes for the sub-topics radiating outwards.
	**9 Advance** The diagram provides for three major points, but you could insert more. Start at the base with an event, person, discovery, invention, etc. You could place a relevant photograph at the base to illustrate the topic. Place labels along the arrow in terms of key development steps, influence, impact, significance or perhaps how a small insignificant event, discovery, observation rises to produce a key theoretical, scientific, engineering advance etc.

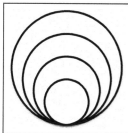	**10 Ripples** A variation on the previous exercise. Insert a key event, person, object in the base circle and identify the major outward ripples. Ideally you are charting the spread of a new idea, theory or discovery. Perhaps the spread of an epidemic, rises in global temperature, growth in retail sales, growth of the European Union member states with, in all cases, related descriptive detail, etc.
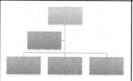	**11 Hierarchy** There is a wide choice of hierarchal charts in Word, and you can select the one that best suits your purpose. Perhaps in the Health Care chart the structure of the Health Service from secretary of state down to individual health trusts, or the police force or typical business organisation or in land-based flora and fauna groupings/families, etc. In each place the appropriate description and explanation. It might also reflect a sequence of linked consequences. Perhaps the first box has the title a rise in global temperatures by two degrees. What are the key consequences and then for each major consequence the linked issues, etc.
	**12 Links** This is a variation on the hierarchal chart. Place the topic in the first bar and below the linked concepts or related sub-topics. You might also use a topic label to create a title bar and use sticky notes to build up the hierarchy.
	**13 Jigsaw** Create a handout by printing the topic title across the top of an A4 page followed by the jigsaw image with four questions or issues linked to the topic title. On the reverse print four large squares to capture the answers or conclusions. Establish four separate groups – A, B, C and D – with four students in each group to examine each sub-topic with a brief to arrive at an answer. Once the groups have completed their research recast the four groups but with one person from each original research group so that within each group there is an A, B, C and D group member. Each person in turn briefs the rest on their group's conclusion and all discuss, raise points for clarification and record a summary.
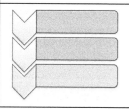	**14 Process** Invite the groups to confirm the best/correct order for a sequence of steps e.g. instructions for operating a machine, preparing a meal, completing a task, a chronology of developments, events, a sequence of consequences – A leads to B and B leads to C, etc.

Daily News Our headline / Relevant Photograph Text, Text, Text, Text, Text, Text, Text, text Text.	**15 Front page** Invite the students in small groups to write up a key topic, theory, development, event, discovery, etc., linked to your subject as though they were reporting the news. This will encourage concise writing and creativity in the reporting style adopted. You might also invite to write an obituary for a famous individual, artist, scientist, engineer, etc. Each group can choose a different standard newsletter template from Word or, better still, if you have Microsoft Publisher with its many more design options.
	**16 Biography** Once opened in Word, as an A4 document the circle contains a prompt for inserting a photograph. Select a list of key people linked to your subject for study e.g. key scientist, poet, writer, artist, engineer, hairdresser, sports star. Drop in their photograph and complete the text box with a short sharp summary of the individual's importance, contribution, theories, etc. The groups could research an individual each and provide feedback as in the jigsaw model. The feedback could be a PowerPoint or other presentation but ultimately reduced to a short, sharp summary to be recorded by all into the textbox. Clearly the textbox will expand and so you can decide in designing the worksheet whether to have two or three mini biographies to a side of A4 or perhaps print onto A3 paper to give more space. Decide a series of standard subheadings to report against e.g. place of birth, education, career highlights, etc. Instead of biographies, the same approach might be taken with events, objects, places, etc.
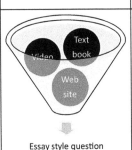 Essay style question	**17 Funnel** Print a topic title and the funnel diagram at the top half of an A4 page and place a text box in the bottom half of the page. At the top of the text box print a question to answer or select a past exam question. To support the answer identify a video, library textbook, periodical article or reference book and a website as information sources. Rotate the groups around each resource and provide prompt questions against each resource to guide thinking. Invite all to write and compare short, sharp answers to the question and if need be spill over onto the back of the handout. However, it is best to specify a word total as a test of the ability to develop sharp, concise writing.
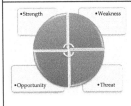	**18 SWOT analysis** SWOT encourages analysis by looking at an issue from the different viewpoints. Key bullet points can be placed into the relevant segment of the circle. On the reverse, divide the A4 page into four quarters to capture more depth of comment. The students could be divided into four groups to take charge of one aspect each and then draw together using the jigsaw model of reporting. A case study often supports this activity well.

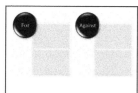

19 Debate
Set a key question for debate and invite all to review and investigate both sides of the argument by creating two vertical columns of key debating points. Draw lots to divide into 'for' and 'against' teams of no more five students per team. The rest of the class should form the audience. Issue the audience with a blank copy of the A4 handout, and as the teams present, the audience members should list the key arguments presented and consider questions they would like to ask. After both presentations and an opportunity to ask questions the audience should place their vote on slip of paper and post into a ballot box for counting. The teacher should announce the winning team.

Question	Personal opinion
For/Positives	Against/ Negatives
Group consensus	Answer

20 Judgment
This table is designed to support a step-by-step critical thinking designed to arrive at a group consensus. To use the table write the issue for debate and judgment into the first box. Next give five minutes of individual thinking time and invite the students to enter their personal opinion into the second box. Next enter into a group discussion to share individual opinions and to confirm the key points to enter into the 'for' and 'against' boxes. When all points are exhausted, the group should examine the evidence and arrive at an overview group consensus. Finally, enter a succinct final answer to the original question.

Essay question
Introduction 100 words
Key points – one paragraph per point

Para 1	Para 2	Para 3
Para 4	Para 5	Para 6

Conclusion 200 words
Finished essay 800–1000 words

21 Academic skeleton essays
Invite students to write skeleton essays as a paired or small group task and if wished, complete the whole essay individually outside of the classroom. This will quickly lift the performance of marginal students and especially if working with more able others. First enter the essay question and underline the key 'instruction' words. Discuss and confirm the instruction words with the class i.e. what is the question asking? Next all should write an introduction of a maximum of 100 words or essentially three sentences. Then discuss and enter one key point per paragraph box – the significant arguments, reasons, etc. Space is provided for six points but there may be more or fewer. Finally write the conclusion in a maximum of 200 words. If the students are directed to write only the introduction and conclusion in full several exam questions can be covered within one lesson. Different pairs or groups can tackle different questions and present their skeleton answers to the class. Or select one skeleton answer and invite the students in groups to write up one key paragraph each. The overall essay when fully written should be 800 to 1000 words.

Image 8.2

Interdisciplinary projects

Group tasks can be beneficially recast as major interdisciplinary projects across several weeks for a more in-depth study focus. Crossing subject boundaries is not a new concept. As highlighted in Chapter 1, Wilhelm von Humboldt recommended combining the arts and sciences as a major part of Prussia's university reforms circa 1820. Rather than simply applying collaborative learning within a single class or curriculum area, creating interdisciplinary project teams can mirror real-world projects. Subject knowledge can be combined and different insights applied to arrive at solutions and viable outcomes to realistic cases studies and/or 'big questions' as presented in Chapter 15. It is an approach adopted by the UK's newest university, the London Interdisciplinary School (LIS). The LIS opened in 2020, and in line with Humboldt's original vision it promotes a fusion between different disciplines: "our innovative interdisciplinary approach teachers the most fundamental theories, research methods and models from across the arts and sciences, then trains the mind to make new connections and find new solutions."[23] Similarly, 'The Engineering and Design Institute' (TEDI) launched in London 2021 also adopts an interdisciplinary approach: "our curriculum takes an interdisciplinary global design approach to engineering . . . the mixture of individual and group projects will allow you to develop teamwork, problem solving, project management and leadership skills and give you the opportunity to study areas that interest you."[24] In October 2020, Dame Nancy Rothwell, the chairwoman of Britain's elite universities, the Russell Group, criticised the early specialisation encouraged by the British education system and recommended increasing the opportunities for interdisciplinary projects.[25] Young people worldwide are very aware of global issues in what is often dubbed the Greta effect, in recognition of the influence of Greta Thunberg. Rather than waiting to be 'educated', children, let alone students, have self-educated from YouTube and regularly interact online (and often on their feet) with society and government on a full range of social, political and economic issues. Who could have predicted even a few years ago that a school child would address the United Nations (UN)? Interdisciplinary projects can channel despondency over major concerns like climate change, plastic pollution, air pollution bio-diversity threats, species extinction, etc., into solution-focussed mindsets. This thinking underpins the Earthshot Prize (www.earthshotprize.org) announced by the Duke of Cambridge, Prince William, in October 2020. In a deliberate echo of the 1960s Moonshot, the Earthshot prize is designed to combat global environmental challenges by awarding five £1 million prizes per year from 2020 to 2030 amounting to £50 million. The prizes will be awarded to individuals or organisations with innovative solutions to help resolve some of the world's most pressing environmental problems. Increasingly individuals can and do make a difference. In 2016, ten-year-old Caillin Patterson designed a poster and initiated a campaign in Ullapool, Scotland, to protect an endangered population of red squirrels. Her environmental focus subsequently shifted to preserving the local reefs from ocean bottom scallop trawling and combatting plastic pollution. Together with her sister Maia and many other local children she established the campaign group 'Ullapool Sea Savers,'[26] which successfully lobbied the Scottish government to establish a local marine conservation park. The translation of problems into challenges by posing 'big questions' can be highly motivational and direct creative energy into relevant citizenship, community and charitable endeavours, and in the case of the Earthshot, to address major global challenges. The WEF 'Schools of the Future' report recommended, "Move from process-based to project- and problem-based content delivery, requiring peer collaboration and more closely mirroring the future of work."[27] Many schools like School21 (school21.org.uk) in East London already involve pupils in applying their subject knowledge by engaging with Real World Learning Projects (RWLP):

> Every student starting in Year 10 is required to successfully complete a Real World Learning Project. . . . Spending half a day a week for a term and a half students are tasked with solving an authentic problem for a real organisation. . . . The projects can take any form. . . . This could be a piece of research, a social media campaign, the redesign of a process, promotional videos, the creation of a piece of art or the planning and delivery of a community event etc. It should be something that would be of genuine value to the organisation.[28]

The International Baccalaureate (www.ibo.org) also involves students in selecting and completing a Creativity, Activity or Service (CAS) project in a similar bid to step beyond the boundaries of single subjects. All those approaches draw students into processing new knowledge by discussing, summarising, comparing, contrasting, etc. This in-depth focus on manipulating and applying new information significantly deepens the relevant memory store, as confirmed by Craik and Lochhart (1972), in terms of shifting learning from shallow to deep retention.[29] Essentially, the more students process information in different ways the greater the recall. Slavin, in reviewing the extensive literature on cooperative learning, commented, "Research on cooperative learning is one of the greatest success stories in the history of educational research."[30] More recently Hattie's summary of educational research evidence confirmed the benefits of peer co-operation: "there seems a universal agreement that cooperative learning is effective . . . cooperation was superior to competition in promoting achievement across all subject areas."[31] Collaborative learning adds significant value not just in relation to building and consolidating knowledge but in developing life and personal competences and contributing to social cohesion.

References

1 Johnson, David W. and Johnson, Roger T., Theory into practice, *Building Community Through Cooperative Learning*, vol. 38, no. 2, Spring, 1999, pg. 72.

2 The Educational Endowment Foundation, *Teachers' Toolkit*, https://educationendowmentfoundation.org.uk/evidence-summaries/teaching-learning-toolkit/collaborative-learning/

3 Johnson, David W. and Johnson, Roger T., Theory into practice, *Building Community Through Cooperative Learning*, vol. 38, no. 2, Spring, 1999, pg. 73.

4 Hattie, John Professor, *Visible Learning for Teachers*, Routledge, 2012, pg. 87.

5 Cullinane, Carl and Montacute, Rebecca, *Life Lessons, Improving Essential Life Skills for Young People*, Sutton Trust, October 2017, pg. 8.

6 Advisory Panel to Government Chaired by Rt. Hon Alan, Milburn M.P., *Unleashing Aspirations: The Final Report of the Panel on Fair Access to the Professions*, HM Government, July 2009.

7 Kirschner, P. A., et al., From cognitive load theory to collaborative cognitive load theory, *International Journal of Computer-Supported Collaborative Learning*, vol. 13, 2018, pg. 213, https://doi.org/10.1007/s11412-018-9277-y

8 Ibid.

9 Slavin, Robert E., *Research on Cooperative Learning and Achievement: What We Know, What We Need to Know*, Center for Research on the Education of Students Placed at Risk, Johns Hopkins University, October 1995, pg. 5.

10 Heywood, John, 1546, www.phrases.org.uk/meanings/two-heads-are-better-than-one.html

11 Johnson, David W. and Johnson, Roger T., Theory into practice, *Building Community Through Cooperative Learning*, vol. 38, no. 2, Spring, 1999, pg. 72–73.

12 Wiliam, Dylan, *Embedded Formative Assessment*, Solution Tree Press, 2011, pg. 137.

13 Danieslon, Charlotte, *The Framework for Teaching, Evaluation Instrument*, 2013, pg. 69, https://www.nctq.org/dmsView/2013_FfTEvalInstrument_Web_v1_2_20140825

14 Marzano, Robert J., *The New Art and Science of Teaching*, Solution Tree Press, 2017, pg. 31.

15 Muijs, Daniel, Kyriakides, Leonidas, van der Werf, Greetje, Creemers, Bert, Timperley, Helen and Earl, Lorna, State of the art – teacher effectiveness and professional learning, *School Effectiveness and School Improvement: An International Journal of Research, Policy and Practice*, vol. 25, no. 2, 2014, pg. 231–256, https://doi.org/10.1080/09243453.2014.885451

16 Hirsch, E. D., *The K-8 Sequence*, The Core Knowledge Foundation, www.coreknowledge.org/our-approach/core-knowledge-sequence/k-8-sequence/

17 Liberty Common Elementary School, *Core Knowledge School of Distinction*, 11th October 2012, https://3o83ip44005z3mk17t31679f-wpengine.netdna-ssl.com/wp-content/uploads/2016/10/Liberty-Common-School.pdf

18 Grayhawk Elementary School, *Core Knowledge School of Distinction*, 3rd June 2014, https://3o83ip44005z3mk17t31679f-wpengine.netdna-ssl.com/wp-content/uploads/2016/10/Grayhawk-Elementary-School.pdf

19 Nestojko, John F., et al., Expecting to teach enhances learning and organisation of knowledge in free recall of text passages, *Journal of Memory and Cognition*, vol. 42, no. 7, 2014, pg. 1038–1048.

20 Slavin, Robert E., *Research on Cooperative Learning and Achievement: What We Know, What We Need to Know*, Center for Research on the Education of Students Placed at Risk, Johns Hopkins University, October 1995, pg. 1.

21 Wiliam, Dylan, *Embedded Formative Assessment*, Solution Tree Press, 2011, pg. 135.

22 Marzano, Robert J., *Classroom Instruction That Works*, Association for Supervision and Curriculum Development, 2001, pg. 73.

23 London Interdisciplinary School (LIS), *Overview*, 2020, www.londoninterdisciplinaryschool.org/overview/

24 The Engineering and Design Institute (Tedi), *About*, 2020, https://tedi-london.ac.uk/learn/about-tedi-london/

25 Pupils should mix arts and science, says woman leading top universities, *The Times*, 24th October 2020.

26 https://ullapoolseasavers.com/

27 World Economic Forum, *Schools of the Future*, World Economic Forum, January 2020, pg. 4.

28 www.school21.org.uk/rwlp

29 Craik, Fergus and Lockhart, Robert, Levels of processing: A framework for memory research, *Journal of Verbal Learning and Verbal Behaviour*, vol. 11, no. 6, 1972.

30 Slavin, Robert E., *Research on Cooperative Learning and Achievement: What We Know, What We Need to Know, Center for Research on the Education of Students Placed at Risk*, Johns Hopkins University, October 1995, pg. 1.

31 Hattie, John, *Visible Learning*, Routledge, 2009, pg. 212.

9

Online teaching

The unexpected closure of schools following the coronavirus pandemic propelled online teaching from the periphery and the realm of the tech enthusiast to the centre of knowledge access and acquisition. It is often remarked that more progress was made in developing online teaching and learning in the five months March to July 2020 than in the preceding five years. The flurry of developmental activity generated significant advances but also exposed the differences between online teaching and online learning. The former was an emergency measure that transferred teachers online via Zoom, Teams or Meet to conduct lessons in real time. As an emergency measure, it succeeded, but only for the minority who had both a laptop and access to the internet. This was as low as 5% in some disadvantaged areas of the UK as reported by the Sutton Trust.[1] Remote 'real-time' teaching also exported many of the limitations of the classroom online and should not be confused with the blended or flipped learning pedagogy. However, remote teaching raised the benefits and familiarity of both teachers and students with digital tools, online resources and particularly video for self-paced anytime and anywhere learning as originally envisaged in the 2006 Vision 2020 report.

Vision 2020

The Vision 2020 report, published in 2006, envisaged internet-based learning as an integral feature of students' programmes by 2020: "changes to the traditional school day and greater access via the internet to interactive learning opportunities, enabling 24-hour access to learning . . . the use of domestic digital technology as a learning tool, including home access to the internet."[2] The report was written by an expert panel chaired by a past chief inspector of Ofsted, Christine Gilbert and commissioned by the then Department of Education and Skills (DfES). The stimulus was the fast pace of technological change and in particular the potential of online resources to extend learning beyond timetabled lessons. The central

DOI: 10.4324/9781003132783-12

recommendation was for the introduction of a personalised learning curriculum, to promote progression by outcome, rather than chronology. Vision 2020 presented the following goals for the development and application of online learning:

- broadening the range of learning material children are able to access, either guided by a teacher or as part of self-directed learning
- enabling quick interactive assessments, for example, using 'voting' technology
- promoting development of a broad range of knowledge, skills and understanding, in new contexts and with virtual access to experts
- facilitating collaboration with peers (in the same school and in other schools) increasing the variety of learning resources, software and communication tools, through new media
- helping schools to use a wider range of readily available resources and software to enhance learning, including making software available to children to use at home
- blurring distinctions between informal and formal learning – giving children the ability to choose what they learn and when they learn it
- increasing motivation, through pace and variety
- increased relevance, through greater links between children's experience of school and of the technology-rich world outside.[3]

These goals have stood the test of time and still embrace good practice considerations i.e. promoting self-directed learning, introducing digital tools for formative assessment, online peer collaboration, access to online resources and enabling online home study. The reference to "virtual access to experts" was also prescient given the rise of expert TED Talks, podcasts, YouTube channels and massive open online courses (MOOCs) to stretch and challenge students. Vision 2020 was never resourced or pursued following a change in government but given the events of 2020 the following goal, in particular, represented a missed opportunity: "They [Government] should consider how technology might be used to enhance pupils' access to learning resources and key software packages from home."[4] In 2019 the Department of Education renewed interest in integrating digital technology with the classroom with the publication of a digital technology strategy: "We are living in a digitally enabled world where technology is increasingly part of our society. We owe it to our young people, and to anyone who wants to upskill, to do more to explore and reap the benefits that technology can bring."[5] Similarly, the Organisation for Economic Co-operation and Development (OECD) report 'Learning Compass 2030' highlighted the importance of preparing young people for living and working in a digital society. The goals for 2030 were amplified in an OECD webinar November 2020[6] with an emphasis upon digital integration with the classroom rather than a digital 'bolt-on' and the promotion of a holistic pedagogy centred on knowledge, skills, attitudes and values.

Digital learning pedagogy

The stand-alone timetabled lesson with a start, middle and end is a deeply embedded construct that has defined learning for over 200 years, but over the last five years artificial intelligence (AI) has transformed how learning is accessed, presented and assessed. Learning is no longer bound by time or location or reliant on the curriculum knowledge of an individual teacher. Consequently, it is essential that our classroom-focussed pedagogy adjusts to embrace learning beyond as well as within the classroom by addressing the following key elements of knowledge acquisition and comprehension.

Image 9.1

Goals – Students need to know what to study, in what order and to what depth and this raises a requirement for student-facing rather than staff-facing curriculum planning. Ideally, advance organisers should replace traditional schemes of work to share the study goals along with recommended resources as detailed in Chapter 10.

Knowledge – An online knowledge library can promote high-quality teaching and learning by stepping beyond the experience and knowledge of an individual teacher in favour of the expertise of a curriculum team with links to wider expert opinion including the latest innovations and research. Curriculum teams should curate a wide range of stimulating resources to support each key unit.

Questions – Introduce pre-questions and key questions in place of objectives to prompt a focus on arriving at answers and underpin a learning agenda that can extend online.

Elaboration – Focus lessons on dialogic learning by applying flipped learning pedagogy. Place core subject knowledge online and reserve class time for a mix of individual, paired and group tasks to elaborate and interrogate new information. Utilise digital collaborative and presentation tools to support and extend peer support.

Feedback – Adopt a coaching role by using digital tools to provide each student with clear, precise improvement actions with additional support and/or acceleration as appropriate. Feed forward more than feedback with precise improvement actions to apply in future assignments with the aim of step-by-step refinement.

Challenge – Attach a challenge task to every key unit with encouragement for all to have a go rather than associating challenge with the more able. Identify related online resources to raise horizons and to promote critical thinking.

These items present a 'digital edge' 'to the core elements of effective teaching and learning practice as introduced in Chapter 1 and raise the importance of blended learning.

Blended learning

Blended learning is an umbrella title for all forms of digital learning activity whether digital tools within a lesson, accessing online resources, online collaborative forums or the application of flipped learning. The term blended learning arose within the business training industry during the 1990s as a description for instructional programmes involving a 'blend' of different learning experiences e.g. direct instruction, individual task and group task. The term was subsequently adopted by distance learning providers to describe achieving a motivational balance or blend between classroom, textbook, video and learning pack resources. Following the steady migration of learning resources online, the term 'blended learning' followed and was increasingly attached to any study programme combining classroom with computer-based resources. Bonk and Graham in their authoritative survey of blended learning (2006) provided the following widely quoted definition, "blended learning systems combine face to face instruction with computer-mediated instruction."[7] However, opinions vary as to whether the *computer-mediated instruction* should be within or beyond the lesson. The practice of distance learning providers was to avoid taking up valuable lesson time studying resources that could be absorbed outside the classroom. Consequently, we should distinguish between digital tools that enhance the process of teaching and learning and a digital resource like a video that could be viewed outside the classroom. This principle is even more relevant in the digital era given that online resources are accessible twenty-four hours per day but class time is strictly limited. Whereas blended learning focuses on enhancing the process of teaching and learning with digital tools and resources, flipped learning addresses advance preparation for lessons.

Flipped learning pedagogy

The concept of flipped learning evolved from the redesign of the traditional university lecture by Professor Eric Manzur, from Harvard University. His concern was not only the passive nature of the lecture format but more fundamentally the cognitive processes involved in assimilating unfamiliar concepts and information. To improve the process he experimented with releasing his PowerPoint slides in advance of his lectures along with pre-questions for the students to consider and answer. Within the lecture theatre Manzur invited the students to form pairs to discuss and agree their answers followed by combining the pairs into groups of four to further refine their answers. The random formation of pairs and groups generated a heterogenous mix of students and resulted in beneficial crossovers of different opinions and knowledge and triggered peer-to-peer tuition in an echo of the Monitorial system described in Chapter 1. The traditional lecture theatre format of a formal presentation, passive note-taking and a few tentative questions from the more confident students gave way to in-depth discussion and raised points for clarification which Manzur then addressed. It was adaptive teaching in action because rather than presenting a standard lecture, Manzur identified and corrected misconceptions as they arose. He called his approach peer instruction and published the book *Peer Instruction* in 1997 with the following key recommendations:

1   Instructor poses question based on students' responses to their pre-class reading.
2   Students reflect on the question.
3   Students commit to an individual answer.
4   Instructor reviews student responses.
5   Students discuss their thinking and answers with their peers.
6   Students then commit again to an individual answer.
7   The instructor again reviews responses and decides whether more explanation is needed before moving on to the next concept.

This sequence remains at the heart of flipped learning pedagogy, and it is worth reflecting on how it develops and secures learning. The pre-questions offer valuable thinking time and permit students to formulate answers before entering into dialogue with the tutor, discussion with peers and lastly confirmation of the key learning points. Not only have the students assimilated information in advance of the session and had time to reflect on what they understand and don't fully understand but the session is focused not on listening and receiving new information but on understanding and evaluation. In parallel in 2000 Wesley J Baker from the University of Cedarville developed a similar model he described as 'The Classroom Flip.' Baker was also dissatisfied with the passive nature of the traditional lecture format and particularly students focusing on capturing notes from his slides rather than fully concentrating on and evaluating the content. Today it is common to see students in a lesson photographing PowerPoint slides with their mobile phones. To assist the students Baker routinely posted his PowerPoint presentations online after his lecture to ease the note-taking task. However, like Manzur, it occurred to him that posting his slides in advance of the lecture would be of greater benefit both to ease the cognitive load and to encourage the students to enter the lecture theatre with pre-prepared questions:

> A key component for the 'flipped' class is the movement of lecture material out of the classroom through online delivery . . . classroom discussion is extended . . . discussion gives a voice to many students who are silent during in-class discussions. Experience has shown that these students want time to prepare, edit and rewrite their comments before submitting them to peer review. Their contributions to the discussion are usually well thought out and carefully articulated.[8]

Baker's research is archived but may be accessed at www.classroomflip.com. Baker's 'flip' was facilitated by the release by Microsoft of the option to save PowerPoint slides as video and the emergence of software like Camtasia for capturing and uploading videos onto Virtual Learning Environment (VLE) platforms.

Developing flipped learning

The use of video as a primary means of supporting learning arose from the initiative of Jonathan Bergmann and Aaron Sams. Bergmann and Sams both taught chemistry in Woodland Park School in Colorado, and in 2010 they experimented with capturing key topic information and lab experiments on video and posting online for their students to view in advance of their lessons. After some weeks of trials they perfected, short, sharp video explanations, instructions and lab experiments and collaborated to cover their whole chemistry curriculum. The immediate benefit for the students was being able to absorb the information at their own pace and with the ability to rewind, re-watch, pause, make notes and identify aspects of personal difficulty for later clarification in the classroom. The option to 'pause the teacher' was reported by the students to be their favourite feature of the new strategy; the equivalent of being handed the TV remote. This popularity of this option was later confirmed by Professor John Hattie because it allowed students to re-watch and re-listen as many times as they wished to fully absorb key points.[9] Bergmann and Sams experimented further and noted that their students made faster and deeper progress if they reversed or 'flipped' the standard pattern of teaching and learning.

The common approach to teaching and learning, as illustrated, is using lesson time for note-taking from direct instruction, a textbook or watching video, etc., to build key topic information which pupils or students record as notes. Homework is typically set against this information base with the tasks and questions designed to promote reflection, analysis and evaluation. In practice, the focus of the classroom was on lower-order information gathering tasks while the

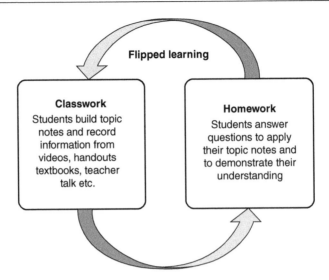

Image 9.2

homework presented higher-order evaluative tasks. Many students struggled with the latter, and in the absence of a teacher to help, it was common for students to turn to their siblings, parents and/or their friends for help or to simply give up and offer variations of 'the dog ate my homework' or in the modern age, 'my laptop crashed.' The failure of many students to submit homework was often not so much a case of poor behaviour, but rather poor understanding. The flipped learning pedagogy 'flips' the less demanding note-taking tasks out of the classroom to form the homework tasks and reserves the classroom for a mixture of explanatory direct instruction and collaborative tasks to evaluate and analyse the topic information with the added advantage of teacher support. The key advantage for both teachers and students is time to focus lessons on the cognitive gap i.e. Piaget's step up from concrete factual reasoning to higher order conceptual reasoning. Hattie ranked Piagetian Programs as second in his overall rank order of 150 influences on achievement. Consequently, far from being redundant by the march of technology teachers' subject expertise and supportive interventions are vital to coach and lift all students forward. As Couros was keen to emphasise, "Technology will never replace great teachers, but technology in the hands of great teachers is transformational."[10] Although the term 'homework' is used in the diagram, it should be interpreted more broadly as extended learning. In 2012 Bergmann and Sams published *Flip Your Classroom* as a guide to implementing what quickly became dubbed flipped learning. Their learning strategy has since expanded into a major international learning initiative with a substantial research and practitioner base. Bergmann co-founded and currently leads the Flipped Learning Global Initiative which now governs the development and application of quality standards for flipped learning across forty-seven countries (www.flglobal.org).

Creating a learning sequence

To put blended and flipped learning into practice, the key is to plan a sequence of learning across a topic rather than planning for a lesson at a time. It is about achieving a learning 'flow' from the classroom to online and back again. The aim is a single, stimulating learning experience, with each lesson contributing to the achievement of the learning goals for a topic as a whole. The following is an illustration of a learning sequence across five lessons and in practice involving appropriate digital tools and resources.

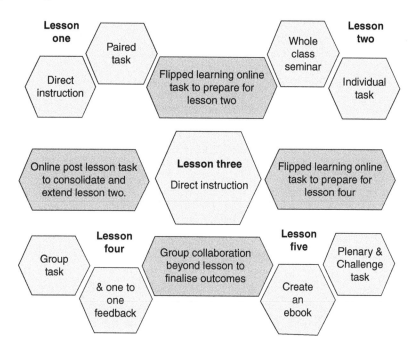

Image 9.3

★Creating an e-book using bookcreator.com is an example. See Chapter 10 for a wide range of reporting techniques e.g. an information display, a video, a presentation, a podcast, a report, a photo slide show. Those reporting techniques permit outcomes to be developed and completed beyond the lesson. No more rushed in-lesson student report backs and no more low stakes inconsequential tasks – high standards should be modelled and secured.

The planning of both pre-lesson and post-lesson learning extensions releases class time to check and deepen learning. It removes the concept of learning confined to a fixed timescale in a fixed location and counters the all too common student mindset that learning ends when the lesson ends. Success will involve coaching and fostering self-regulated learning (SRL) to develop and equip students as confident, independent learners. SRL correlates with high success rates and is a notable feature of the skillset of Chinese and Indian heritage students who routinely top national examination success tables as detailed in Chapter 13. Our significant goal is to prompt and support our more dependent students to equally apply themselves beyond the classroom. The shaded learning extensions must avoid the trap of being 'bolt-on' tasks, but rather they either carry forward the learning developed in a lesson with a consolidation task (post-lesson) or a flipped learning task for advance preparation for the next lesson (pre-lesson).

This two-way learning extension identifies lessons as components within an overall sequence of learning and promotes students as active participants in their own learning. Rather than waiting to receive and note information in each lesson, students enter ready to report and/or engage in collaborative analysis and evaluation. This shift liberates teachers from spending most of their lesson time presenting core subject information as highlighted by the Education and Training Foundation:

> Technological advances and more specifically the internet facilitate a "shift from thinking about teaching as providing information to thinking of learning and creating learning environments." This in turn creates a relationship shift between teachers and learners as the teacher is no longer the sole information holder and promotes an "evolution toward inquiry-based learning and toward the development of a learner-centred environment.[11]

The effectiveness of blended and flipped learning is often questioned, but research evidence indicates that it is as effective as standard classroom instruction.

Research evidence

The Education Information Resources Center (ERIC)[12] has recorded 34,196 research studies against the research search term 'online learning' with a further 415 reported in 2020. A search by 'flipped learning' yields 1047 research studies with 44 published in 2020. The consensus is that online learning and/or flipped learning strategies produce outcomes comparable with teacher-led lessons. Neither is markedly superior, but in terms of learning experiences self-paced learning records high satisfaction scores. This no doubt relates to the popularity, as reported earlier, of pausing, rewinding and re-watching direct instruction on video rather than trying to keep pace with classroom-based instruction. Professor John Hattie's review of teaching strategies observed, "it does seem that many computer packages may be of better instructional quality compared to many teachers' instructional methods."[13] Robert J. Marzano has also acknowledged the contribution of online learning resources "with the advent of free internet-based materials . . . blended learning is no longer the future of classroom instruction, it is the present."[14] In 2020 the principal of Basingstoke College of Technology reported the outcomes of a trial project using AI-enabled personalised learning techniques to support the teaching of maths as follows:

> We were pleased to see that the results showed that when students used AI to help revise for their maths GCSE resits for as little as 10 minutes a week, they improved their results twice as much as the national average. Those who used AI to revise for over one hour a week saw improvements of over 10 times the national average. Overall, we found that the technology empowers students to take more ownership of their learning which enables students, who may have been less engaged in a more traditional school classroom environment, to be more involved in achieving their goals.[15]

The project was supported by UFI Tech Ed and Century Tech and demonstrated the ability of AI to pinpoint students' misconceptions and to cue additional support. The Education Endowment Foundation (EEF) also published positive research conclusions in relation to remote teaching initiatives in April 2020. The central conclusion was that "teaching quality is more important than how lessons are delivered." This conclusion was amplified as follows:

> Pupils can learn through remote teaching. Ensuring the elements of effective teaching are present – for example clear explanations, scaffolding and feedback – is more important than how or when they are provided. There was no clear difference between teaching in real time ("synchronous teaching") and alternatives ("asynchronous teaching"). For example, teachers might explain a new idea live or in a pre-recorded video. But what matters most is whether the

explanation builds clearly on pupils' prior learning or how pupils' understanding is subsequently assessed.[16]

The focus is firmly on pedagogy rather than technology.

Curating a knowledge library

Knowledge is but a question away. Knowledge is no longer the preserve of individual teachers or limited to the information available from one or two class textbooks as it was for past generations. Ask Google, Cortana, Alexa or Siri a question and gain an immediate answer:

Q What is the square root of 24?
A *4.899*

Q What is the capital of Slovakia?
A *Bratislava*

Q What time is it in New York?
A *It is currently 4.15 p.m. in the UK and 11.15 a.m. in New York.*

Q What is graphene?
A *Graphene is an allotrope of carbon in the form of a two dimensional atomic scale lattice in which one atom forms each vertex.*

Q How deep is the ocean?
A *Challenger Deep in the Western Pacific is the deepest known point at 36,200 feet.*

Q What is the difference between inflation and deflation?
A *Inflation occurs when the price of goods and services rise while deflation occurs when those prices decrease.*

Q What were the causes of the First World War?
A *The immediate cause was the assassination of Archduke Franz Ferdinand on 28 June 1914 but historians believe that the rivalry between the Great Powers precipitated the wider world war. To discover more follow this web link.*

The internet first went live to the public 6 August 1991 following its development in 1989 by the British Scientist Tim Berners-Lee to solve the problem of large data transfers between scientists working on the CERN project in Geneva, Switzerland. The early internet was a 'read only' environment with many resources of dubious merit, but the internet of today offers fully interactive learning resources, from authoritative sources, across all disciplines, both surface and deep. However, it is important to distinguish between the internet and online learning. Online learning relates to a controlled learning environment commonly referred to as a VLE but increasingly with the addition of progress tracking and adaptive learning software reference to a learning management system (LMS) or a personalised learning platform (PLP) would be more accurate. The internet remains a vast unregulated store of fact, fiction and opinion. The answers provided by the internet (as illustrated earlier) are in many cases incomprehensible without wider knowledge of the subject as demonstrated by the definition of graphene. The internet can also produce inaccurate, fragmented, or superficial knowledge. Distinguishing not just reliable but expert online knowledge is key, but a wealth of authoritative resources is just a click away. The aim is to curate a stimulating mix of resources to not only support but to extend and stretch students beyond their immediate study goals.

Universities	E-books	TV channels
Research organisations	Apps	Blogs/vlogs
Museums	Websites	World-class experts
Art galleries	Newspapers	Business organisations
Encyclopaedia	Periodicals	Industry
Charities	Trade unions	Government
Examination boards	Journals	Video channels
Photographs	Infographics	Statistics
Cartoons	Maps	Slideshows

Image 9.4

The scale of the information revolution is overwhelming with any one of these sources involving thousands of research reports, articles, images, video, etc. In terms of educational apps there are at the time of writing over 75,000 available for download from Apple and 45,000 on Google Play. There is a 'gee-whiz' danger to consider that in earlier times was applied to classroom games and team activities. It is a question of remaining focussed on learning outcomes and ensuring that any app or resource selected is not simply of novelty value but helps to advance learning. Curriculum teams should review and adopt digital tools and apps that have a clear beneficial learning edge i.e. pedagogy before technology.

E-book revolution

The rise of e-books has transformed the humble textbook into a potent interactive resource with embedded video links, the ability to highlight text, insert bookmarks, conduct a text search and even convert selected information into flashcards for revision. Many e-books like the Pearson enhanced e-book collection include in-built assessments at the end of each chapter. The rising generations are increasingly switching from physical books to e-books. In 2010 Pearson alone sold 21 million textbooks to university students in the United States, but today sales are less than 3 million and falling. Visit Pearson, Kortext, Kognity, Bibliu and Vitalsource to view the extensive range and benefits offered by e-books. In addition, rather than buying an e-book Perlego.com offers access to a vast library of e-books in exchange for a monthly subscription fee. As with other apps and online resources the choices can be overwhelming and it emphasises the importance of curriculum teams guiding selections, checking provenance and channelling online resources into learning pathways.

EFT guidance

The Education and Training Foundation (ETF) includes the following guidance for curating online knowledge libraries as part of its overall digital professional standards:

- Formulate appropriate search strategies to identify digital resources for teaching and learning
- Select suitable digital resources for teaching and learning, considering the specific learning context and learning objective
- Critically evaluate the credibility and reliability of digital sources and resources
- Consider possible restrictions to the use or re-use of digital resources (e.g. copyright, file type, technical requirements, legal provisions, accessibility)
- Assess the usefulness of digital resources in addressing the learning objective, the competence levels of the learner group as well as the teaching approach chosen.
- Adapt and edit existing digital resources, where permitted
- Combine and mix existing digital resources or parts of them, where permitted
- Create new digital educational resources
- Jointly create with others digital educational resources.
- Consider the specific learning objective, context, teaching approach, and learner group, when adapting or creating digital learning resources.[17]

Teachers are also increasingly supplementing online resources with their own direct instruction videos. Students respond well to seeing their teachers on video. It helps to reinforce and strengthen the relationship and permits teachers to target and address precise aspects of instruction. Within the vocational curriculum e.g. science, catering, hairdressing, construction, video can easily capture a demonstration or a particular vocational skill or process and grant students the option to view as many times as wished to reinforce and consolidate the technique. In addition, video should encompass the 'process' of learning just as much as information 'content' i.e. creating 'how to' videos, both generic and specific, in relation to the study demands of a programme e.g. how to layout an assignment, how to revise, how to write a lab report, how to write an essay or more basically the correct use of the apostrophe. Many teachers are also increasingly taking the next step and sharing their video resources worldwide via YouTube or Loom or perhaps opening an e-shop on the Times Educational Supplement (TES) website to sell their resources.

Maths leading the way

Maths was the first subject to significantly benefit from the online learning revolution with the development of the Khan Academy in 2008. It is worthy of note that the Khan Academy was not developed by a teacher or a teacher trainer or a professor of education or an educational consultant or a writer of educational textbooks, but by Salman Khan a hedge fund analyst of Mountain View, California. Within the last decade the Khan Academy has expanded to become the world's largest online school with 10 million logins per month across 400,000 lessons translated into thirty-six languages. The real-time dashboard applies mastery learning principles by monitoring progress, pinpointing misunderstandings, offering further practice and/or advancing to the next step as appropriate. The Khan Academy has since stepped beyond maths into sciences, computing, humanities and economics underpinned by financial support from Bill Gates and with a stated mission to "provide a free, world class education to anyone, anywhere."[18] In 2015 the Khan Academy established its first terrestrial presence with the opening of the Khan Lab School (KLS) in San Francisco. The school employs not teachers but learning advisers who monitor and direct each pupil's PLP. Nor are the pupils grouped by age but by their levels of learning independence/ability. Beyond the Khan Academy, the following are some of the most popular and reliable sources of online maths tuition:

The most recent addition, drfrostmaths.com, was launched by the maths teacher Jamie Frost in 2016 following in the footsteps of Colin Hegarty. Hegarty is an Oxford graduate with a first-class degree in mathematics who was shortlisted for the Global Teacher Award for outstanding contributions to teaching in 2016.

Subscription access	Free access
Ezyeducation.co.uk	Corbettmaths.com
Mymaths.co.uk	Studymaths.co.uk
Mangahigh.com	Mei.org.uk
Matheletics.co.uk	Mathigon.org
Mathsbank.co.uk	Math-quiz.co.uk (but pay for extras)
Mathscentre.ac.uk	Eddie Woo (YouTube channel)
Mathswatch.co.uk	Citizenmaths.com
Hegartymaths.com	Drfrostmaths.com

Image 9.5

Frost also gained a First at Oxford, and like Hegarty, his website covers the maths curriculum from primary to sixth-form level. The comparison doesn't end there because, in turn, Frost was nominated for the Global Teacher of the Year Award in 2020, and although he never won the top prize, he was awarded the special prize of Covid Hero for the support offered to students during the coronavirus pandemic in 2020. Frost's website provides a comprehensive programme of maths support utilising the latest AI tracking and assessment software to offer a highly personalised learning experience. Maths is leading the way but similar developments across the curriculum are increasingly offering all students access to expert knowledge. Try youtube.com/crashcourse for a swift overview of an expanding range of topics.

Capture and record worksheets

To fully integrate online resources with the classroom, it is important to consider how the resource will support or further extend knowledge of a topic. Consider the information you expect your students to gain from viewing a video, visiting a website or reading a chapter of an e-book, etc., and design a worksheet to capture and record the relevant information. Equally design worksheets to step beyond mere recording of information by employing SmartArt templates to prompt and scaffold appropriate analysis and evaluation e.g. cataloguing, ranking, summarising, comparing. The visual learning templates presented in Chapter 8 may be easily applied or adapted for this role. Alternatively gain stimulation and many free template downloads from https://templates.office.com or design your own worksheets to ensure that students fully engage with the specified resources to avoid passive access.

Cornell note-taking

The Cornell note-taking system provides a straightforward but highly effective way to not only capture and record notes but to prompt metacognitive thinking. It was first developed by Professor Walter Pauk of Cornell University circa 1956 and can be used to fully engage students with note-taking from direct instruction or any online resources e.g. textbook, journal article, website.

Key points	My notes
After you have recorded your notes, re-read them and use this space to summarise with key bullet points.	Use this space to record all your notes whether from a lecture, a textbook, video, article, etc.
My questions Use this space to record questions you want to ask or simply points for clarification.	

Image 9.6

Invite the students to rule an A4 page following the layout provided here. The students should record overview notes in the main section and reduce their notes to four or five key bullet points in the left-hand column to introduce an immediate element of evaluation and analysis. The last 'My questions' section encourages the students to reflect upon their understanding and importantly to gain the confidence to raise questions for clarification. The ability to self-question is an important step towards developing SRL and overall metacognition.

Creating video slide shows

One of the simplest and most effective ways to support and develop blended and flipped learning pedagogy is to create video slide shows via PowerPoint or similar for self-paced learning with embedded teacher video instruction. All teachers are familiar with slide shows, and by adding video instruction they can support high-impact teaching and learning. The key is to select a single aspect of subject knowledge to ensure a sharp 'bite size' focus rather than a longer multi-issue slide show. Online resources are easily embedded into slides by adding hyperlinks to the appropriate video, e-book or website, etc. Ensure your slides avoid lists of bullet points by applying dual coding principles and aim for a stimulating mix of photographs, infographics, quotations, video, text, etc. Interspace with slides specifying tasks for completion and relevant 'capture and record' diagrams to copy into notebooks. Create a bright title slide and introduce the video with a full screen 'talking head' video presentation for maximum visual impact. As you move through the slides alternate full screen video teacher instruction with smaller video windows placed alongside relevant text and graphics.

Create single issue slideshows including direct instruction.	Use the 'convert to Smartart' option to alter bullet point lists for visual impact.	Apply dual coding with high visual impact images, infographics, tables, video etc
Introduce audio voiceover or video- whole screen or small video windows.	Use the 'action' option to introduce a menu for slide navigation	Use the 'link' option to make a hyperlink to a website, eBook, or a video etc.
Use different animations for text and objects to slide in or appear.	Click 'Add On' and select useful apps e.g. interactive assessment polls.	Set transitions for slides to auto advance and save as video if wished*

Image 9.7

You can stretch or shrink video windows in the same way as text boxes and by clicking on 'video format' in the ribbon menu at the top of the screen select border options or opt to place the video within a shape. The above prompts relate to Power-Point 365 and highlight options to create a high-impact presentation.

If you are not familiar with some of these options, help is but a click away. Simply search for 'PowerPoint' on YouTube and you will discover multiple channels providing step-by-step guidance from beginner through to many impressive, advanced features. The latest version of PowerPoint is PowerPoint 365, and it offers the advantage of direct in-slide video recording and editing rather than the need to create and import a video file. This option provides a simple way to experiment with creating teacher instruction videos, and you will find step-by-step instructions in Chapter 3.

Finally, the experience of remote learning during the coronavirus pandemic revealed the extent of student dependency on teacher direction and the major disparity in SRL skills between students. Coaching SRL is a vital foundation step if all students are to thrive and take advantage of online learning.

References

1 Sutton Trust, *Learning in Lockdown*, Sutton Trust, 21st January 2021.
2 Department for Education and Skills, *Vision 2020, Report of the Teaching and Learning in 2020 Review Group*, Department for Education and Skills, 2006, pg. 26.
3 Ibid, pg. 27.
4 Ibid, pg. 28.
5 Department for Education, *Realising the Potential for Technology in Education*, Department for Education, April 2019, pg. 3.
6 Sutton Trust, *Learning in Lockdown*, Sutton Trust, 21st January 2021.
7 Bonk, C. J. and Graham, C. R., *The Handbook of Blended Learning: Global Perspectives*, Pfeiffer, 2006, pg. 5.
8 Baker, W. J., *The Classroom Flip*, www.classroomflip.com/files/classroom_flip_baker_2000.pdf
9 Hattie, J., *The Times*, 16th March 2019.
10 Couros, George, https://georgecouros.ca/blog/archives/tag/technology-will-not-replace-great-teachers
11 Education and Training Foundation, *EdTech Strategy*, Education and Training Foundation, 2018–2021, pg. 5.
12 Education Information Resources Center, https://eric.ed.gov/
13 Hattie, J., *Visible Learning*, Routledge, 2009, pg. 224.
14 Marzano, R. J., *The New Art and Science of Teaching*, Solution Tree Press, 2017, pg. 110.
15 Bravo, Andrew, *Times Educational Supplement*, Is AI the Secret to Improving GCSE Resit Pass Rates, 5th January 2020.

16 Education Endowment Foundation, *Remote Learning, Rapid Evidence Assessment*, Education Endowment Foundation, April 2020, pg. 4.

17 Education and Training Foundation, *Digital Teaching Professional Framework*, www.et-foundation.co.uk

18 The Khan Academy, *Mission Statement*, www.khanacademy.org/about

10

Online learning

At 6. p.m. on 29 June 2007, Apple released the iPhone and ignited a revolution both in social interactions and access to information. As we enter the 5G era with chips as small as three nanometres to power the Internet of Things (IOT), phones will become primary hubs for the management of all aspects of our lives. Generation Z and Millennials have already entered parenthood, and it is the iPhone generation, or Generation Alpha, who are seated in our primary classrooms and increasingly entering our high school classrooms. Alpha are immersed in a bright online treasure house of knowledge, music, games, video, shopping, travel and entertainment and it is a world they have always known. Their parents helped them to drift off to sleep by listening to the Baby Soothe app from the Apple Store and as soon as Alpha could grasp an object they reached for the iPhone or equivalent. Toddlers have been observed trying the swipe the pages in a book, and most knew the alphabet before they entered their reception classes from apps like Alpha Blocks. The UK Office for Communications (Ofcom) monitors the upward and downward digital trends, and in February 2020 they reported the following access to internet-connected devices for the age group twelve to fifteen years.

Ofcom noted "between the ages of nine and ten, smartphone ownership doubles from 23% to 50% – representing an important milestone in children's digital

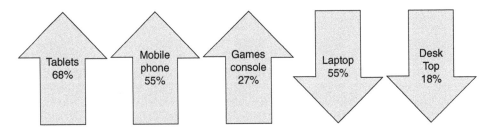

Image 10.1 The arrow indicates an upward or downward trend along with current percentage usage.

DOI: 10.4324/9781003132783-13

independence as they prepare to transition to secondary school. At age 15 almost all children own their own smartphones"[1] In 2020 smartphone ownership in the UK was 96% for people ages fifteen and up, and YouTube was preferred over terrestrial television, with 89% watching YouTube videos for an average of eleven hours per week and 71% maintained a social media profile.[2]

The outcome has been an explosion in online data with access to data now treated as a basic utility as vital as water, gas and electricity supply. Any interruption to the data flow makes for headline news. In 2019 the average daily data consumption was as follows:[3]

- 500m tweets
- 294bn emails
- 4PB Facebook
- 5bn searches per day with 3.5bn via Google
- 95m Instagram videos and photos
- 65bn WhatsApp messages
- 4TB from connected cars
- 28PB from wearable technology

Data units
KB Kilobyte 1,000 bytes
MB Megabyte $1,000^2$ bytes
GB Gigabyte $1,000^3$ bytes
TB Terabyte $1,000^4$ bytes
PB Petabyte $1,000^5$ bytes
EB Exabyte $1,000^6$ bytes
ZB Zettabyte $1,000^7$ bytes
YB Yottabyte $1,000^8$ bytes

All of this is a world away from the first cell phone launched by Motorola in 1973. It weighed 1.1 kg, measured 228 × 27 × 44mm and had a battery life of

Image 10.2

thirty minutes with no memory facility for telephone numbers, let alone anything else. Motorola executive Martin Cooper was credited with making the world's first cell phone call on 3 April 1973. Today the significant majority, not simply Generation Alpha, are comfortable online and are avid consumers of online information, entertainment, goods and services as regularly cued by Google, Facebook, Amazon, Twitter, Instagram, YouTube, Tik Tok, apps, blogs and podcasts. Given this ready access to information twenty-four hours per day and seven days per week, the concept of learning being confined to three or four lessons per week is entirely anachronistic. This reality was acknowledged by the Education and Training Foundation:

> It (ed-tech) should be seen as an inseparable thread woven throughout the processes of teaching and learning. It is senseless to pretend it isn't something that every teacher and every learner uses every day. What we should concentrate on is when and in which ways it is best deployed to support these processes.[4]

Online subject knowledge to support and extend learning beyond the classroom is a common feature of school and college learning platforms, but as detailed in Chapter 11, the sum of education is more than qualifications. All aspects of personal development should be promoted and supported online by developing an opportunity-rich learning portal.

Creating a holistic learning portal

The five major aspects – Knowledge, Community, Challenge, Enrichment and Create – are broad labels to illustrate an online focus on holistic personal development as follows. The sub-topics as illustrated are far from exhaustive. The aim is to curate a comprehensive range of support services, opportunities and resources to underpin all aspects of personal development. Many schools and colleges not only ensure comprehensive support but also introduce a weekly online 'spotlight' feature or similar to advertise an event, promotion, campaign or innovation of general interest. Curriculum teams need to become adept at stirring curiosity and using social media to nudge and draw students into participation. Ideally, encouraging a whole school or college identity by promoting interaction between different year-groups and disciplines, including regular social media outreach to parents or guardians. The focus is opportunity to counter disadvantage by stepping beyond immediate community and life experiences to provide a window on the world. The significant purpose is to reinforce the benefit of education as a portal to a better and fulfilling life. If the portal can be characterised as 'hardware,' then self-regulated learning (SRL) is the 'software' and without attention to developing SRL students will fail to take advantage of the opportunities offered.

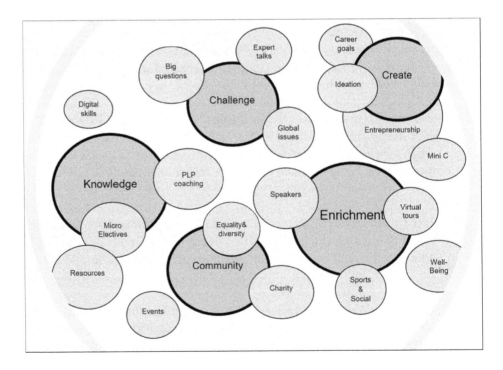

Image 10.3

Closure of schools

The absence of SRL became evident during the closure of schools in 2020 when high numbers of students failed to meet study targets or even log in to online lessons. Within the UK concerns were expressed for a 'lost generation' and the emergence of a 'learning gap' that might take six or more months to bridge. Much of the concern was prompted by research published by Professor Francis Green from University College, London. Green's research revealed that one in five pupils had completed no schoolwork at all or managed less than an hour a day during the lockdown, and he concluded that the closure of schools "constituted a potential threat to the educational development of a generation of children."[5] The political and academic reaction centred around introducing more 'catch-up' class time with proposals for extending the school day, the school week, summer classes or stepping back to repeat a year. The alternative summarised by the popular adage, 'do you give a person a fish a day or do you teach people how to fish' was absent from the debate, yet our most successful students; the independent learners have always studied beyond the classroom. The study skills and metacognitive competencies of independent learners need to be normalised by actively coaching and scaffolding SRL i.e. the ability to set, monitor and ultimately achieve personal learning goals.

Independent learning

Independent learning is not a modern-day, liberal concept but was identified as early as 1904 by the British Board of Education as a primary goal: "Self-education should be the key note of the older children's curriculum . . . instruction will have its fullest effect when the teacher realises that his chief task is to teacher the scholars to teach themselves and adapt his methods steadily to that end."[6] Long before the internet, the Public Libraries Act 1850 funded libraries in every British town and city to promote and encourage self-education and later funded the 'library hour' in every school to extend and consolidate classroom learning from recommended textbooks. The Board of Education further commented: "to develop in them [pupils] such a taste for good reading and thoughtful study as will enable them to increase that knowledge in after years by their own efforts."[7] At university level 'reading for a degree' was not simply an expression but an expectation. Reading lists were issued, and students were expected to read the relevant texts in advance of a seminar or to extend and deepen the information presented in a lecture. In addition, many parents, well into modern times, invested in a set of encyclopaedias with Britannica the most well-known and sought-after brand. Britannica's last printed edition was in 2010, but its tradition as an authoritative source of information is maintained online (www.britannica.

com). In my personal case, my working-class parents bought a twelve-volume set of Newes Pictorial Knowledge from a travelling encyclopaedia salesman with monthly payments spread out over two years. I still have them on my bookshelf and I well remember the extensive knowledge I gleaned on Roman Britain well in excess of what was covered in the three lessons available to my history teacher, Mr Beckett. As we progress deeper into the digital era with its ease of access to online resources, it is vital to take active steps to develop our students' capacity for SRL and to raise an expectation for day-to-day independent study. Singapore, in words redolent of the earlier Board of Education, has placed SRL at heart of its current 'Desired Outcomes of Education' strategy: "Self-directed learners who take responsibility for their own learning and question, reflect and persevere in the lifelong pursuit of learning."[8] It is a strategy calculated to 'future proof' Singapore as remote working coupled with regular online upskilling becomes a norm across the growth sectors of the knowledge age economy.

Self-regulated learning

SRL is an umbrella concept that draws together elements of self-efficacy, motivation, metacognition and social cognition and is most associated with the research and writings of Professor Barry J. Zimmerman. Zimmerman (2000), identified SRL as a cyclical process involving three phases: forethought, performance and self-reflection.[9]

In essence this involves first setting learning goals, followed by selecting and applying learning strategies and finally evaluating and reflecting upon progress. The emphasis is upon recognising rather than ignoring personal stumbling blocks and identifying and applying improvement actions: "If a student fails to understand some aspect of a lesson in class, he or she must possess the self-awareness and strategic knowledge to take corrective action."[10] The ability to 'stand back' and to consciously evaluate, select and review the effectiveness of different learning strategies was dubbed metacognition by the psychologist John Favell in 1976, and it is regarded as a trait of our most successful independent learners. The Education Endowment Foundation has confirmed SRL and associated metacognitive thinking skills as a 'high impact, low cost strategy' with a positive influence on achievement, "Metacognition and self-regulation approaches have consistently high levels of impact, with pupils making an average of seven months' additional progress."[11] The key as emphasised by Zimmerman is the importance of students accepting and undertaking responsibility for their own learning:

> Self-regulation is not a mental ability or an academic performance skill; rather it is the self-directive process by which learners transform their mental abilities

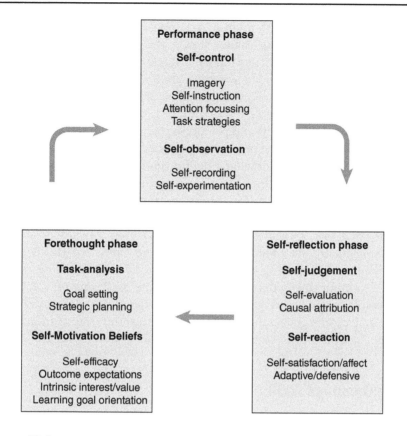

Image 10.4

into academic skills. Learning is viewed as an activity that students do for themselves in a proactive way rather than as a covert event that happens to them in
reaction to teaching . . . These learners are proactive in their efforts to learn
because they are aware of their strengths and limitations and because they are
guided by personally set goals and task-related strategies.[12]

Consequently in addition to offering guidance on the content of an assignment, it is important to offer guidance on how to research, write and present the assignment. Students should be encouraged to share their study
approaches and how to manage their time and complete within a deadline.
The fact that student 'Study Tubers' attract millions of subscribers to their
study channels on YouTube as detailed in Chapter 8 reveals the absence of
sufficient 'how to study' support in our schools and colleges. Precise guidance on how to revise should also be offered in the run-up to examinations with structured support for setting and managing revision timetables.

Too many students are last-minute crammers and apply ineffective techniques like reading and rereading their notes, highlighting text in books and often spending a whole revision session on a single topic or subject. Strategies like interleaving and retrieval-based testing are known to be much more effective and should be addressed. Revision and support services like Senecalearning. com can also offer valuable study and revision support and help to embed SRL by monitoring targets and prompting step-by-step progress. Self-reliance and self-direction will become more significant as we move deeper into the Knowledge Age as acknowledged by Singapore. Remote working, managing own workloads and bidding for and accepting 'side' contracts or additional jobs within the gig economy are fast becoming employment norms along with an increased trend towards self-employment. The Pearson learner survey revealed that 73% of the respondents have already discounted working for a single employer for their entire career,[13] and two-thirds stressed the importance of developing "self-discipline, motivation and time-management skills."[14] Zimmerman identified SRL as a life skill and one that is readily transferable beyond managing study goals to the achievement of wider social, sports and career goals, and this reinforces the importance of establishing a holistic learning portal to prompt wider personal development.

Learning Compass 2030

The Learning Compass 2030 report published by the Organisation for Economic Co-operation and Development (OECD) is an aspirational vision for future education with 'student agency' or essentially SRL at its heart: "The metaphor of a learning compass was adopted to emphasise the need for students to learn to navigate by themselves through unfamiliar contexts, and find their direction in a meaningful and responsible way, instead of simply receiving fixed instructions or directions from their teachers."[15] The goals embrace personal development across knowledge, skills, attitudes and values with an emphasis upon personal decision making and coaching individuals to apply an Activation-Action-Reflection (AAR) cycle. The AAR cycle promotes metacognitive thinking and is defined as follows, "an iterative learning process whereby learners continuously improve their thinking and act intentionally and responsibly, moving over time towards long-term goals that contribute to collective well-being. Through planning, experience and reflection, learners deepen their understanding and widen their perspective."[16] The focus is firmly on the decision-making process by encouraging students to articulate their intentions, weigh options, consider the potential impact on self and others and reflect on outcomes with an eye to future refinement. It also steps beyond personal development to address innovation and creativity that might add value to society and perhaps the wider world community. The AAR cycle is essentially a tool to drive critical thinking and raise metacognitive skills to a high level akin to the development of human intelligences as elaborated by Rosemary Luckin, president of the International Society for Artificial Intelligence and Education.[17]

Self-efficacy

The OECD concept of student agency extends the theory of self-efficacy first articulated by Professor Albert Bandura in 1977 and is defined as follows, "students have the ability and the will to positively influence their own lives and the world around them. Student agency is thus defined as the capacity to set a goal, reflect and act responsibly to effect change."[18] Self-efficacy is rooted in our personal life experiences. Different community, parental, peer and personal influences can colour our judgements and choices throughout life, as discussed in Chapter 13. In the context of education students with high self-efficacy will set study goals, review their progress and seek and act on feedback, whereas students with low self-efficacy will be more likely to regard a task (or subject) as beyond their ability and give-up too early without sufficient effort to succeed. Self-efficacy is one of the most studied concepts in psychology and runs deep through Vygotsky's Zone of Proximal Development (1932), Favell's Metacognition (1976), Zimmerman and Schunk's Self-Regulated Learning (1989), Dweck's Mindset (2006) and Duckworth's Grit (2016). However, be wary of elevating Mindset and Grit. Both lean towards psychological traits that elude replication rather than concrete improvement strategies. Equally be wary of linking expertise with 10,000 hours of deliberate practice. The 10,000-hour rule was popularised by Gladwell (2008) and based on research published by the late K. Anders Ericsson in 1993. Ericsson recorded a range of different times for the development of expertise in different fields ranging from 2,000 to 25,000 hours of effort and application but he never specified 10,000 hours as a benchmark for expertise. Ericsson expressed his disappointment that Gladwell had misrepresented his research. The figure of 10,000 hours is an arbitrary number and not a target we should be encouraging our students to adopt. However, we should encourage (appropriate) effort and not discount the importance of self-belief. Too many students dwell in the past and permit the shadow of past underachievement to develop into a fixed mindset as articulated by Dweck i.e. the tendency to ascribe a learning difficulty to an innate inability to understand maths, etc., rather than a measure of time and effort applied. The underpinning concept has a long history. Henry Ford's quote, 'whether you think you can, or you think you can't – you're right'[19] is a popular quotation based on the Latin motto, "Possunt quia posse videntur," translated as 'they can' because 'they think they can.' Similarly, the superintendent of Schools in Alabama, John Herbert Phillips, famously exhorted his students to apply self-belief in an address in 1905,

"Have faith in yourself; develop confidence in your own power, reliance upon your own resources. If you believe you can, you will; if you think you can't, you will fail."[20] The concept also underpins Vygotsky's theory of the Zone of Proximal Development. Vygotsky advanced that it was not a question of 'can do' or 'can't do' but rather 'can do' or 'can't do yet.' In relation to the latter he emphasised the importance of timely interventions to offer a resolution and a pathway forward when a student hits a learning difficulty. Essentially, there is no 'can't do' but rather 'can do' with help. Promoting agency and ensuring timely interventions can act to counter the inner voice of learned helplessness. Dweck offered the pertinent point, "success is not coming to you, you must come to it"[21] and warned of the danger of low expectations: "test scores and measurements of achievement tell you where a student is but they don't tell you where a student could end up."[22] Similarly, Professor Deborah Eyre who led the UK National Academy for Gifted and Talented Youth (NAGTY) 2002–2007 commented, "The fact that a child is not a high performer right now does not indicate that they are unable to become one."[23] Those positive encouraging messages are useful tools to apply, but they must be allied with concrete improvement actions to ensure our students gain not only a sense of personal progress but know they are making progress. This is an important counter to self-handicapping deflections i.e. focussing on reasons why a goal is impossible rather than identifying strategies to achieve the goal. The 'Deans for Impact' consortium of American universities summarised the research evidence and guidance for developing self-belief as follows:

- Teachers should know that students are more motivated if they believe that intelligence and ability can be improved through hard work.
- Teachers can contribute to students' beliefs about their ability to improve their intelligence by praising productive student effort and strategies (and other processes under student control) rather than their ability.
- Teachers can prompt students to feel more in control of their learning by encouraging them to set learning goals (i.e., goals for improvement) rather than performance goals (i.e., goals for competence or approval).[24]

Essentially agency is not a personality trait, but something that can be taught and developed and this raises the significance of introducing of advance organisers to scaffold and underpin study goals.

Student-facing advance organisers

Students cannot apply agency and develop SRL if they do not know what to study, in what order and to what depth. In addition, study is no longer confined to the classroom but extends online. Consequently, curriculum planning needs to adapt and evolve from teacher-facing schemes of work to student-facing advance organisers. Schemes of work have been the standard form of course planning for well over 100 years but they guide and inform teacher rather than student actions. Schemes of work are rarely shared with students and even if they were, they would provide little in the way of illumination because of the barrier of educational language and the regular use of abbreviations. Shifting to student-facing curriculum planning is essential for developing SRL because without clear study guidance, students are locked into dependency on lesson-to-lesson teacher direction. Self-paced learning is the key advantage of online learning, and care must be taken not restrict the pace. This raises the significance of applying curricular knowledge as described in Chapter 4 to distinguish between core, advanced and challenge level resources linked to each major topic. Those levels present students with a clear learning agenda with the ability to advance at their own pace and for the most able and/or motivated to engage with specified challenge tasks. During school closures 2020–2021 many students discovered the advantages of self-paced learning on personal learning platforms (PLPs) like www.drfrostmaths.com, www.senecalearning.com or the more well-known www.khanacademy.org along with options for additional support and acceleration at each level.

Advance organisers

Advance organisers offer the 'big picture' and transparent topic by topic study guidance. Professor David Ausubel (1918–2008) identified two major forms of advance organisers: either comparative to help students to assimilate new learning through attachment to existing schemata or expository in relation to presenting an overview of the study goals to cue discussion of existing prior knowledge. In both cases Ausubel provided little in the way of clear definitions or criteria for the design or content of an advance organiser, but this may also be a strength in relation to adopting a best fit with different learning situations. Hattie's review of effective teaching and learning strategies affirmed the benefits of advance organisers: "good teachers often provide overviews of what we are to learn and these are referred to as advance organisers which serve to activate prior knowledge and so enable us to acquire new information efficiently."[25] In addition, Marzano in reviewing the research evidence for the impact of advance organisers reported, "all produce fairly powerful results . . . expository has the largest effect size."[26] Within our schools and colleges advance organisers should be regarded as replacements for schemes of work, rather than as supplements, to avoid any undue increase in teachers' workloads.

Knowledge organisers

Knowledge organisers should not be confused with advance organisers. As the title suggests, they focus on summarising and listing the key knowledge associated with a particular topic or lesson. They have emerged from schools adopting the core knowledge curriculum as a bright, attractive graphic organiser for easy referral to key vocabulary, concepts, events, etc. In this context they are a resource attached to a topic, whereas an advance organiser is an overall curriculum guide.

Learning plan

The learning plan, as described later, adopts and adapts the recommended expository form of an advance organiser to guide and support SRL. It is presented here as an A4 document, but the key components are easily replicated in different forms online. All learning management systems (LMSs) offer curriculum guide functionality and a wide range of collaborative tools along with the benefit of clickable links to resources. If your school, college or organisation does not have an LMS, then Google Classroom is a popular alternative. An A4 handout may appear to be wholly redundant in this context, but a physical handout remains the most straightforward, flexible and accessible resource of all. Physical handouts are also essential for those students who do not have a laptop and/or an internet connection at home. A learning plan offers a host of learning advantages:

- A standout, bright, clear divider within student files to introduce each major topic,
- A series of pre-questions offering scaffolded support for meeting the programme standards,
- Recommended resources to build and consolidate learning,
- Facilitation of spaced and retrieval practice by returning to earlier learning plans to test retention,
- Facilitation of interleaving and spiral curriculum concepts by moving between different learning plans,
- Facilitation of effective student revision by switching between different learning plans during revision sessions,
- Support for flipped learning by identifying factual knowledge questions for investigation and answer in preparation for the next lesson,
- Support for post lesson learning to prompt depth of study,
- Informing a progress dialogue with mentors and/or classroom support assistants in relation to personal difficulties and stumbling blocks as each student engages with the questions,
- Promoting metacognitive thinking and SRL,
- Setting challenge tasks to stretch the most able and/or most motivated.

Creating a learning plan is a beneficial first step towards developing online learning by prompting consideration of the relevant pre-questions and resources to support a topic. Once trialled and perfected, the A4 learning plan can be retained or wholly embedded online.

Learning plan calendar

The first step in developing a learning plan is to present students with the overall 'big picture' in the form of a simple course calendar printed on the reverse of an A4 title page as illustrated.

Aim for a bright, attractive title page dominated by an eye-catching photograph or infographic that reflects the curriculum. On the reverse print a simple calendar grid. In the left-hand column of the grid enter the week commencing date and against each week, in the centre column, the planned key topic. If a topic takes two or more weeks to teach, then simply repeat the topic heading as many times as required down the column. Once completed the students will be able to see at a single glance the overall balance of the curriculum and the relative importance/depth of each topic i.e. one week allocation as against three weeks. This identifies the expected pace.

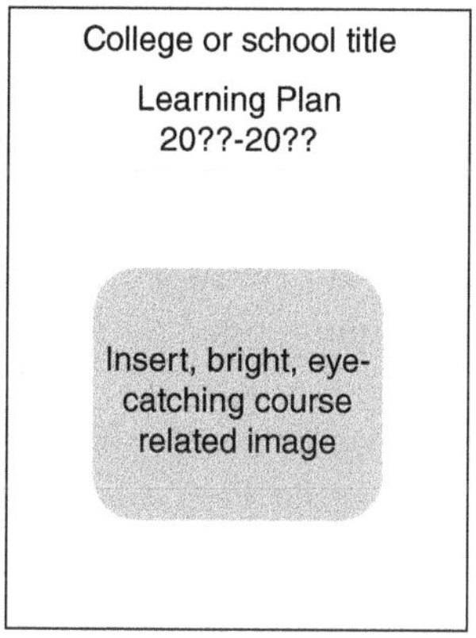

College or school title
Learning Plan 20??-20??
Insert, bright, eye-catching course related image

Week	Topic	Events
1		
2		
3		
4		
5		
6	Half Term	
7		
8		
9		
10		
11		
12	Christmas holidays	

Image 10.5

Wider events

In the right-hand column enter events for the students to look forward to across social, sports, charitable, careers and citizenship themes e.g. visiting speakers, concerts, drama events, sports events, charitable fundraising events, Black History month, Holocaust Memorial day, International Women's day, key faith celebrations like Diwali, Eid, Christmas and national and local community celebration events, etc. Reflect the cultural backgrounds of your students, but note that it is also important within monocultures to raise the awareness of other faiths and traditions. Ensuring a wide range of events and experiences is significant. The influential Life Lessons report published by the Sutton Trust raised the importance of students from disadvantaged backgrounds accessing social and cultural experiences that are often considered a norm within more advantaged homes:

> Schools should focus on ensuring a wider range of their pupils develop a broad array of non-academic skills, through both classroom strategies and extra-curricular enrichment activities such as debating, cultural visits and volunteering. There should be a particular focus on increasing take-up by those from a disadvantaged background.[27]

The completed calendar may be printed or if preferred placed online. The latter would hold the advantage of clickable links for more information. The course calendar is perhaps best issued term by term so as not to overwhelm and to allow for adjustments in relation to curriculum pace and the currency of events. Upcoming events may be promoted on social media with updates, alerts, and information shared with parents and the wider community. This regular contact can nudge both parents and students into positive engagement with the curriculum as detailed in Chapter 13. The second major step is to create an individual learning plan for each topic as listed on the calendar page.

Learning plan topics

The key topics listed in the calendar page should be supported with individual learning plans to share the study targets and recommended resources. The learning plan is presented as two sides of A4 printed back-to-back as illustrated.

Place your school or college heading at the top of the title page followed by the title of the learning plan e.g. Engineering Learning Plan 1 or Biology Learning Plan 3. On the immediate top left list, the individual lessons planned for the topic along with the lesson titles and/or focus. Learning is fluid and should be envisaged as a sequence of learning across the lessons allocated to a topic rather than a lesson-by-lesson focus. Learning develops over time rather than within the neat confines of a single lesson, and even after the conclusion of a topic it may be the regular application of spaced practice and a return to earlier topics that reveals misconceptions, consolidates and confirms learning. Under the list of lessons enter a single overarching aim for the topic as a whole. The 'Big Picture' box should provide a concise narrative overview of what the topic will cover, and more space can be gained by stretching the box across the page as required. This reflects the common practice for academic papers to open with an overview abstract and likewise for official reports to start with an executive summary. On the right-hand side insert a bright photograph or infographic to reflect the theme of the topic to make it more

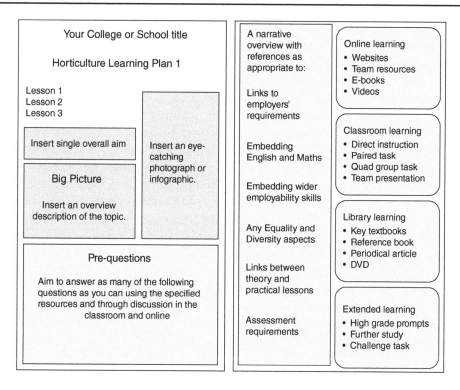

Image 10.6

visually appealing. A Quick Response (QR) code may also be added to permit students with a smartphone or tablet to access a relevant YouTube video or website straight from the handout.

Pre-questions, not objectives

On the lower half of the page, list pre-questions in place of specific objectives as detailed in Chapter 4. Objectives are summative rather than formative and assume achievement i.e. 'by the end of this unit of study you will be able to . . .' whereas pre-questions cue a quest for answers from the identified resources both within and beyond the classroom. Pre-questions scaffold learning by promoting self-assessment and metacognitive strategies i.e. the ability to gauge the gap between answers and the programme standards and to proactively seek advice and guidance.

Resources page

The resources page identifies four types of learning: online, classroom, library and extended. The order reflects a flipped learning pedagogy with students ideally accessing the resources specified in the online learning box before entering the classroom. In the case of vocational programmes, the category, 'library learning' may be altered to 'practical learning' or 'workshop learning' to reflect the division between classroom-based theory lessons and practical skills development within a joinery workshop, hairdressing salon or catering kitchen, etc. In that situation any key library resources might be referenced in the extended learning box. The immediate visual message is that attending lessons is only one part of a student's learning commitment to challenge the mindset, held by some students, that learning ends when the lesson ends. The classroom box should focus on learning activities and direct instruction. Class time is valuable, and videos and other resources can be accessed online to reserve class-time for dialogue. The library box should be used to promote a reading habit because books remain our primary source of authoritative in-depth information. An estimated 10% of British homes do not have any books and at the other end of the scale 7% of households have more than 500 books. Possession of 200 books and a related reading habit correlate with higher academic performance, but a generational divide is emerging as younger people tilt towards Google rather than a bookshelf. The average number of books owned by sixteen- to twenty-four-year-olds is 59 compared to 131 for over those over age fifty-five. However, many teenagers still love a good book, as evidenced by teenagers Mireille and Elodie-Lee. They have gained over 200,000 followers for their loveofliterature book review posts on Tik Tok. Videos tagged with the hashtag booktok have been viewed 5.9 billion times, highlighting that reading can be successfully promoted. Identify recommended books to support each major topic or as applicable a single chapter or even a relevant page range. As Willingham has noted, reading extends both knowledge and vocabulary: "books expose children to more facts and to a broader vocabulary than virtually any other activity and persuasive data indicate that people who read for pleasure enjoy cognitive benefits throughout their lifetime."[28] Finally, the 'Extended Learning' box should reference resources or opportunities to stretch and challenge students beyond the immediate study goals with perhaps encouragement to gain micro credentials from an online platform as detailed in Chapter 15. Include regular challenge tasks to promote a 'have a go' culture. A small prize might be appropriate and/or at least recognition in the form of establishing a 'challenge winners' noticeboard in your classroom or online to record successful completion. To complete the learning plan use the blank column on the left-hand side to capture a brief narrative overview of the topic along with assessment or relevant assignment details. Any opportunities to develop and build English, maths, employability and life skills may also be highlighted plus any links to workshop or workplace learning in the case of vocational courses. Print this page back-to-back with the title page and issue as a handout to your students as you approach each topic to scaffold the learning expectations and as a practical tool to promote and develop SRL.

How to study

Translating SRL into practice will also involve clear guidance on *how* as well as *what* to study. Generation Alpha are confident navigators of all things digital and by posting short, 'How to. . .' videos we can significantly advance online learning. There are three major categories of 'how to' videos to consider as self-access resources:

- **Curriculum standards** – It is common for curriculum teams to have preferred ways of working and common standards for the completion of reports, projects, essays, lab reports, data, etc. However, all too often those standards are not shared in advance but revealed in feedback with a low mark. Individual teachers may also have own preferences. Curriculum teams need to arrive at a consensus and confirm their standards and preferably capture on video. Each video may only be three to five minutes but the modelling of how to layout an assignment or a lab report, etc., has high value. The standard is demystified, and feedback is significantly strengthened by referral to a relevant video if a student submits work below the standard.
- **Generic study skills** – Extend your 'how-to' video library beyond curriculum guidance to address generic study skills e.g.

One of the most important but overlooked of the study skills is note-taking. Note-taking is often regarded as a matter of personal choice, but there are significant qualitative and quantitative differences. Some students will make regular and extensive notes, others will capture a few key points and many others will largely doodle. This becomes an issue when students approach assignments or examinations and draw upon their notes and in many cases carry forward misconceptions and/ or partial information. Ideally our lesson planning should involve consideration of how key information should be recorded by introducing subheadings, review pauses and end summarisation. There is also a major difference between recording and processing new information and all too often the former dominate. **Notebook or laptop?** There is a notable rise in students using their laptops or other digital devices for note-taking, but research published by the University of Tokyo in 2021 demonstrated a superior memory imprint and improved information retrieval when students captured notes by hand rather than keyboarding.[29] Magnetic resonance imaging (MRI) scans revealed that the act of writing triggers increased brain activity across memory, language and spatial centres and results in a stronger memory store. Essentially writing promotes processing and thinking whereas keyboarding is centred on recording. Mueller and Oppenheimer (2014) similarly concluded that note-taking on a laptop promoted verbatim note-taking because keyboarders can keep pace with a presenter. In contrast students writing notes tend to listen and select key points to record. There is also a major distraction issue to consider. Few students with an open laptop or smartphone can ignore the temptation to dip into social media or to respond to messaging. The doodlers swiftly become online dabblers. Banning laptops is perhaps not a realistic option but by employing subheadings and review pauses we can promote information processing rather than mere recording whether students are using a traditional notebook or a laptop. Beyond guidance on these major aspects of study skills invite the English team to post 'style guide' videos on individual aspects of good English e.g. how to use the apostrophe, key grammar pitfalls and perhaps for academic writing how to use the Harvard referencing system, etc. Invite the maths team to similarly post guidance on how to crunch and present data and create high impact charts and diagrams.

- **Digital skills** – Whereas Alpha possess confident digital skills, their experience with business-level software applications across Microsoft Office and other specialist software applications may be limited. Post 'how to' videos across not only the obvious Word, Excel and PowerPoint functions but higher professional and career-relevant software applications. Students may wish to take advantage of the free digital skills updating modules available from Trailhead https://trailhead.salesforce.com.

Overall, populating a learning portal with comprehensive study and personal development opportunities will transform the life chances of our students by mitigating disadvantage, raising ambition and most significantly stepping away from the pace of a class to self-paced learning.

As Generation Alpha rise through our education system, we are watching a major revolution as the new rather than the older generation become the seers and the guides to the future. It is notable that the dominant names and products of the internet era e.g. Microsoft, Apple, Dell, Google, and Facebook emerged not from some corporate research department after many years of research but from the creativity of individual students. Bill Gates was 13 when he first dabbled in computers, Steve Jobs was 16, Michael Dell was 19, Larry Page and Sergey Brin were both 23 and Mark Zuckerberg was 20 and a student at Harvard University when he first hit upon the idea of creating an electronic version of the university 'Facebook' of students' pen portraits. Beyond the world of digital innovation the simple soaring and ethereal power of words to inspire was memorably demonstrated by Amanda Gorman at the inauguration of President Joe Biden, January 2021, "If we merge mercy with might and might with right then love becomes our legacy . . . there is always light if only we are brave enough to see it if only we are brave enough to be it."[30] Gorman was named a US National Youth Poet Laureate at nineteen. Generation Alpha are setting the pace for the 21st century, and as Tapscott prophesised, "there is a new generation emerging that will change the world as never before."[31]

References

1 Ofcom, *Children and Parent: Media Use and Attitudes Report 2019*, Ofcom, 4th February 2019, pg. 1.
2 Ibid, pg. 5.

3   Future of data supplement, *The Times*, 26th March 2019, pg. 8–9.

4   Education and Training Foundation, *Taking Learning to the Next Level, Digital Teaching Professional Framework*, Education and Training Foundation, pg. 21, www.et-foundation.co.uk/wp-content/uploads/2018/11/181101-RGB-Spreads-ETF-Digital-Teaching-Professional-Framework-Full-v2.pdf

5   www.ucl.ac.uk/news/2020/jun/children-doing-25-hours-schoolwork-day-average

6   Board of Education, *Handbook of Suggestions for Teachers*, Board of Education, 1927, pg. 57.

7   Ibid, pg. 8.

8   Singapore, Ministry of Education, *Desired Outcomes of Education*, www.moe.gov.sg/education-in-sg/desired-outcomes

9   Zimmerman, Barry J., Becoming a self-regulated learner: An overview, *Theory into Practice*, vol. 41, no. 2, June 2002, pg. 67, College of Education, The Ohio State University.

10 Ibid, pg. 65.

11 Education Endowment Foundation, https://educationendowment-foundation.org.uk/evidence-summaries/teaching-learning-toolkit/meta-cognition-and-self-regulation/

12 Zimmerman, Barry J., Becoming a self-regulated learner: An overview, *Theory into Practice*, vol. 41, no. 2, June 2002, pg. 67, College of Education, The Ohio State University.

13 Pearson, *Global Learner Survey*, Pearson, August 2020, pg. 35.

14 Ibid, pg. 41.

15 OECD, *Future of Education and Skills 2030, Conceptual Learning Framework, Learning Compass 2030*, OECD, pg. 1, https://www.oecd.org/education/2030/E2030%20Position%20Paper%20(05.04.2018).pdf

16 OECD, *Future of Education and Skills 2030, Conceptual Learning Framework, Skills for 2030, AAR Cycle*, OECD, https://www.oecd.org/education/2030-project/teaching-and-learning/learning/learning-compass-2030/OECD_Learning_Compass_2030_Concept_Note_Series.pdf

17 Luckin, Rosemary, *Machine Learning and Human Intelligence*, UCL Press, 2018.

18 OECD, *Future of Education and Skills 2030, Conceptual Learning Framework Student Agency for 2030*, OECD, pg. 1, https://www.oecd.org/education/2030-project/teaching-and-learning/learning/student-agency/Student_Agency_for_2030_concept_note.pdf

19 Ford, Henry, www.goodreads.com/quotes/978-whether-you-think-you-can-or-you-think-you- can-t-you-re

20 Herbert, Philips John, *Speech to High School Students*, Alabama, 1905, https://quoteinvestigator.com/2015/02/03/you-can/

21 Dweck, Carol Dr., *Mindset*, Robinson, 2012, pg. 195.

22 Ibid, pg. 66.

23 Eyre, Deborah Professor, *Room at the Top, Inclusive Education for High Performance*, Policy Exchange, 2011, pg. 13.

24 Deans for Impact, *The Science of Learning*, Deans for Impact, 2015, pg. 3, https//:deansforimpact.org

25 Hattie, John Professor and Yates, Gregory, *Visible Learning and the Science of How We Learn*, Routledge, 2014, pg. 115.

26 Marzano, Robert J., et al., *Classroom Instruction That Works*, Association for Supervision and Curriculum Development (ASCD), 2001, pg. 118.

27 Cullinane, Carl and Montacute, Rebecca, *Life Lessons, Improving Essential Life Skills for Young People*, The Sutton Trust, October 2017, pg. 5.

28 Willingham, Daniel T., *Why Don't Students Like School*, Jossey Bass, 2009, pg. 49.

29 Umejima, Keita, et al., Paper notebooks vs mobile devices: Brain activation differences during memory retrieval, *Frontiers in Behavioural Neuroscience*, vol. 15, 19th March 2021.

30 Gorman, Amanda, *The Hill We Climb*, 2021, recited at televised Presidential inauguration 20th January 2021.

31 Dontapscott.com/speaking

Feedback

Personal development

Harari posed the following thought-provoking question in 2018:

> A baby born today will be thirty-something in 2050. If all goes well that baby will still be around in 2100 and might even be an active citizen of the twenty-second century. What should we teach that baby that will help him or her to survive and flourish in the world of 2050 or of the twenty-second century?[1]

His question reflects the rapid transformation of work and society as AI transforms everything it touches. The pace of change has prompted an international re-evaluation of how well existing education systems equip young people for the future. The emerging consensus arising from the world's highest performing education systems Singapore, Finland, South Korea, Shanghai and Canada is the need for a shift from academic exam grades as *the* measure of educational success to *a* measure within the development of more holistic curricula focussed on overall personal development. Singapore is often celebrated for the excellence of its education system in recognition of its regular dominance of the Programme for International Student Assessment (PISA) international rankings. In the past it has been associated with traditional classroom practice but its current national education strategy, 'Desired Outcomes of Education' has replaced examination grades as the primary measure of personal progress with more holistic goals as follows:

At the end of secondary school students should:

- Have moral integrity.
- Believe in their abilities and be able to adapt to change.
- Be able to work in teams and show empathy for others.
- Be creative and have an inquiring mind.
- Be able to appreciate diverse views and communicate effectively.
- Take responsibility for their own learning.
- Enjoy physical activities and appreciate the arts.
- Believe in Singapore and understand what matters to our country.

DOI: 10.4324/9781003132783-15

At the end of post-secondary education students should:

- Have moral courage to stand up for what is right.
- Be resilient in the face of adversity.
- Be able to collaborate across cultures and be socially responsible.
- Be innovative and enterprising.
- Be able to think critically and communicate persuasively.
- Be purposeful in pursuit of excellence.
- Pursue a healthy lifestyle and have an appreciation for aesthetics.
- Be proud to be Singaporean and understand Singapore in relation to the world.[2]

South Korea has similarly announced a drive to replace rote learning and memorisation of facts for examinations with a focus on creativity, innovation and personalisation.[3] Finland has defined personal development as the overriding goal of education:

> the objective of general upper secondary education is to promote the development of students into good, balanced and civilised individuals and members of society and to provide students with the knowledge and skills necessary for further studies, working life, their personal interests and the diverse development of their personalities.[4]

Within the UK the Chief Inspector of Ofsted, Amanda Spielman, has equally emphasised the importance of a shift away from exam results as the hallmark of educational success:

> One of the areas that I think we sometimes lose sight of is the real substance of education. Not the exam grades or the progress scores, important though they are, but instead the real meat of what is taught in our schools and colleges: the curriculum. To understand the substance of education we have to understand the objectives. Yes, education does have to prepare young people to succeed in life and make their contribution in the labour market. But to reduce education down to this kind of functionalist level is rather wretched. Because education should be about broadening minds, enriching communities and advancing civilisation.[5]

Personal development focus

This reappraisal of educational priorities was reflected in the UK by the publication of the Life Lessons report by the Sutton Trust, "it is easy to focus on academic results as the primary consideration for a young person's success in life.

But education is, and should be, about a lot more than that."[6] The report identified that 94% of employers thought skills were as important, if not more important, than academic or vocational qualifications: "With increasing automation, it is the ability to show flexibility, creativity and teamwork that are increasingly becoming just as valuable, if not more valuable, than academic knowledge and technical skills."[7] The much earlier 2009 government commissioned report, 'Unleashing Aspirations,' similarly reported:

> One survey showed that soft skills such as adaptability were more valuable to employers than education or qualifications. . . . Employers may then give increased attention to other indicators in making employment decisions . . . social and people skills, personal style, adaptability, team working and other softer skills have become more important to employers, driven in part by the growth in service sector employment.[8]

The stumbling block is the primacy accorded to examination results as the principal measure of educational and personal success. The headmaster of Eton College, Tony Little, commented in 2015 "the message we have given our children is that assessments and exams are no longer milestones on a journey, but the sole purpose and destination."[9] More recently in September 2020 the current headmaster of Eton, Simon Henderson, in common with many other leading UK academics, signed a letter to the *Sunday Times* recommending an end to the current system of single-subject General Certificate of Secondary Education (GCSE) examinations. The letter criticised the narrow repetition of basic factual knowledge and the absence of opportunities to build and develop personal skills: "no credit is given to those who are skilled communicators, thoughtful team players, clever problem solvers or creative thinkers; in short the stuff that helps you thrive in life and makes you invaluable to employers."[10] The future of learning envisaged is not so much about leaving school with a set of neatly wrapped parcels of knowledge but helping each individual to pursue and develop their personal passion whether academic study, vocational skills, sporting prowess, artistic talents, musical ability, etc. The Sutton Trust specified the importance of personal fulfilment and an education for life rather than simply employment:

> Adult life requires a range of skills in order for people to flourish, both in the workplace and in their daily lives, from the confidence and motivation to seek challenges and complete tasks, to the interpersonal skills that aid teamwork and other social interactions. These essential life skills are crucial to people achieving their potential, and therefore it is natural that they should also lie at the heart of our education system.[11]

Given the knowledge that 30% to 40% of each cohort underachieve, it is important for schools and colleges to seek to foster an intrinsic interest in learning.

Why learn

The answer to the question 'Why learn' is commonly expressed in utilitarian terms i.e. the prospect of securing a future high salary. Universities regularly make this a feature of their degree publicity, and career advisers often highlight the high starting salaries commanded by STEM (science, technology, engineering, math) as opposed to humanities graduates. However, students tend to follow their hearts rather their heads and are motivated not by the prospect of financial reward but what they find enjoyable, interesting and stimulating. They instinctively lean towards intrinsic rather than extrinsic reward and this tendency is often reflected in student surveys. In 2020 the Pearson Global Learner Survey revealed that the goal "to have a better life" was ranked first by the majority of the respondents as their primary motivation for engaging in education. The goal "to feel confident" was ranked third and the goal "to create well-rounded citizens" was ranked fifth and placed above the goal "to earn more money" which was relegated to sixth position.[12] The survey results evince Abraham Maslow's (1908–1970) hierarchy of needs, which identified self-actualisation as the highest goal of personal development.

Maslow's hierarchy

Maslow' hierarchy, first published in 1943, identified five needs for personal well-being: physiological, safety, love, esteem and self-actualisation. Whereas the robustness of Maslow's evidence base has been questioned and particularly how far each step is dependent on the preceding step, his concept of self-actualisation remains widely endorsed as the highest reach of self-development. However, it should be noted that Maslow qualified his research in his final years. He singled out the values of mysticism and spiritualism as the very pinnacle of self-actualisation and worthy of separate categorisation as 'self-transcendence.' Maslow was not responsible for the famous triangle, but it has a new peak. The overall import is that our actions are driven not by the anticipation of reward but by the personal satisfaction derived from engagement alone. Witness any young person who enjoys a particular hobby, sports or social activity, and they will devote hour after hour to the pursuit of karate, swimming, tap-dancing, *Fortnite*, playing the clarinet, painting, football, drama, *Minecraft*, keeping tropical fish, etc. What drives them is an intrinsic interest – an inner drive – and commitment to that hobby, sport or social activity. This intrinsic interest can produce sports stars, pop stars, inventors, writers, artists, actors, entrepreneurs, etc. In the case of Mya-Rose Craig, an early childhood experience of birdwatching ignited a passion for birds and their habitats. At age twelve Craig began blogging her interest and observations as 'Birdgirl' and topped 4 million views. In 2020 the blog was converted into a book and at aged eighteen Craig found herself in the centre of a bidding war between fourteen different publishers. Coming from a mixed heritage background, Craig also established 'Black2nature' as a campaign to attract more underrepresented ethnic minority groups into countryside pursuits and associated environmental activism. Craig is far from alone in the pursuit of a personal interest, as illustrated by the further examples in Chapter 15, and they collectively reveal the value and transformational impact of intrinsic motivation.

Promoting intrinsic motivation

Intrinsic motivation is associated with the highest learning outcomes because it drives effort and sustained application. Our goal is to trigger an intrinsic interest in academic and/or vocational study i.e. why study English or history or biology or why pursue a career in catering, hairdressing or engineering, etc. The impetus is elusive but rather than a single strategy the evidence points to multiple overlapping strategies centred on enabling personal choice:

- **Choice** – From earliest childhood we lean towards the freedom to choose. Offering students regular choices and options promotes a sense of personal control e.g. deciding the order of study of sub-topics, selecting different case studies/examples/theories/ themes to explore – jigsaw learning approaches and a choice over presentation methods. The OECD commented, "When students are agents in their learning, that is, when they play an active role in deciding what and how they will learn, they tend to show greater motivation to learn and are more likely to define objectives for their learning."[13]
- **Purpose** – Specify the importance, significant and benefits of a particular subject or aspect of study. Highlight what the students will gain. Why study . . . ?
- **Relevance** – Highlight the relevance of study topics to real life, current areas of research, new innovations, significant issues/challenges for society and the wider world.
- **Challenge** – Introduce extended learning and 'big question' or 'big idea' challenge tasks to intrigue and raise interest beyond the immediate study goals as illustrated in Chapter 15.
- **Recognition** – Offer regular positive feedback valuing contributions, praising standards of work, personal effort and successful completion of tasks.
- **Opportunity** – Present a wealth of opportunities across social, sports, health, fitness, citizenship and charitable endeavours to promote positive well-being and levelling up 'cultural capital'.

All of these factors in combination can drive a high level of commitment, if not intrinsic motivation, and are preferable to the more common focus on introducing extrinsic rewards. Parents often offer monetary rewards, treats and presents as incentives and as children rise through the school system prizes and awards are common-place tools to promote positive behaviours, full attendance and study progress. Extrinsic rewards do boost performance, most notably with low-performing students, but the impact tends to be temporary because the reward works in the negative i.e. the reward is the motivation rather than a personal commitment/ interest or an altruistic act. Sanctions occupy the same territory by producing conformity with a specified behaviour rule to avoid a punishment for non-compliance. Triggering intrinsic motivation is the preferable goal because it can generate not only high achievement but in many cases foster Maslow's self-actualisation.

Behavioural influences

Personal development is subject to life experience. As early as age ten, the following four primary influences will have generated a positive or negative attitude to learning and present schools and colleges with a significant challenge to 'sell' the benefits of engaging in learning.

Influence	Experience
Community	Some of our communities are blighted by vandalism, limited sports and social facilities and a sense of danger rather than safety. Living in a deprived community can significantly harm motivation and distort behavioural norms through negative role models, regular street crime, drug abuse and surviving rather than thriving households. The seminal research study 'Broken Windows' (1982) concluded that a downward spiral follows the first broken window, "As buildings, streets or even entire districts are allowed to become dirty, litter strewn and covered in graffiti, this gives rise to the perception that since no one else really cares about this area, "why should I."[14] The positive and negative impacts of different communities has been confirmed by much more recent research but qualified by the degree of parental care, "when children live in deprived communities and also experience limited parental warmth and monitoring, they are most likely to become anti-social."[15] The practical outcome of this research has been the importance attached by councils and transport authorities, etc., to cleaning graffiti as soon as it appears, removing litter and repairing broken windows, etc. School and college site maintenance policies should similarly ensure a bright, clean attractive environment to encourage a pride in belonging along with the existent of clear rules and boundaries to promote a place of safety and security.
Home	Some homes provide children with unqualified emotional support and positive encouragement during their formative years, whereas others at the opposite extreme may involve neglect, psychological or even violent physical abuse. Many children are also dependent on the free hot school dinner as their main nutritious meal of the day, and some are in caring roles for parents or siblings. In addition, some homes will confer a material learning advantage and others a material learning disadvantage coupled with significant differences in social, cultural and enrichment experiences. Those differences in 'cultural capital' can have a marked impact on individual social awareness, personal confidence and social interactions.

Influence	Experience
Peer	During adolescence it is common for many teenagers to question their parents' or guardians' values, and the result is tension in the home and a changing relationship that either helps or hinders learning. Navigating this tension can be turbulent for all concerned, and many parents feel a loss of not just influence but of control over their son or daughter's behaviour. At age fourteen and up, teenagers largely prioritise peer group values and opinions over parental guidance, and those values will either support or reject the benefits of engagement in learning. Ultimately there is such a thing as 'bad company' and today we must be alert to the fact that those negative influences can be more often online rather than sitting on the street corner.
Personal	The random allocation of nature across height, weight, colour, hair, teeth, sight, speech, accent, skin condition, etc., become a focal point of self-identity and self-perception during teenage and early adulthood. Some of those factors may seem trivial areas of concern compared to those coping with learning difficulties, disabilities or medical conditions but even a minor blemish or perceived imperfection can harm self-esteem and impact personal confidence. A careless remark by a parent, teacher or peer can cause significant hurt. Today's students are also at high risk from negative social media interactions and can fall victim to online grooming. Whereas bullying once stopped at the school gates, it can now enter the home and be a constant presence 24/7. Many young people will suffer in silence, and this raises the importance of regular dialogue with a mentor and the need for all teachers to read and react to body language with interventions as necessary to offer appropriate guidance and support. Poor behaviour is not innate; it has a trigger.

Image 11.1

Those negative influences can be mitigated by promoting a wide range of enrichment opportunities, career pathways and challenges to acknowledge the primary goal 'to have a better life.'

Opportunity-rich learning culture

Examination results are a moment in time, whereas positive experiences can last a lifetime and enhance life chances. Adults remembering their school days do not dwell on an exam failure but will remember a school trip abroad, climbing a mountain, acting in a play, singing in a choir, listening to a visiting speaker, visiting a major museum, white water kayaking, etc. Our significant purpose is to mitigate disadvantage by improving life skills and building our students' cultural capital. The Unleashing Aspirations report published in 2009 referred to higher 'cultural capital' as a key character trait in relation to entry into our elite universities and as an invisible entry criterion for our top professions:

> Cultural capital, in the form of attitudes, values and aspirations. . . . Studies have shown that a lack of familiarity with particular forms of culture and a lack of sophisticated cultural vocabulary can limit people's confidence in certain social settings and deny them access to opportunities that might contribute to upward social mobility.[16]

Cultural capital is developed through an opportunity-rich informal learning environment. The Harris Federation, with forty-four academies in England, promotes regular enrichment experiences:

> In the long term, we see the programme shaping future leaders in all walks of life. Students are exposed to a wealth of high-end cultural experiences, ranging from world class art auctioneering with Christie's Auctioneers to a trip to the Royal Opera House; from a day of Science in Action at Imperial College, London University, to a bespoke day of lectures at Oxford University.[17]

The Newham Collegiate Sixthform Centre serving one of the most deprived districts in the UK has introduced its 'Code breaker' course to equip students with the social skills to navigate the elite professions within the nearby City of London. The course includes the basics of confident conversation, appearance and formal restaurant dining. The related 'super curriculum' of electives designed to drive ambition has resulted in 95% progressing to a Russell Group university including 30% Oxbridge entry. To address those more holistic goals, ensure a wide range of opportunities across the following four key aspects of personal development.

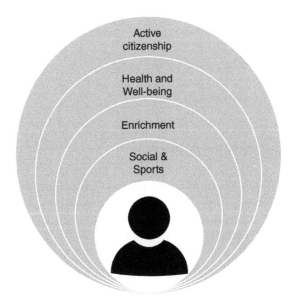

Image 11.2

Promote social awareness by ensuring that the interests, languages, customs, diet and festivals of different ethnic groups and cultures are acknowledged and celebrated in your college or school. How did your school or college mark Black History month last year or Eid-ul-Fitr or Diwali or Chinese New Year or the Harvest Festival or significant events like Holocaust Memorial Day, etc? Test your provision by conducting an 'opportunity walk' from your school or college foyer, down the corridors, into the refectory, the learning centres, the classrooms and not forgetting an electronic walk through the school or college website and any online learning platform. What visible evidence can you find of the following opportunities and guidance:

- Role model case studies
- Exam successes
- Learners' of the Month
- Prize/award winners
- Subject/topic displays
- Visiting speakers
- External cultural visits
- Foreign travel/trips
- Work experience placements
- Latest curriculum related research, innovations
- Local and national employment opportunities
- European and world employment opportunities
- Self-employment guidance
- Applications to Oxford or Cambridge
- Applications to a Russell Group university
- Applications to a European or US university
- Regional and national competitions
- World Skills championships
- Annual commemorative days/events
- Charitable/fundraising events
- Sports and social activities
- Healthy eating and lifestyles
- Personal fitness
- Safeguarding
- Fundamental British Values (FBVs)
- Cultural and faith events
- Committee memberships
- Community events/organisations
- Recommended websites and apps
- Student council/union activities

In the case of schools, colleges, training providers or adult education venues with limited facilities identify and promote all the sports, social and community groups operating within the local area. Place links on your LMS and encourage membership and invite the different organisations and sports clubs to provide stalls and to mount displays at the start of term and during progress evenings, etc. Our goal is to 'level up' and especially in areas of community deprivation. Exposure to opportunities displayed on a noticeboard might be fleeting as a student passes down a corridor but as highlighted in Chapter 2, our implicit memory subconsciously registers the images and words. Something you buy this weekend may well be the result of passing a billboard advertisement, an image on Instagram or simply an impulse buy resulting from an attractive in-store promotion. Clearly advertising works or manufacturers would not spend billions of pounds per year advertising their products. Blank walls, empty foyers and random posters on noticeboards are missed opportunities.

Why not Oxford University?
Why not enter the short story competition?
Why not enter the catering department's 'bake-off' competition?
Why not join the Business Studies trip to the Ocado distribution centre?
Why not sign up to hike the Three Peaks?
Why not audition for a place in the *Mamma Mia* drama production?
Why not target a Gold Duke of Edinburgh Award?

This is perhaps a scattergun approach, but different students will be motivated by different opportunities.

Mentors should monitor participation and encourage involvement in enrichment opportunities. The Sutton Trust highlighted the significance of the informal curriculum in relation to social mobility:

> Unequal access to opportunities for developing life skills plays a role in the over-representation of those with independent school backgrounds of the UK's top professions. Giving young people from all backgrounds a greater opportunity to develop those skills can therefore be an engine for opportunity and social mobility.[18]

It is about a nudge to overcome inertia and to help step beyond comfort zones. Clearly there are cost factors and therefore it is important for the discreet application of hardship funds to open up opportunity for all. Personal development is ultimately a process of nurture to build confidence and positive self-belief and a sense of belonging and membership of a wider caring community. The many YouTube videos posted under the title 'This is the greatest school' capture this spirit well. Personal development should take account of and monitor exposure to social media. Over the last decade in line with the expansion of social media there has been a 141% surge in young people and children seeking help for depression. Research conducted by Dr Ann John revealed,

Girls were three times as likely to be diagnosed with depression or put on anti-depressants as boys and children from the most deprived areas were twice as likely as those in the least deprived to be given anti-depressants. Children from poorer areas were twice as likely to be offered the drugs.[19]

Social media can substantially undermine personal confidence and may damage mental health. Many young people are only as happy as their last text message or 'likes' in relation to their latest post. Data from the Millennium Cohort Study 2021 has revealed that 16.1% of children aged up to seventeen years reported 'high psychological stress' and of greater concern 7.4% had contemplated suicide. Guidance should be offered in relation to engaging with social media and helping young people to control rather than to be controlled by their online activity.

Maintaining personal health

We are perhaps used to the concept of regular exercise and a balanced diet to maintain a healthy body, but our brains also respond well to exercise and diet. The key elements for overall good personal health are:

- Healthy diet,
- Aerobic exercise,
- Deep sleep,
- Cognitive stimulation.

Our aim is not just to help students pass examinations but to live long and healthy lives.

Healthy diet

The students entering our schools and colleges are part of the unhealthiest generation ever to sit in our classrooms. They are the product of a perfect storm of the rise of labour-saving devices in our homes, door-to-door car transport, screen time and not just a calorie-laden fast-food takeaway culture but the less remarked sugar-rich supermarket ready meal. There is a simple equation: activity burns calories and inactivity stores calories as harmful fat. Research published by the Nuffield Trust in 2019 has revealed that the UK has "the highest rates of obesity for 15- to 19-year-olds among 14 European comparator countries" and "low rates of engagement in exercise by 11-year-olds in England and Wales."[20] We have reached a stage where school uniforms are available in extra-large as our fast-food eating culture displaces more balanced meals. We are also witnessing the emergence of type 2 diabetes among primary school children due to obesity. By their thirties – not even middle age – many of our students will be in frequent ill health and pain and queuing for hip replacements, knee replacements and seeking treatment for liver failure, arthritis, cardiovascular disease, strokes, high blood pressure as well as diabetes. There are 11 calories in an Americano from Starbucks and 326 in a tall mocha with whipped cream. There are 350 calories in an iced chocolate-filled doughnut from Krispy Kreme and 336 in a cheese steak sub from Subway. How far do we raise awareness? Perhaps the starting point is for our schools and colleges to take the lead by displaying prominent posters at the start of the refectory queue highlighting the recommended daily calorie intake for an adult followed by labels displaying the calorific value against each food choice or snack item so that students and teachers can engage in their own arithmetic while they queue. It is not usual for refectories to not only serve lasagne but to offer chips as an accompaniment! A token poster on the refectory wall promoting 'five a day' and a bowl of fruit by the till are entirely ineffective if there is a 'chips with everything' eating culture rather than promoting and encouraging a Mediterranean diet.

Promoting a Mediterranean diet

The association between a Mediterranean diet and good health has been well established over the last thirty years, but within recent years neuroscience has identified links to higher cognitive functioning. A Mediterranean diet is primarily based around the consumption of fish, nuts, fruit, vegetables and olive oil with minimal consumption of meat, dairy products, sugar and saturated fats. In 2017 research published in the journal *Neurology* by Professor Ian Deary of University of Edinburgh concluded:

> Increased adherence to the MeDi has been linked with lower inflammation, better cognitive function, and reduced risk of Parkinson disease and Alzheimer disease and mortality from cardiovascular disease and cancer. . . . When examining individual food groups, their results indicated that higher fish and lower meat intake were the primary contributors to the observed effects on brain structure.[21]

This research confirmed similar findings from the University of Columbia published in Neurology in 2015. Dr David Nabarro, who led the World Health Organisation's response to Ebola (2014–2016), has described the spread of Western diet habits as more dangerous to world health than Ebola. His major concerns are rising rates of obesity and diabetes which are shortening life spans, and he has urged all governments to take action to promote healthy eating. Fish, in particular, is recommended as the chief component in a healthy diet. Fish provides high concentrations of polyunsaturated omega 3 fatty acids and vitamins A, D and K, all firmly linked to reducing cardiovascular disease, neuroinflammation and neural death. The National Health Service (NHS) 'livewell' website recommends two portions of fish per week, one of which should be oily fish e.g. salmon, mackerel, sardines, herring, fresh tuna (not canned) and trout. Fish oil capsules are a good alternative for those not keen on eating fish.

Aerobic exercise

More and more doctors are prescribing aerobic exercise for all-round health benefits and in particular guarding against strokes, cardiovascular disease and combatting the debilitating impact of obesity. Aerobic exercise relates to physical effort that makes your heart beat faster, makes you breathe faster and makes you sweat. Aerobic exercise, ideally performed for thirty minutes per day, improves oxygen and glucose circulation to the brain and has been shown to promote the growth of new neurons and faster processing speeds. Harvard Medical school reports, "the parts of the brain that control thinking and memory (the prefrontal cortex and medial temporal cortex) have greater volume in people who exercise versus people who don't."[22] Sustained exercise stimulates the release of brain-derived neurotrophic factor (BDNF), a molecule which encourages neurons to grow and protects against stress. The most effective form of aerobic exercise is jogging but otherwise undertake regular exercise in your own home. During the coronavirus lockdown from 2020 to 2021 Jo Wicks sprang to prominence with his daily aerobic workouts and you can find and follow his workouts on YouTube.

Time to stand up

The UK Chief Medical Officer (CMO) published the first national guidelines for physical activity in 2011:[23]

- Children and young people (5–18 year olds): 60 minutes and up to several hours every day of moderate to vigorous intensity physical activity. Three days a week should include vigorous intensity activities that strengthen muscle and bone.
- Adults (19–64 years old) and older people (65+): 150 mins – two and half hours – each week of moderate to vigorous intensity physical activity (and adults should aim to do some physical activity every day). Muscle strengthening activity should also be included twice a week.

The recently published British Active Students Survey 2017–2018 detailed the activity levels of UK university students and revealed that just over half (53%) met the CMO guidelines. The survey identified the following benefits of regular weekly activity,

> Participation in regular physical activity as well as sports participation and gym membership was found to improve students' personal well-being, mental well-being, social inclusion and perceived academic attainment and employability.[24]

To raise awareness of inactivity, invite each student to calculate their sitting hours starting from eating breakfast, travelling to school or college, time seated in the refectory, classroom, learning centres, travelling home, eating dinner, evening at home and finally their sleeping hours. On a sheet of flipchart paper draw a simple chart and ask the students to calculate their total inactive as opposed to active hours and identify the mode as a discussion point. Hippocrates (460–370 BC) recognised the benefits of a good walk and gave advice that might be beneficial for all, "If you are in a bad mood go for a walk. If you are still in a bad mood go for another walk."[25] Hippocrates's observation is now supported by scientific research. A study conducted in 2016 by Professor Shannon Taylor of the University of Central Florida identified walking 8,000 to 10,000 steps per day as correlating with a positive mood, "We think exercise acts as a counterbalance, because it promotes healthy brain functions needed to properly regulate emotions and behavior."[26] An exercise 'work-out' before a challenging task enhances performance. Consequently, during revision periods and in advance of examinations our students should be encouraged to undertake regular aerobic exercise to break-up study periods and to improve their mental alertness.

Encourage physical activity by investing in a set of pedometers e.g. Fitbit and invite students to apply the 10,000 step challenge every day for a month. It is the equivalent of five miles. However, three ten-minute brisk walks per day are known to generate the same health benefit. Encourage your students to walk rather than taking the bus or get off a stop earlier or if driving to park farther away. Students and staff should always take the stairs and not the lift and opt for a more circuitous route to the classroom by going up or down an extra floor to get the steps in. Set up a fitness circuit around the school or college grounds with different stations for sit-ups, pull-ups, running on the spot, etc., and introduce a physical challenge task each term. Abseil from the roof or a 'stair climb' challenge in the nearest tower block or a 5K fun run or regular 'Three Peak' hikes, etc. Set up cross-college sports tournaments and provide regular opportunities to try something entirely new like rock climbing, orienteering, tackling an assault course, rafting, kayaking, tree top walking or zooming down a zip line, etc. All these simple pursuits can be invigorating and generate a feel-good factor and will build resilience and grit faster than any classroom discussion. Encouraging the Duke of Edinburgh award, Scouts or Outward-Bound activities can also build those experiences into wider, valuable social interactions.

Deep sleep

The brain needs sleep. It needs time to process information without the distraction of new stimuli. Going without sleep is quickly debilitating for normal cognitive functions on a par with drinking too much alcohol. Concentration levels quickly fall, and we find it difficult to process even basic tasks. We regularly rotate through five stages of sleep. It is stage five deep sleep, or rapid eye movement (REM) sleep, that is most significant for learning. During REM sleep there is evidence from electroencephalography (EEG) monitoring of high levels of active mental processing as significant bursts of action potentials and chemical neurotransmitters relay information and create new connections or synapses between neurons. The brain also enters into 'housekeeping' mode removing dead cells – the by-products of metabolism – and the sticky beta-amyloid proteins associated with Alzheimer's disease. Sleep deprivation is known to disrupt those processes and will impair the consolidation of new information within memory. However, even a relatively short power nap of forty-five minutes to an hour has been shown to have beneficial effects on consolidating new learning. Research published in 2017 by Dr Anne Skeldon of Surrey University in conjunction with Harvard Medical School has identified as a myth the widespread belief that the circadian cycle of sleep/wake alters so significantly in teenagerhood that it raises a requirement for them to sleep late. Teenagers living in pre-industrial societies without electricity (the dominant form of society around the globe) fall asleep once dusk turns to night and wake with the dawn without any difficulty. Teenagers and adults in industrial society artificially extend the day with bright electric light and by staring at brightly lit TV, tablet and smartphone screens. Electronic devices emit a short wavelength blue light that signals the retina that it is not yet nightfall thereby supressing the release of the sleep-promoting hormone melatonin. The darkness which ordinarily triggers sleep is absent. Skeldon concluded:

> adolescents are not 'programmed' to wake up late and that by increasing exposure to bright light during the day, turning lights down in the evening and off at night should enable most to get up in time for work or school without too much effort and without changing school timetables.[21]

In addition research published by Wood et al. in 2013 revealed that looking at your phone within an hour of going to bed increased the likelihood of getting less than five hours sleep threefold.[22] In other words the much observed sleep deprivation in teenagers is not a quirk of nature but reflects a preference for staying up late interacting on social media and/or playing online games on phones and tablets. A 2016 survey of 2,750 children aged eleven to sixteen conducted by Digital Awareness UK in conjunction with the UK Headmasters and Headmistress's conference revealed the following social habits after bedtime:

- The survey found that almost half (45%) of students admit they check their mobile device after going to bed. Of those:
- A quarter (23%) check their mobile device more than 10 times a night
- A third (32%) of these students' parents are not aware that they check their mobile device after going to bed
- Almost all (94%) of these students are on social media after going to bed
- 70% of boys are playing games after going to bed
- 10% of students said they'd feel stressed about missing out if they didn't check their mobile device before going to sleep
- 38% of students said they'd be curious to know what's happening if they didn't check their mobile device before going to sleep.[27]

Nor is this overexposure to screen time just a teenage problem. A survey conducted by Childwise revealed that 73% of toddlers aged six months to four years had access to tablets and smartphones with 29% owning their own tablet. Playing a last game on a tablet rather than reading a last chapter in a book is becoming all too normal for so called 'I-tods'. To improve sleep everyone, not just children or teenagers, should dim the lights with the TV, mobiles and tablets switched off to simulate dusk an hour before going to bed.

Cognitive stimulation

The recommendations for regular cognitive stimulation to help ward off dementia has resulted in a rash of 'brain training' products appearing in the marketplace. Most of these products make significant claims for improving cognitive function but there is little, if any, scientific evidence to underpin such claims. The Stanford University Centre for Longevity released the following statement in 2014:

> We object to the claim that brain games offer consumers a scientifically grounded avenue to reduce or reverse cognitive decline when there is no compelling scientific evidence to date that they do. The promise of a magic bullet detracts from the best evidence to date, which is that cognitive health in old age reflects the long-term effects of healthy, engaged lifestyles. In the judgment of the signatories below, exaggerated and misleading claims exploit the anxieties of older adults about impending cognitive decline. We encourage continued careful research and validation in this field.[28]

This statement was signed by seventy-five world-wide leading neurologists engaged in dementia research. Essentially engaging with the relevant training videos or online exercises improves your ability to complete the relevant task(s), but this is simply the result of repetition. We get better at the specific task but it does not have transfer effect on improving memory or wider cognitive functions. However, cognitive stimulation is beneficial and one of the most effective of all according to Elizabeth Stinemorrow, professor of psychology at University of Illinois, is simply reading.[29] Following the news, reading a daily newspaper, reading new books, learning something new and social interaction are the keyways to maintain cognitive alertness. Cognitive challenge releases noradrenaline which helps to form new neural connections and promotes brain plasticity. Teachers can encourage a reading habit by nominating a 'book of the week' which may be subject specific or of wider potential interest. This will not just improve learning and understanding but over time build higher-order thinking and reasoning skills and contribute to greater density of grey matter. The leading neuroscientists Ian Dreary, Alexander Weiss and David Batty identify that longevity itself may be enhanced by raising awareness of how to maintain a healthy brain:

teaching all children and adults, regardless of intelligence, techniques for maintaining a healthy lifestyle, developing nutritious eating habits and avoiding stressors could minimize the overall accumulation of cellular defects that impinge on longevity and long term mental functioning. Indeed, the findings of cognitive epidemiologists such as ourselves bolster what all of us have known all along – that instilling good habits and healthy behaviors may lead to a lifetime of protection from the ravages of age.[30]

Education has a major role to play in raising students' awareness of how to maintain and improve their personal health and fitness and cognitive function. The essence of education is educating for life.

Developing character

The development of 'character' often explains the ascendancy of independent school alumni more than examination results or parental networking. The best-known independent school in England, Eton, specifies the following aims and values:

- Promoting the best habits of independent thought and learning in the pursuit of excellence,
- Providing a broadly-based education designed to enable all boys to discover their strengths, and to make the most of their talents within Eton and beyond,
- Engendering respect for individuality, difference, the importance of teamwork and the contribution that each boy makes to the life of the school and the community,
- Supporting pastoral care that nurtures physical health, emotional maturity and spiritual richness,
- Fostering self-confidence, enthusiasm, perseverance, tolerance and integrity.[23]

There is no universal definition of character, but it relates to an unselfish view of the world in terms of concern and consideration for others, a desire for self-improvement, honesty, modesty, resilience in the face of setbacks, confident communication and open to challenge and endeavour. Character development attracts and retains public support. This was underlined in the United States in February 2015 when the governor of the state of Wisconsin, Scott Walker, proposed altering the mission statement of the University of Wisconsin from the century old, a "search for the truth" and to "improve the human condition" to the more utilitarian "meet the State's workforce needs."[24] The proposal sparked considerable controversy and was subsequently dropped and explained away as a "drafting error." Within the UK, the Board of Education's *Handbook for Teachers*, first published in 1904, detailed character development as the primary purpose of England's schools:

> The purpose of the Public Elementary School is to form and strengthen the character and to develop the intelligence of the children entrusted to it . . . to implant in the children habits of industry, self-control and courageous

perseverance in the face of difficulties; . . . to strive their utmost after purity and truth . . . instil in them that consideration and respect for others which must be the foundation of unselfishness and the true basis of all good manners . . . to develop in them such a taste for good reading and thoughtful study as will enable them to increase their knowledge in after years by their own efforts.[21]

Over one hundred years later in 2017, the successor to the Board of Education, the Department of Education, restated the central importance of character development within UK schools:

There has been increasing recognition of the role that certain character traits or attributes such as resilience, self-regulation, and emotional and social skills can play in enabling children and young people to achieve positive health, education, employment and other outcomes. . . . Across all school types, the character traits most highly prioritised were honesty, integrity and respect for others.[22]

Many of our newly formed academies are renewing the importance of character development by setting clear aspirational goals in relation to personal development and promoting a wide range of enrichment experiences to build self-confidence. One of the UK's newest academies, the Kensington Aldridge Academy (kaa.org.uk), London opened in September 2014, with the motto, "*Intrepidus*," meaning undaunted, fearless and bold. The school also promotes the values of excellence, creativity, resilience and citizenship, "we will develop students into confident, rounded individuals, equipped for anything that life throws at them."[27] Whereas different theorists and educational preferences can fall in and out of favour, values transcend time.

Top five regrets

Finally, the importance of friendships and pursuing something you enjoy was highlighted by Bronnie Ware in her best-selling book, *The Top Five Regrets of the Dying*. Ware was a nurse in Australia who provided palliative care for those with only weeks left to live. Regrets were a common topic of conversation as the end drew near, and the terminally ill patients discussed and reflected upon their lives Ware identified five common regrets:[28]

1 I wish I had pursued my dreams and aspirations and not the life others expected of me.

   Ware recorded this as the most common regret of all – accepting limitations and not following personal interests.

2 I wish I didn't work so hard.

   Feeling the pressure of being the breadwinner and putting in too many working hours at the expense of time with family.

3   I wish I had the courage to express my feelings and speak my mind.

Supressing true feelings to keep the peace rather than confronting difficult situations or objecting to offensive behaviour or opinions.

4   I wish I had stayed in touch with my friends.

Allowing friendships to fade because of the pressures of working and family life.

5   I wish I had let myself be happier.

Happiness is about everyday experiences rather than the pursuit of possessions or position.

In the 1980s Japan gave us the concept of *kaizen* in relation to a focus on efficient working practices, but it is *ikigai* that may dominate the 21st century. The Japanese concept of *ikigai* translates as 'what do you live for' – essentially the pursuit of personal happiness.

References

1   Harari, N. Y., *21 Lessons for the 21st Century*, Jonathan Cape, 2018, pg. 259.
2   www.moe.gov.sg/education/education-system/nurturing-students
3   www.ajanews.asia/archives/3424
4   www.finnwaylearning.fi/finnish-education-system/secondary-general-academic-education/
5   Spielman, A., *Enriching the Fabric of Education*, Speech to the Festival of Education, 23rd June 2017, www.gov.uk/government/speeches/amanda-spielmans-speech-at-the-festival-of-education
6   Cullinane, C. and Montacute, R., *Life Lessons: Improving Essential Life Skills for Young People*, Sutton Trust, October 2017, pg. 2.
7   Ibid, pg. 2.
8   Milburn, Alan, *Unleashing Aspiration: The Final Report of the Panel on Fair Access to the Professions*, Cabinet Office, July 2009.
9   Tony, Little, *An Intelligent Person's Guide to Education*, Bloomsbury, 2015, pg. 21.
10   *The Sunday Times*, 27th September 2020, pg. 22.
11   Cullinane, C. and Montacute, R., *Life Lessons: Improving Essential Life Skills for Young People*, Sutton Trust, October 2017, pg. 2.
12   Pearson, *The Global Learner Survey*, Pearson, August 2020, pg. 34.
13   OECD, *Future of Education and Skills 2030, Conceptual Learning Framework, Student Agency for 2030*, pg. 2, www.oecd.org/education/2030-project
14   NASUWT, *One More Broken Window the Impact of Physical Environment on Schools*, NASUWT, 2008, para 2.12.
15   Belsky, Jay, et al., *The Origins of You, How Childhood Shapes Later Life*, Harvard University Press, 2020, pg. 197.

16 Advisory Panel to Government Chaired by Rt. Hon Alan Milburn M.P., *Unleashing Aspiration: The Final Report of the Panel on Fair Access to the Professions*, HM Government, July 2009, pg. 3.

17 The Harris Federation, www.harrisfederation.org.uk/211/the-harris-experience-is-a-two-fold-programme-over-five-years

18 Cullinane, Carl and Montacute, Rebecca, *Life Lessons: Improving Essential Life Skills for Young People*, Sutton Trust, October 2017, pg. 4.

19 John, Ann Dr., *Speaking at the British Science Festival Swansea*, 9th September 2016, www.independent.co.uk/news/science/antidepressants-childhood-children-use-statistics-30-per-cent-10-years-unhappiness-a7231756.html

20 Shah, Hagell and Cheung, R., *International Comparisons of Health and Well-Being in Adolescence and Early Childhood*, Nuffield Trust, February 2019, pg. 6.

21 Chief Medical Officer, *UK Physical Activity Guidelines*, 11th July 2011, www.gov.uk/government/publications/uk-physical-activity-guidelines

22 British Universities and Colleges Sport, *British Active Students Survey*, British Universities and Colleges Sport, 2017–2018, pg. 4.

23 Hippocrates (460–370 BC), www.goodreads.com

24 Taylor, Shannon Professor, http://today.ucf.edu/study-shows-exercise-sleep-keys-keeping-employees-bringing-home-work-frustrations/

25 Eton College, *Aims*, www.etoncollege.com/EtonsAims.aspx?nid=7228fed0-c26f-4dd6-ae1d-db79bdcac748

26 Scott, Walker, *Budget Speech*, Governor of Wisconsin, 5th February 2015.

27 Board of Education, *Handbook of Suggestions for Teachers*, Board of Education, 1927, pg. 8.

28 Department for Education, *Developing Character Skills in Schools*, Summary Report, Department for Education, 2017, pg. 3–6.

29 Kensington Aldridge Academy, https://kaa.org.uk/wp-content/uploads/2018/02/KAA-Mission-Statement.pdf

30 Ware, B., *The Top Five Regrets of the Dying: A Life Transformed by the Dearly Departing*, Amazon, 2012.

12

The skills agenda

The knowledge or skills debate has dominated educational discussions since the 1980s, but it is a false dichotomy. Effective teaching and learning involve both knowledge and skills. The two are indivisible, and either in isolation would be a poor preparation for future life and employment. E. D. Hirsch, who established the Core Knowledge Foundation to champion the importance of a knowledge-based curriculum, also stressed the importance of embedding skills with knowledge: "effective Core Knowledge teachers know that both content and skills are essential; they embed the teaching of critical skills within the content they share with their students."[1]

The same conclusion emerged in the UK in 2009 when a government commissioned 'expert panel' reported:

> The Panel believes that while academic performance is important, qualifications alone do not necessarily equip young people with the soft skills that will help them go on to succeed in accessing a professional job. We know that there has been much debate about whether schools are too narrowly focused at present on simply delivering exam results, or whether they should be focusing instead on citizen development the Panel believes that it is not a question of 'either/or'. It is both.[2]

Over ten years later this guidance is increasingly entering mainstream thinking with a focus on the importance of personal skills and competencies.

Fusing knowledge and skills

High standards of knowledge are paramount but allied with high personal competencies i.e. applying critical thinking, collaborating with others, thinking divergently and developing confident interpersonal and intrapersonal skills. The Partnership for 21st Century Learning (P21) initiative emphasised a fusion between knowledge and skills as illustrated next.[3]

DOI: 10.4324/9781003132783-16

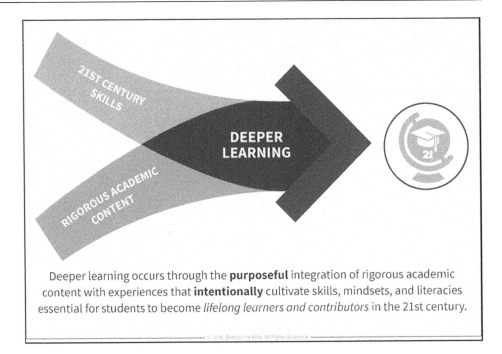

Deeper learning occurs through the **purposeful** integration of rigorous academic content with experiences that **intentionally** cultivate skills, mindsets, and literacies essential for students to become *lifelong learners and contributors* in the 21st century.

Image 12.1 Used with permission of Battelle for Kids and the Partnership for 21st Century Learning.© 2019, Partnership for 21st Century Learning, a network of Battelle for Kids. All Rights Reserved.

The significance of rebasing curricula to develop personal competences as well as knowledge was emphasised in 2018 by the Organisation for Economic Co-operation and Development (OECD): "the next generation of young citizens will create jobs, not seek them, and collaborate to advance humanity in an increasingly complex world. That will require curiosity, imagination, empathy, entrepreneurship and resilience, the ability to fail constructively to learn from mistakes."[4] The OECD's comment reflected the onset of the Fourth Industrial Revolution as described in Chapter 3 with the emergence of an economy where individuals rather than taking twenty or more years to climb the corporate ladder can opt to pursue their personal entrepreneurial goals via internet-based companies or a single app and trade worldwide. The online business trend was set in the earliest days of the internet era in 1994 when Jeff Bezos, operating out of his garage, established Amazon as a company to sell books online. Today Amazon is a world-famous emporium, employing some 647,500 people and catapulted Jeff Bezos from a standing start to a multi-billionaire. A new business can arise from a simple observation and entrepreneurial spirit. In 2004 while out walking on Clapham Common, London Anna Gibson observed a child taking great delight in whizzing along on a micro scooter. On a whim she flew to Switzerland to meet with the manufacturer and secured an exclusive contract to market and sell the micro-scooters in the UK, and today Gibson leads a major business (www.micro-scooters.co.uk). More recently in 2012 nineteen-year-old Ben Francis founded the sportswear company Gymshark in his parents' garage while studying at Aston University by day and delivering pizzas by night. As a keen gym member, he experimented with designing and making his own gym wear, having first taught himself how to use both a sewing machine and a screen printer from YouTube videos. He successfully used Instagram to showcase and promote his brand and in 2020 gymshark.com was valued at over one £1 billion. More and more individuals like Ben are discovering the ease of publishing and sharing what they have written, drawn, designed, painted, programmed, photographed, manufactured and composed online or, like Anna Gibson, capturing the market with a new product. It can lead to major business success, as illustrated, but also beneficial community enterprise, social advances and/or simply high levels of personal fulfilment and enhanced well-being. This shift from corporate to individual endeavour as a locus of economic development emphasises the importance of our schools and colleges developing not just subject knowledge but wider personal competencies, skills and importantly entrepreneurship. The skills question has been hotly debated since the 1980s but over the past decade the focus has shifted from treating skills like knowledge i.e. a specified list of employability skills 'bolted-on' to the curriculum to a more holistic focus on overall personal competencies. The former prioritised the employer as the client rather than the individual whereas individual creativity and innovation is increasingly driving job creation. This switch of focus is reflected in the significant skills and competencies specified by World Economic Forum (WEF) for individual advancement,

- **Global citizenship skills**: Include content that focuses on building awareness about the wider world, sustainability and playing an active role in the global community.
- **Innovation and creativity skills**: Include content that fosters skills required for innovation, including complex problem-solving, analytical thinking, creativity and systems analysis.
- **Technology skills**: Include content that is based on developing digital skills, including programming, digital responsibility and the use of technology.
- **Interpersonal skills**: Include content that focuses on interpersonal emotional intelligence, including empathy, cooperation, negotiation, leadership and social awareness.[5]

OECD Learning Compass 2030

The OECD Learning Compass 2030 vision similarly elevated personal competences over the narrower employability skills focus of business and industry:

- **Cognitive and metacognitive skills**, which include critical thinking, creative thinking, learning-to-learn and self-regulation
- **Social and emotional skills**, which include empathy, self-efficacy, responsibility and collaboration

- **Practical and physical skills**, which include using new information and communication technology devices.[6]

The Learning Compass vision placed personal competences within the context of global citizenship and importance of promoting ethical and moral decision-making, "principles and beliefs that influence one's choices, judgements, behaviours and actions on the path towards individual, societal and environmental well-being."[7] The well-established International Baccalaureate (IB) provides a good example of how those broad aspirations can be translated into educational goals:

- Follow their chosen education and career pathways in life
- Combine academic subjects with their personal and professional interests and skills
- Engage in learning that makes a positive difference to their community
- Think critically and creatively
- Communicate clearly and effectively in a variety of situations
- Work independently and in collaboration with others
- Consider new perspectives and other points of view
- Develop greater self-confidence and self-awareness
- Demonstrate high levels of resilience and flexibility
- Be internationally-minded and globally aware
- Apply their knowledge to real-world scenarios and situations.[8]

The development of personal skills was endorsed by students worldwide as reported by the Pearson 2020 global learner survey, "People will need to develop more of their soft skills such as critical thinking, problem solving and creativity." Against an average 89% agreement with this statement, the percentages for the seven countries surveyed were as follows:[9]

USA	UK	Aus.	Canada	Brazil	China	India
90	85	91	91	91	90	86

Image 12.2

Traditional curricula need to adjust to create more opportunities to develop skills and competences and increasingly the answer is through immersion in interdisciplinary studies, big questions, global development themes or creative and challenge projects as detailed in Chapters 15 and 16.

Future trends

Future economic growth is linked to two key drivers: digital applications and creativity. Artificial intelligence (AI) in the form of a variety of robotic applications and data management algorithms is increasingly undertaking routine tasks and replacing human labour. The World Economic Forum has projected that 75 million jobs will be lost to AI during the 2020s but crucially 133 million jobs will be gained across the expanding service sector with a concomitant demand for a workforce with high personal skills:

> 'Human' skills such as creativity, originality and initiative, critical thinking, persuasion and negotiation will likewise retain or increase their value, as will attention to detail, resilience, flexibility and complex problem-solving. Emotional intelligence, leadership and social influence as well as service orientation are also set to see particular increase in demand relative to their current prominence today.[10]

The OECD remarked, in relation to the scale of automation affecting all aspects of work and society, "we have to find and refine the qualities that are unique to our humanity and that complement not complete with capacities in our computers."[11] The chairman of the world's largest retailer Alibaba, Jack Ma, commented in similar terms during a discussion session at the World Economic Forum in 2018, "We have to be teaching something unique so that the machines can never catch up with us values, believing, independent thinking, teamwork and care for others."[12] In essence, people should not to try to compete with the higher accuracy and speed of robotic applications but focus on what humans do best i.e. creative pursuits and social interaction. However, even this bastion may be under assault. A survey conducted by the University of Colorado Boulder in February 2021 revealed that a random sample of 200 people could not distinguish between human artist and computer-generated paintings both landscapes and abstract. In addition, in July 2021 an AI design application named Dabus has become the first non-human to be awarded a patent for inventing an improved stackable food container to speed production.

Emerging technology

The WEF has identified the following top ten emerging technologies of interest to employers for future economic growth and the maintenance of a competitive edge.

The steady expansion and reliance on digital applications will increasingly raise a demand for employees with confident and adaptable digital and entrepreneurial skills i.e. the ability to recognise and exploit applications to improve existing products, services and systems or to design new and novel applications. The ability to keep abreast of change will be significant given estimates that the knowledge acquired within the first year of a four-year technical degree will be outdated by the time of graduation. Four years is a long time in relation to digital developments and applications. Individuals will need to keep investing in and updating their skills and knowledge and this is already becoming a norm.

No.	Digital technology	% employers likely to adopt
1	User and entity big data analytics	85
2	App and web-enabled markets	75
3	Internet of Things	75
4	Machine learning	73
5	Cloud computing	72
6	Digital trade	59
7	Augmented and virtual reality	58
8	Encryption	54
9	New materials	52
10	Wearable electronics	46

Image 12.3

Update modules on all aspects of business services and skills are available from one of the many online learning providers as described in Chapter 16. The CBI's Learning for Life, report published in October 2020 has predicted, "Nine in ten workers will need some form of reskilling by 2030, this is an issue that affects everyone. Virtually every job will change – some incrementally, some radically."[13] It would appear that the futurist Alvin Toffler's prediction circa 1980 was prophetic: "the illiterate of the 21st Century will not be those who cannot read and write but those who cannot learn, unlearn and relearn."[14] Whereas skills have always been a requirement for employment the significant difference between the 21st-century and 20th-century economies is the high demand for digital and creative competencies. This is reflected in the following top ten list of capabilities and skills published by the WEF:[15]

Rising skill needs

- Analytical thinking and innovation
- Active learning and learning strategies
- Creativity, originality and initiative
- Technology design and programming
- Critical thinking and analysis
- Complex problem-solving
- Leadership and social influence
- Emotional intelligence
- Reasoning, problem-solving and ideation
- Systems analysis and evaluation

Those skills and competences step well beyond the 20th-century focus on traditional English, maths, teamwork, etc. The importance of digital skills was acknowledged by the UK Department for Business, Innovation and Skills in 2016: "As a minimum, all children should leave school digitally literate, with the skills needed in the workplace and to realise social outcomes. To this end, digital literacy should be seen as a core skill alongside English and Maths."[16]

Defining skills

Beyond the consensus on the importance of digital and creative skills there are many different opinions on the wider skills and the personal attributes schools and colleges should seek to develop. This has been compounded by a constant re-branding of the skills agenda over the past forty years as different theorists, organisations and government ministers introduce their personal stamp e.g. core skills, common skills, communication skills, key skills, functional skills, generic skills, transferable skills, people skills, soft skills, personal skills, world-class skills, 21st-century skills and most recently of all life skills. The result can be a confusing clutter of ill-defined skills sets. However, at the heart of the different initiatives four common qualities and competences frequently surface albeit in different words, Creativity, Communication, Collaboration and Critical thinking. Those four skills were memorably branded the '4Cs' of employability by the Partnership for 21st Century Learning (P21) initiative in 2002.

Partnership for 21st Century Learning

P21 was established in the United States to review and make recommendations for curriculum reform following the sharp decline in employment in traditional industries and a corresponding rise in service sector employment. Over the last thirty years the same economic shift has rippled across the Western world. Within the UK the service sector has eclipsed traditional industries and accounts for 80% of employment. The skills and behaviours required by the 'people-facing' service sector, in comparison with employment on the factory floor, are markedly different. The 2009 UK Unleashing Aspiration report commented:

> In a knowledge-based economy, education is the motor that drives social mobility. . . . Those without skills get left further and further behind, with profound implications for social cohesion. . . . It is no longer sustainable for our education system to produce youngsters who lack the skills to compete in the modern labour market."[17]

P21 published a 'Framework for 21st Century learning' and summarised its recommendations for curriculum reform within the following rainbow arch.[18]

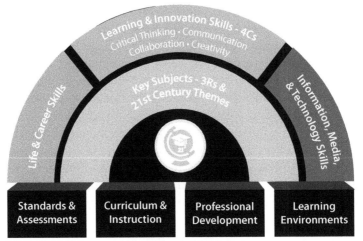

21st Century Student Outcomes & Support Systems

The P21 Framework for 21st Century Learning was developed with input from educators, education experts, and business leaders to define and illustrate the skills, knowledge, expertise, and support systems that students need to succeed in work, life, and citizenship.

The Framework continues to be used by thousands of educators and hundreds of schools in the U.S. and abroad to put 21st century skills at the center of learning. All elements of the Framework are critical to ensure 21st century readiness for every student.

When a school, district, or state builds on this foundation, combining knowledge and skills with the necessary support systems of standards, assessments, curriculum and instruction, professional development, and learning environments, students are more engaged in the learning process and graduate better prepared to thrive in today's digitally and globally interconnected world.

Image 12.4 Used with permission of Battelle for Kids and the Partnership for 21st Century Learning.© 2019, Partnership for 21st Century Learning, a network of Battelle for Kids. All Rights Reserved.

The rainbow model presents a summary of how the different elements of a reformed curriculum might interlock to create a holistic programme of personal, career, academic and skills development. The keystone identified the 4Cs as the core employability skills:

- Critical thinking,
- Communication,
- Collaboration,
- Creativity.

The 4Cs have been widely adopted over the last decade and were extended by Michael Fullan to form the 6Cs as an analysis of the key factors underpinning deep learning. The distinction between creative and critical thinking is significant. Both are closely intertwined as described in Chapter 15, but whereas the former emphasises divergent thinking, the latter emphasises convergent thinking. Willingham in 2007 warned against treating critical thinking as a general transferable skill. Critical thinking is not a generic skill but domain specific in relation to the differing processes underpinning historical enquiry, scientific method, literary criticism, etc. In 2019 Willingham reiterated this point in a paper written for the New South Wales Department of Education: "It is not useful to think of critical thinking skills, once acquired, as broadly applicable . . . analysis, synthesis and evaluation mean different things in different disciplines."[19] Critical thinking can be taught but within the context of each discipline and by applying domain specific processes and knowledge to arrive at a solution to a problem.

The 6Cs of deep learning

Michael Fullan is the director of the Deep Learning consultancy, and his 6Cs for developing 'deep learning' have been adopted by over 1,000 schools across seven countries, including Ontario.[20]

6Cs of deep learning	Descriptors
Character	Learning to deep learn, armed with the essential character traits of grit, tenacity, perseverance, and resilience; and the ability to make learning an integral part of living.
Citizenship	Thinking like global citizens, considering global issues based on a deep understanding of diverse values and worldviews, and with a genuine interest and ability to solve ambiguous and complex real-world problems that impact human and environmental sustainability.
Communication	Communicating effectively with a variety of styles, modes, and tools (including digital tools), tailored for a range of audiences.
Critical thinking	Critically evaluating information and arguments, seeing patterns and connections, constructing meaningful knowledge, and applying it in the real world.
Collaboration	Work interdependently and synergistically in teams with strong interpersonal and team-related skills including effective management of team dynamics and challenges, making substantive decisions together, and learning from and contributing to the learning of others.
Creativity	Having an 'entrepreneurial eye' for economic and social opportunities, asking the right inquiry questions to generate novel ideas, and leadership to pursue those ideas and turn them into action.

Image 12.5

Fullan's 6Cs extended the original 4Cs with the addition of character development and citizenship to spotlight the importance of individual responsibility and social cohesion respectively. Ontario's Ministry of Education has endorsed the 6Cs and confirmed a future focus on skills development: "Communication, problem-solving, critical thinking, creativity and global citizenship are skills that will help Ontario students thrive as they grow up in a changing, interconnected world."[21]

Improving digital skills

Most young people are digitally active and competent but often their competence is higher in relation to surfing social media, shopping and gaming apps rather than familiarity with data management, coding and the application of Microsoft Office and/or the Apple equivalent software. A House of Lords report highlighted the significance of building digital skills as follows:

> Digital technologies are the present and the future of these 21st century children. They will define their opportunities as workers and as citizens. We agree with the Digital Skills Committee that no child should leave school without an adequate standard of digital literacy. It is the view of this Committee that digital literacy should be the fourth pillar of a child's education alongside reading, writing and mathematics, and be resourced and taught accordingly.[22]

Our students should seek to improve their digital skills both to take full advantage of online learning opportunities and to match future employment expectations. Consequently, in addition to the normal range of diagnostic tests, our schools and colleges should administer a digital skills questionnaire to benchmark students' digital competencies. Our minimum 'digital' target should be familiarity and confidence in using Microsoft Word, PowerPoint, Publisher and Excel and/or the Apple equivalents as appropriate. Beyond skills, our students need to be able to discriminate and evaluate the provenance, usefulness and credibility of digital information sources given the widespread prevalence of 'fake news,' hacking and phishing scams and within employment being alert to the legal requirements governing data protection. Similarly, all students should be aware of the importance of guarding their own personal data and carefully vetting online contacts to ensure personal safety and to be vigilant for indications of grooming in relation to sexual or financial exploitation and terrorism. Our students should also apply social responsibility in relation to their personal posts and information sharing and be aware that employers often conduct social media searches as part of their employment application processes. An ill-advised tweet, Instagram post, etc., may be personally forgotten but it will still exist online and may harm future employment prospects and/or personal relationships.

Developing employability skills

Employers regularly highlight the difference between exam results and the skills required to advance business growth and personal advancement. Essentially exam results win the interview, confident personal skills win the job and creativity within the workplace wins promotion. Whereas knowledge is important it must be realised that employers are not waiting for General Certificate of Secondary Education (GCSE), A-Level, Business and Technology Education Council or even degree-level subject knowledge to walk through their doors. That knowledge already exists within their walls. A business studies student may be able to recite all the key facts about the Stock Exchange or explain the differences between inflation and deflation, but how often will a future employer invite them to do so? It is more likely at a junior level of employment to be expected to work well in a team, to respect different opinions, to display cultural and social awareness, to be well acquainted with Microsoft Office applications (or Apple equivalents), to work to deadlines, to write clearly with correct spellings and punctuation, to speak with confidence, to interpret charts and tables, to process data and to be committed and reliable. At a more senior level of employment, it is common to be asked to lead a team, to chair a meeting, precis a complex report, articulate and sustain own opinion, negotiate a favourable outcome, write a crisp clear report, analyse data, research a topic, give a persuasive presentation, apply critical thinking, display creativity and increasingly possess the ability to identify and apply digital solutions.

CBI employability skills

The importance of those practical employability skills was confirmed by the tenth annual employment skills survey published by the Confederation of British Industry (CBI) in conjunction with Pearson, "Formal qualifications are valuable indicators of achievement and ability. But businesses are clear that the biggest drivers of success for young people are attitudes and attributes such as resilience, enthusiasm and creativity."[23] The survey of employers' opinions ranked the personal 'attitude and aptitude' of applicants well above qualifications, as presented in the following table.[24]

Most important factors in recruiting school leavers	
Attitudes towards work/character	86%
Aptitude for work	63%
Academic results	43%
Qualifications obtained	34%
Basic literacy and numeracy	28%
Relevant work experience	21%

Image 12.6

The same rankings emerged from surveys related to graduate recruitment with 90% of employers specifying 'attitude and aptitude' as their most important recruitment consideration well above degree classification at 65% and degree subject at 62%. The Department for Education has raised an expectation for universities, just as much as schools and colleges, to foster employability skills:

> We expect higher education to deliver well designed courses, robust standards, support for students, career readiness and an environment that develops the 'soft skills' that employers consistently say they need. These include capacity for critical thinking, analysis and teamwork, along with the vital development of a student's ability to learn.[25]

The CBI has specified the following seven employability skills as significant competencies across all sectors of employment:[26]

Self-management – readiness to accept responsibility, flexibility, time management, readiness to improve own performance.

Teamworking – respecting others, cooperating, negotiating/persuading, contributing to discussions.

Business and customer awareness – basic understanding of the key drivers for business success and the need to provide customer satisfaction.

Problem solving – analysing facts and circumstances and applying creative thinking to develop appropriate solutions.

Communication and literacy – application of literacy, ability to produce clear, structured written work and oral literacy, including listening and questioning.

Application of numeracy – manipulation of numbers, use of statistics, general mathematical awareness and its application in practical contexts.

Application of information technology – basic IT skills, including familiarity with word processing, spreadsheets, presentation and data management software.

The president of Pearson UK, Rod Bristow, commented in relation to these skills, "Some say it is not the role of schools to provide these skills. So whose role is it? And to what extent should we shape our qualifications to reflect these skills? That's a debate we need to have."[27]

The steady rise of digital natives within the workplace is influencing the digital infrastructure as companies respond to how the rising digital generations message, interact, create and share information on social media. Businesses are increasingly adopting cloud-based platforms like Zoom, Google Meet, Microsoft Teams, Facebook Workplace or Workfront.com for research, collaboration and communication as opposed to email and stand-alone software packages. For many students it is also represents a seamless transition from interacting with their teachers and peers via a school or college learning management system (LMS).

Applying T-shaped skills

T-shaped skills should not be confused with the introduction of T-Level qualifications in the UK. Rather, it is a straightforward tool for school and college curriculum teams to discuss and capture key employability skills to prioritise within their programmes. The first task is to populate the horizontal of the T with generic employability skills followed by specific vocational employability skills down the vertical of the T. The latter should involve discussion with relevant employers and reflect future career pathways and the promotion of wider personal competences of value to the individual. Creativity has been entered because of its prominence as the key employability skill for the 21st century, but different opinions may prevail. The diagram can be expanded or contracted and used to develop a team

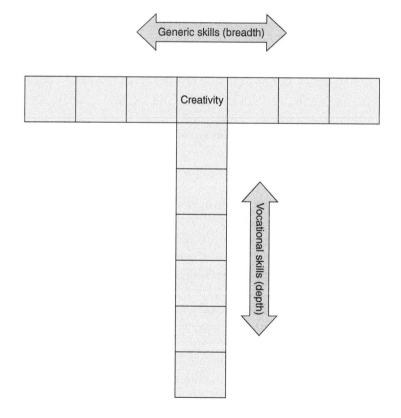

Image 12.7

consensus. The aim is not only to discuss and agree the skills but to identify the opportunities and strategies to promote and develop the skills over the course of a study programme.

The greatest gift

Finally, the greatest gift we can offer our students in terms of life skills is the gift of confident oracy. The common hallmark of those who rise to the top of our professions is 'presence' i.e. the ability to command a room, to articulate ideas and to share opinions in a clear, fluent and persuasive manner. Confidence can be taught, but all too often our efforts are directed towards improving written rather than spoken English. The significant exception within the UK is the independent school sector. The articulate and confident nature of students from independent schools is often commented upon along with their successful onward progression to dominate Oxbridge admissions and employment across the legal profession, journalism, politics, finance, banking, business, drama, etc., as highlighted in Chapter 8. Many of our leading comedians and actors also attended independent schools. However, coaching effective public speaking does not have to be the preserve of the independent sector. School 21 in East London provides an excellent example of how public speaking can be coached and developed if it is sufficiently prioritised within the curriculum. Visit YouTube and view the school's video, *Public Speaking: Oracy Skills for the Real World* and see how their 'Find Your Voice Programme' invites the students to develop and refine their abilities to debate and give formal presentations.

Environment and upbringing play a part in this success, but parents who damage their children's confidence by ignoring or rejecting their opinions exist across the social and income spectrum. Our responsibility as teachers is to lift all forward, and when we detect low confidence and communication apprehension (CA), we need to consider how best to build personal confidence. Education is a portal to a better future, and central to this is helping all to find their voice. This is not an easy task. Public speaking rather than snakes and spiders regularly tops surveys of personal fears. The primary reason is a lack of familiarity. Our classrooms offer too few opportunities to practise public speaking. Like any skill or knowledge, the more it is practised, the more familiar and confident we will become. CA, as detailed in Chapter 5, can be personally debilitating and limit life chances. Feedback on how to speak and how to deliver an effective presentation should be a teaching norm:

■ Demonstrate how to stand and use body language – Avoiding the fig leaf stance (hands clasped in front) and the so-called power stance (legs wide apart). Maintain open palms and move hands primarily at waist level. Gestures are effective to emphasise key points because they trigger visual memory but keep within bounds. Avoid pacing up and down and finally identify and control any nervous tics, physical and oral. We all have them.

- Coach the nerve calming technique of breathing in through the nose until the full chest expands followed by a slow, controlled exhale – It is a norm to be nervous. Do this up to three times to control and relax breathing.
- Coach use of voice in terms of volume, speed, pitch and tone.
- Promote the effective use of PowerPoint i.e. bright, high-impact relevant photographs and diagrams with minimal text in large fonts to support key points. Direct the attention of the audience to look at a particular slide and gain a micro pause to help settle any nerves. Take a breath.
- Use the text on PowerPoint or the invisible notes feature as your prompts rather than looking down at notes.
- Speak to your prompts rather than trying to read a pre-prepared script.
- Make and break eye contact with appropriate movement and aim to direct eye contact towards all members of your audience.
- Applying the TED Talk rule of three – i.e. a significant headline with only three sub-points in support.
- Sip water as your audience responds to a slide change to avoid a dry mouth.

These guidelines should be modelled for the students and routinely coached and reinforced during student presentations. Make it fun. We can't ensure that every student will become a first-class presenter, but we can try.

The traditional curriculum information focus of lessons granted little space and time for the development of personal skills but as curriculum information is increasingly accessed online attention can switch away from presenting to processing information and a multitude of opportunities to build and refine the 4Cs of employability.

References

1 Core Knowledge Foundation, *Core Knowledge Sequence, Content and Skills Guidelines for K-8*, Core Knowledge Foundation, 2013, pg. 3.
2 Advisory Panel to Government Chaired by Rt. Hon Alan Milburn M.P., *Unleashing Aspiration: The Final Report of the Panel on Fair Access to the Professions*, HM Government, July 2009, pg. 78.
3 Battelle for Kids, *Partnership 21 Initiative*, www.battelleforkids.org/networks/p21
4 Schleicher, A., *World Class, How to Build a 21st Century School System*, OECD Publishing, 2018, pg. 251.
5 World Economic Forum, *Schools of the Future*, World Economic Forum, January 2020, pg. 4.
6 OECD, *Future of Education and Skills 2030, Conceptual Learning Framework. Skills for 2030*, OECD, https://www.oecd.org/education/2030-project/#:~: text=OECD%20Future%20of%20Education%20and,of%20Education% 20and%20Skills%202030&text=The%20Future%20of%20Education%20 and,in%20and%20shape%20their%20future

7   OECD, *Future of Education and Skills 2030, Conceptual Learning Framework. Skills for 2030, Attitudes and Values for 2030*, OECD, pg. 2, https://www.oecd.org/education/2030-project/#:~:text=OECD%20Future%20of%20Education%20and,of%20Education%20and%20Skills%202030&text=The%20Future%20of%20Education%20and,in%20and%20shape%20their%20future

8   www.ibo.org/programmes/career-related-programme/curriculum/

9   Pearson, *The Global Learner Survey*, Pearson, August 2020, pg. 40.

10. World Economic Forum, *Future of Jobs*, World Economic Forum, 2018.

11 Schleicher, A. *World Class, How to Build a 21st Century School System*, OECD Publishing, 2018, pg. 247.

12 Ma Jack, World Economic Forum, *YouTube*, www.youtube.com/watch?v=rHt-5-RyrJk

13 CBI, *Learning for Life*, CBI, October 2020.

14 Toffler, A., 1980, www.alvintoffler.net

15 http://reports.weforum.org/future-of-jobs-2018/workforce-trends-and-strategies-for-the-fourth-industrial-revolution/?doing_wp_cron=1537219885.1841690540313720703l2

16 Department for Business, *Innovation and Skills, Success as a Knowledge Economy*, Department for Business, May 2016, pg. 43.

17 Advisory Panel to Government Chaired by Rt. Hon Alan Milburn M.P., *Unleashing Aspiration: The Final Report of the Panel on Fair Access to the Professions*, HM Government, July 2009, pg. 63.

18 Battelle for Kids, *Partnership 21 Initiative*, www.battelleforkids.org/networks/p21

19 Willingham, Daniel T., *How to Teach Critical Thinking*, Department of Education, 2019, pg. 7.

20 Fullan, M., *Deep Learning: An Invitation to Learn*, pg. 2, http://npdl.global/wp-content/uploads/2017/06/npdl-invitationtolearn-1.pdf

21 https://news.ontario.ca/opo/en/2017/09/updated-curriculum-new-report-cards-coming-to-ontario-schools.html

22 House of Lords, *Growing Up with the Internet*, Select Committee on Communications, 21st March 2017, paras 192, 317.

23 CBI/Pearson, *Helping the UK Thrive*, July 2017, pg. 25, www.cbi.org.uk

24 Ibid, pg. 26.

25 Department for Education and Skills, *White Paper 14–19 Education and Skills*, Department for Education and Skills, February 2005, pg. 31, para 4.6.

26 Confederation of British Industry, *Building for Growth: Education and Skills Survey*, Confederation of British Industry, 2011, pg. 16.

27 Bristow, R., President of Pearson UK, *The Right Combination*, CBI/Pearson, July 2016, pg. 5.

Holistic targets and goals

Goals and targets are primarily raised to drive academic achievement, but this is much too utilitarian an objective and at odds with the more holistic drive for an education for life. Education at its best raises horizons and ambitions and more broadly seeks to develop young people into thoughtful, caring and active citizens who leave our schools and colleges ready and able to pursue rewarding and enjoyable lives. This focus on the whole person extends to keeping students safe from harm, including the dangers of drug and substance abuse, gang violence, online safety and caring for their wider health in relation to healthy eating and drinking, personal fitness for long-term good health and finally their emotional and mental well-being. Holistic aspirations are common to schools both old and new. Britain's most famous public school, Eton, founded in 1440, promotes not high examination outcomes but "the best habits of independent thought and learning in the pursuit of excellence; supporting pastoral care that nurtures physical health, emotional maturity and spiritual richness; fostering self-confidence, enthusiasm, perseverance, tolerance and integrity."[1] Similarly one of Britain's newest schools, the Harris Academy Wimbledon, founded in September 2018, places achievement within a wider aspirational context:

> an excellent education in an innovative, inclusive and happy environment. As well as promoting academic achievement across the curriculum and encouraging participation in extra-curricular opportunities, we want to support our students to make decisions wisely, ready for the challenges they will face as adults.[2]

Our core purpose is to stir curiosity, nurture, enthuse, inspire and challenge all young people to improve all aspects of their lives and to achieve a sense of personal fulfilment. This emphasis on the importance of personal values underpins the Organisation for Economic Co-operation and Development (OECD) Learning Compass 2030 initiative which places education within an overall framework of not only developing knowledge but also skills, attitudes and values, defined as, "a sense of purpose and responsibility while learning to influence the people, events and circumstances around them for the better."[3] The starting point for advancing the achievement and life chances of each individual is to capture and build a comprehensive personal profile.

Personal profile

Every student is different. Our students have different community backgrounds, home circumstances, peers, values, interests, ambitions and awareness of how to study and learn. Goals and targets are not context free, and we should be alert to each student's personal circumstances and factors that might hinder rather than promote their personal progress:

- Career goals
- Home background – Living with parent(s), guardians, independently or in care
- Childcare or wider family care responsibilities
- Ethnic, faith, linguistic and gender identity
- Parent(s) or guardian(s) employment or unemployment
- Learning difficulties or disabilities and related support needs
- Health issues
- Part-time employment
- Social and/or sports interests
- Community or charitable involvements
- English and maths attainment
- Further qualifications
- Digital skills/abilities
- Employability skills
- Online personal access e.g. laptop, tablet, smartphone
- Social media activity/interests
- Study and organisational skills
- Attendance and behaviour record

All of these different experiences and influences translate into observable positive and negative behaviours that in turn either promote or hinder progression. Three broad groups of students populate our classrooms, and each group requires different goals, targets and support to address their differing capacities to learn. Hattie refers to proficient, competent and novice learners, but perhaps the terms independent, dependent and directed learners are more descriptive of the differing attitudes and approaches to learning.

Different learners

Curriculum teams need to discuss and agree on the most appropriate strategies to support and challenge the following three groups of learners to help all to achieve their full potential.

Independent learners	Dependent learners	Directed learners
Independent learners will have enjoyed good to high achievement in most of their subjects. They will often hold an intrinsic interest in some of their subjects and wish to specialise. They are likely to have clear career ambitions and be keen to progress to university and may have identi-fied the university they wish to attend. They are confident, well-motivated and possess good study, social and learning skills. They tend to have high cultural capital from regu-lar foreign holidays and wider enrichment from playing an instrument, visiting museums, art galleries, theatre, cinema, concerts, etc. Their par-ents have often attended university, value educa-tion, hold high aspirations and regularly offer effec-tive learning support and guidance. At home they mostly have access to the internet, a laptop, a wide range of textbooks and study aids. In the class-room they will participate to a high level and ask as well as answer questions. Outside the classroom they will engage in regular independent study and make effective use of library, study centres, internet resources and apply significant effort to extend and consolidate their knowledge. They will probably gain high grades.	Dependent learners will have gained some high grades in favoured subjects, but otherwise progress is largely average. They are uncertain about their future career paths and whether to progress to university. They often lack confidence and have underdeveloped study, social and learning skills. Their holidays will be mainly UK with occasional cultural experiences prompted by a particular concert, exhibi-tion or event. Their parents achieved benchmark quali-fications and are supportive but uncertain how best to help and promote learning. At home there is a shared computer and internet access and few books beyond the core textbooks for their subjects. In the classroom they will be cooperative and complete all necessary work. Outside the classroom they will complete specified home-work but are not sufficiently motivated and/or lack the skills for deeper independ-ent study. They are largely dependent on what is covered and issued in the classroom each week. They will probably pass the course but struggle to achieve high grades.	Directed learners will have poor achievement across most of their subjects. They will often have no career goals and a limited idea of higher course or career options. They will commonly display low self-esteem and low personal confidence and lack appropriate study, social and learning skills. They will rarely go on holiday and have a narrow range of cultural interests with rare trips, visits and experiences beyond their local area. Parents may have few or no qualifica-tions and offer very limited guidance or practical sup-port. At home they have no internet or computer access and the home has no textbooks or study aids. In the classroom they will often exhibit behavioural problems and be easily distracted, go off task or even indulge in disruptive behaviour. They will often attend lessons ill-equipped for study and end lessons without completing all set tasks. Outside the class-room they will not under-take any additional study and may need support and encouragement to submit assignments. They will struggle to complete the course and are at a risk of failure.

Image 13.1

All three groups of learners may be present within the same classroom to different degrees, or a classroom may be dominated by single group. The most challenging group to teach are the directed learners because they will need explicit firm boundaries and high levels of 'direction' to engage with their lessons. Hattie confirms, "students need to know the boundaries of what is acceptable or not and what to expect when they move outside these boundaries."[4] Directed learners are more frequently referred to as disadvantaged learners or novice learners, although Marzano prefers the descriptor 'reluctant' learners. Most of these learners will exhibit low self-esteem and a lack of appropriate social, study, organisational and learning skills. Hattie highlights that disadvantaged learners often develop a fixed negative mindset after years of low achievement: "achievement goals will not happen for him or her and that he or she is helpless to change the situation . . . such hopelessness is likely to come from prior academic failure . . . holding beliefs that achievement is not readily changeable, but is more likely to be fixed."[5] Too many students, regardless of backgrounds, have challenging experiences of life:

- Physical or psychological violence in the home
- Medical condition
- Break-up of a close relationship/friendship
- Alcohol dependency and/or binge drinking
- Pregnancy
- Drug abuse
- Victim of crime
- Arrest
- Parental divorce
- Death of someone close
- Bullying
- Caring for an ill family member
- Poor mental health

A negative attitude to life can also be triggered by living in a deprived community blighted by vandalism, street crime, gang culture and surviving rather than thriving households. An initial one-to-one meeting with each student should focus on gaining feedback on four key aspects of their personal profiles:

- Career aspirations
- Prior knowledge of the subject and related progress
- Social and sports memberships/interests
- Home study support

It is important to replace helplessness with choice and to help all to identify a pathway forward. Most students respond very differently in one-to-one encounters compared to their classroom persona, and we should take time to demonstrate our care and support for each individual by ensuring that uniform high expectations govern all aspects of our interactions, standards and targets. Those standard and targets should be consistently applied and driven by curriculum team rather than individual teacher interventions. All curriculum teams should 'publish' common stretch and challenge, study support and behaviour management strategies within an overall teaching and learning policy to ensure consistent standards. The following strategy suggestions offer a broad starting point and should be personalised and translated into appropriate targets for individual students.

The strategies are also not exclusive to each group but reflect common support requirements.

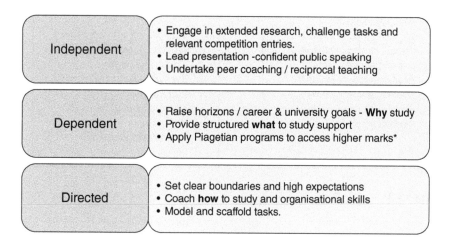

Image 13.2 *Hattie observed that "fewer than 50% of Year 11 and Year 12 students are 'formal operational' thinkers."[6]

Different homes

The different life experiences illustrated earlier raise the significance of home influence on personal development and achievement. Some homes provide children with unqualified emotional support and personal encouragement during their formative years, and others at the opposite extreme may involve psychological or even violent physical abuse. At ages fourteen to nineteen, in particular, many students question their parents' or guardians' values, and the result is tension in the home and a changing relationship that either helps or hinders learning. In addition, some homes will confer a material learning advantage and others a material learning disadvantage with a marked impact on overall personal development.

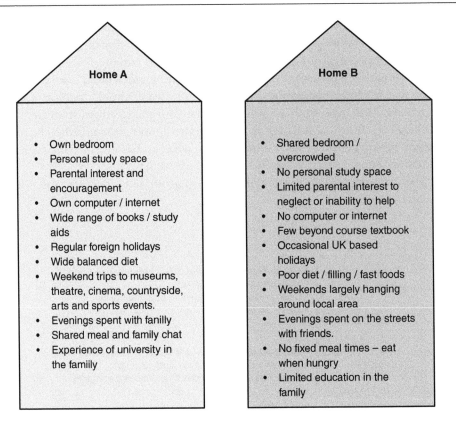

Image 13.3

The UK State of the Nation report 2016 commented, "By the time that students receive their GCSE results, around 32 per cent of the variation in performance can be predicted on the basis of indicators observed at or before age five."[7]

These illustrations of Home A and Home B represent a broad generalisation because there are a host of exceptions and crossovers. There is also a Home C, and for some young people no home at all in the case of 'looked after' children or the homeless living in cramped B&B conditions. In those circumstances Willingham has identified the negative impact of stress as a principal factor affecting the progress of children from low socio-economic status homes.[8] The stress absorbed by parents living in poverty can manifest as harsh parenting and ill-tempered exchanges with significant consequences for cognitive development and self-esteem. Essentially, students from advantaged backgrounds significantly outperform students from disadvantaged backgrounds, with the lowest levels of achievement arising from 'looked after' children. However, research undertaken by Professor Jane Waldfogel concluded that the key home factor influencing progress is not material advantage or disadvantage, but the level of parental support for learning and encouragement to work hard i.e. high levels of ambition and learning support may exist in any home regardless of material advantages. A home may be materially poor but emotionally rich and vice versa:

> the biggest factor in the achievement gap is parenting style . . . it is a question of maternal sensitivity − warmth and nurturing . . . next in importance comes a factor more obviously related to income − home background that includes access to books and computers . . . taken together parenting style and the home learning environment explain between a third and a half of the gap in achievement between the poorest children and their middle class counterparts.[9]

Waldfogel's findings were underscored by research undertaken by Professor Stephen Scott at King's College London who concluded, "Financial poverty is a factor but not a central one . . . it seems to be poverty of the parent-child experience that leads to poor child outcomes rather than poverty of a material kind."[10] Those findings were more recently confirmed by the Education Policy Institute's (EPI's) analysis of underachievement in UK schools referred to as the underperforming 'tail.' The EPI concluded, "over three quarters of the tail are not poor."[11] The issue identified was a poverty of aspiration affecting not just individual households but often whole neighbourhoods. This was an issue President Obama commented upon in a speech to American school children 8 September 2009:

> Maybe someone in your family has lost their job, and there's not enough money to go around. Maybe you live in a neighborhood where you don't feel safe, or have friends who are pressuring you to do things you know aren't right. But at the end of the day, the circumstances of your life − what you look like, where you come from, how much money you have, what you've got going on at home − that's no excuse for neglecting your homework or having a bad attitude. That's no excuse for talking back to your teacher, or cutting class, or dropping out of school. That's no excuse for not trying. Where you are right now doesn't have to determine where you'll end up. No one's written your destiny for you. Here in America, you write your own destiny. You make your own future.[12]

The UK government commissioned report 'Unleashing Aspiration' introduced the term 'cultural capital' as a further factor anchoring low achievement:

> Cultural capital, in the form of attitudes, values and aspirations. . . . Parents' expectations and aspirations for their children are important predictors of educational attainment. Parental interest in a child's education has four times more influence on attainment by age 16 than does socio-economic background. . . . Parental involvement in education and aspirations for their children's future increase children's attainment.[13]

Poor students can and do achieve at high levels. The impact of high aspirations is demonstrated by the career ambitions and the high exam pass rates of children from Chinese and Indian heritage homes. When exam pass rates are filtered by ethnicity, Chinese heritage students top the table followed by Indian heritage students, while students from a white heritage background significantly underperform. This has been a consistent finding for over thirty years and was recently reconfirmed by the 2021 Commission on Race and Ethic Disparities (CRED):

> the educational aspirations of 12 to 14 year olds in inner city comprehensive schools found that Black African, Asian Other and Pakistani children expressed higher aspirations than White British children in the study, who expressed the lowest aspirations. . . . the lower educational aspirations of White British pupils are tied to a lack of academic self-belief and low educational aspirations in the home.[14]

The actor Sanjeev Bhaskar OBE, well known for his role in the detective series, *Unforgotten*, recounted the story that when he told his father of his wish to become an actor, his father replied, "it is pronounced doctor." There are also regular examples of children arriving in the UK as refugees unable to speak or write English but within a few years outperforming and gaining higher exam pass rates than their native English classmates and not only progressing to university but in many cases securing places in Oxford or Cambridge universities. Those households place a high value on education as the pathway out of poverty with daily support for homework and in particular seeking and acting upon regular teacher feedback on how to improve. There is also evidence of 'organised' households with regular mealtimes, bedtimes, discussion of subject and career options, purchase of books and study aids and the value of sustained effort. In 2018 underperforming pupils at Chessington Community School in Kingston-Upon-Thames near London were invited to live with high-achieving classmates to share their home and study routines. The house swaps succeeded not only in boosting exam performance but changing the social habits of the pupils from spending time out on the street until late to staying indoors and interacting with parents around a family meal and engaging in reading and studying with parental encouragement. The 2021 CRED report commented,

> recent immigrants devote themselves more to education than the native population because they lack financial capital and see education as a way out of poverty. . . . Indian students are the ethnic group most likely to complete homework five evenings a week.[15]

The differential performance between children from different households is not only linked to parental support for learning but correlates with parental qualifications: "significant characteristics such as family income, Free School Meals (FSM) and family Socio-Economic Status (SES) are less powerful predictors than parents' qualification levels."[16] This conclusion arising from Institute of Education (IOE), University of London, research highlights that the higher the qualifications of the parents, the richer the support for learning in the home. More significant still is a higher correlation with the qualifications of the mother rather than the father: "there were still very strong effects of mother's highest qualification level and the early years home learning environment (HLE) on academic outcomes."[17] Essentially educated mothers (more than fathers) engage more frequently with their children in a wide range of learning activities. The Joseph Rowntree Foundation (JRF) qualified some of these activities by asking parents:

> How often do you read to your child? How often do you tell stories to your child not from a book? How often do you play music, listen to music, sing songs or nursery rhymes, dance or do other musical activities with your child? How often do you teach your child numbers and counting? How often do you draw, paint or make things with your child? How often do you play sports or physically actives games outdoors or indoors with your child? How often do you play with toys or indoor games with your child? How often do you take your child to the park or to an outdoor playground?[18]

Those rich interactions are linked to building a wide vocabulary and promoting cognitive development. In 1995 Drs Betty Hart and Todd Riley of the University of Kanas courted controversy by quantifying a 'word gap' of 30 million words between children from advantaged and disadvantaged homes. Hart and Riley sampled the exchanges between children and parents within three socio-economic groups – welfare, working class and professional – on a monthly basis from birth to age four. The conclusions were stark. Children raised in professional homes were exposed to 45 million words by age four, compared to 26 million words in working-class families and 13 million in welfare homes. The gap of 32 million words between professional and welfare homes was rounded down to a much quoted 30 million, and although the precision of the number is often questioned, few dispute the correlation with differential school performance as confirmed by Willingham: "the conceptual idea that socioeconomic status and volume of caregiver → child speech has been replicated."[19] In 2018 research conducted by the Massachusetts Institute of Technology (MIT) added to the 'word gap' research by identifying that the most significant factor was not the word count itself, but the extent of back and forth turn-taking dialogue between parent and child. The lead researcher Rachel Romeo, using magnetic resonance imaging (MRI) scanning, identified that dialogue strengthened the connections between the Wernicke's and Broca's regions of the brain responsible for comprehension and speech production:

> The researchers found that the number of conversational turns correlated strongly with the children's scores on standardized tests of language skill, including vocabulary, grammar, and verbal reasoning . . . the conversational turn-taking seems like the thing that makes a difference, regardless of socioeconomic

status. Such turn-taking occurs more often in families from a higher socioeconomic status, but children coming from families with lesser income or parental education showed the same benefits from conversational turn-taking.[20]

More recently in 2019 the UK government, in conjunction with the Literacy Trust, launched the Chat, Play and Read campaign because evidence arising from parental surveys revealed that approximately one third of preschool parents do not regularly chat to their children, play number- or alphabet-based games or read stories to encourage questions and build vocabulary. In reviewing the different factors influencing underachievement the UK State of the Nation report 2016 commented:

> Of these factors, the one that goes the furthest to explaining the difference in cognitive outcomes at the age of three has been termed the 'home learning environment'. This relates to the educational activities that parents engage in with their children. These include such things as reading with children, teaching nursery rhymes, the alphabet and numbers, visits to libraries and other educational trips.[21]

Children from non-learning homes start school with a learning disadvantage, and by the end of their primary reception year an estimated 28%, or 180,000 children in England, have a noticeable language and literacy deficit.[22] The evidence indicates that those children never catch up. For instance, in 2016 39% of disadvantaged children achieved the expected level four Standard Achievement Test (SAT) standard at age eleven as opposed to 60% of non-disadvantaged children. Similarly, at the General Certificate of Secondary Education (GCSE) stage 43.1% of disadvantaged students achieved GCSE grade C or better in English and maths compared to 70.6% of non-disadvantaged students. Those findings were reconfirmed in 2021 by the CRED report, "By 16 years old, disadvantaged children are 18 months behind their peers. In 2018, 18% of school leavers left education at age 18 without reaching Level 2 attainment, with poor children twice as likely to do so."[23] Hattie's (2009) survey of educational research confirmed the significant influences of home and parental background. Against an average points score of 0.40 for influences on achievement, Hattie calculated 'home environment' and 'parental involvement' at 0.57 and 0.51, respectively.[24] In relation to home environment, Hattie also raised the significance of emotional support, "achievement is more closely linked to the socio-psychological environment and intellectual stimulation in the home than to parental socioeconomic status indicators such as occupation and education."[25]

In all cases as a universal strategy there should be a significant effort to engage with parent(s) or guardians as much as possible, with the aim of boosting home support and in a few cases to help moderate any evidence of overly intense pressure in the form of unrelenting study schedules i.e. the so-called tiger mothers. All parents, with few exceptions, want their children to succeed but all too often, progress evenings in our schools and colleges are poorly attended. Unfortunately, some parents/guardians have negative memories of their own time at school and are reluctant to engage with teachers. Consequently, consider linking the progress evening to a curriculum display, a demonstration of a range of crafts or sports, a drama presentation, a computer exhibition, a tour of online resources, a prize draw, a careers exhibition or a motivating speaker. Invite your adult education service to set up displays related to adult education opportunities, including taster sessions, to encourage enrolment. A parent or guardian may also become a student. Finally, remember that many parents/guardians who are keen to assist their son or daughter will often lack the knowledge of what best to do.

Connect newsletter

A termly school or college 'Connect' newsletter can be effective as a means of engaging with parents or guardians and can be published as a physical newsletter or online as a school Facebook page and/or a Twitter or WhatsApp feed with much more frequent guidance. Research published by the UK Education Endowment Foundation revealed that a weekly text to prompt support successfully engaged parents with their children's schoolwork.

Many primary schools make extensive and effective use of tapestry.info or classdojo.com, but a physical newsletter may be a consideration in areas of deprivation with possible limited access to the internet. A successful newsletter might only be four sides of A4 i.e. fold A3 card to yield a title page, two inner pages and a back page to yield a circular presentation. If your college or school has graphics courses, invite the students to design an attractive title page and layout and be sure to include the names of the design team as a footer to give them positive recognition.

It might contain:

- Career opportunities,
- Higher course information, including university,
- Prompts to useful study aids/equipment,
- Indication of recommended independent study time,
- Timetable information,
- Holiday dates,
- Assessment information,
- Exam information,
- College regulations and learner charter,
- Suggestions on how to assist their son or daughter,
- Adverts for adult education programmes,
- Contact details.

The key is a regular flow of information to parents or guardians with nudges and prompts to follow up on and support learning targets. The aim is to gain a 'push' from home as well as a 'push' from school or college.

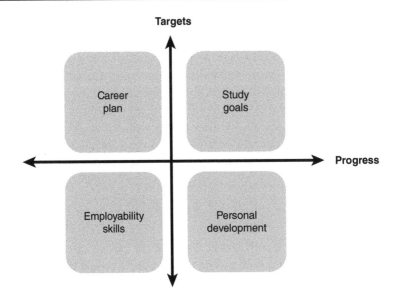

Image 13.4

Personal targets

To advance the progress of each student, personal targets should be agreed to and monitored across the above four major categories of individual performance.

All students should have a named mentor for personal guidance with regular weekly contact to build rapport and to offer constancy and unconditional support. Mentors need to be adept at wearing many different hats e.g. confidant, counsellor, coach, career adviser, intermediary with teaching staff and parent(s) or guardians and in particular a driver of high achievement. With respect to the latter, the mentor should closely monitor progress and intervene as necessary to provide additional support and/or promote effort.

Career goals

Too many of our students lack a clear awareness of the different career opportunities, including apprenticeships and self-employment arising from their subject or course choices. Self-employment is a real possibility given the low start-up costs of the internet. A bias towards academic rather than vocational options is embedded in most schools, and despite the best efforts of our careers service, many pupils may have a limited idea of future employment possibilities. Those with parent(s) or guardian(s) who have been to university and/or held professional employment or founded their own business tend to hold the advantage because they can offer significant guidance and support to their children or know someone who can. They also tend to place a high value on education and promote and expect progression to university. High expectations are not exclusive to professional classes but as noted earlier transcend social and/or income brackets. The website www.icould.com provides a wide range of career pathway information and numerous role model case studies. In addition, the UK charity educationandemployers.org promotes awareness of career pathways and supports schools and colleges with a wide range of information services including the 'speakers for schools' initiative whereby over 1,000 leading business leaders offer free presentations aimed at inspiring young people. A career fall-back position is also recommended in case a favoured pathway cannot be pursued. Research published by the charity in 2019 revealed that pupils who received motivational career talks before sitting their GCSE examinations outperformed control groups who had not received similar careers inputs. It underlines that a clear career goal can significantly boost motivation and help to answer the question 'why learn?'.

Aim to intrigue

Course titles like Biology, Business Studies or Engineering may not convey much to a student and so it is important to raise awareness and prompt enquiry. Our aim is to intrigue and hopefully to spark an interest in knowing more. Try sitting in a student's chair and look around your classroom and/or walk the corridors leading to your curriculum area. What will your students see that might stimulate and raise their interest in studying the subject and perhaps prompt independent investigation beyond the classroom?

- A poster listing 50 or more jobs associated with the subject or course
- Recommended universities
- Future apprenticeship possibilities
- Major employers with internet addresses
- Past student destinations
- Key subject specific websites or apps
- Top ten subject-related books to read
- Key journal articles
- Role model profiles
- Latest research
- Latest innovations/products
- Key subject milestones/discoveries/events, etc.
- Self-employment case studies

Encourage career goals by setting the student targets in relation to discovering more by researching relevant employers, typical vacancies, local, regional or worldwide locations, entry qualifications, associated employability skills, apprenticeships, recommended degree courses, university options including studying abroad, etc. Many of these suggestions could be online with immediate clickable links and inform 'appetiser' presentations at the start of a lesson as described in Chapter 7.

Study targets

Many schools and colleges have adopted well-meaning online systems to record targets, but poorly designed systems often generate overlapping sub-categories leading to multiple entries of the same or similar statements. There is a danger that data capture and 'feeding the machine' becomes the focus rather than the quality of the day-to-day teacher/student dialogue on how to improve. Study targets are preferable to grade targets. A low-grade target based on entry standards or diagnostic testing is counterproductive because it harms motivation. In addition, there is no reliable correlation between past exam performance and future exam performance. At the other end of the scale high grade targets might be expected to be positive and motivational. However, in practice they can introduce pressure to match the grade prediction and raise unnecessary stress. Teachers' grade predictions are also highly likely to mislead. The Universities and Colleges Admission Service (UCAS) in the UK has reported that up to 50% of teachers' grade predications fail to match the grade achieved. This issue was spotlighted during the coronavirus pandemic when a reliance on teacher assessment in place of examinations produced considerable grade inflation. In situations where predictions are required to facilitate applications for higher study or employment, the predicted grade should be set against the outcome of a realistic mock examination rather than teachers' assessment. The exam papers should also, as far as possible, be marked by a neutral colleague to guard against the Pygmalion effect of unconscious bias. Study targets improve performance when they are issued as week-to-week specified tasks for completion. The tasks can be tailored to reflect the students' different levels of motivation, home support, study and organisational skills, as indicated earlier in relation to independent, dependent and directed learners. The aim is to progressively stretch each student via a series of practical improvement steps to build their capacity to learn and to promote higher achievement. Clear, practical study targets allied with precise feedback can accelerate progress by emphasising to all students that what they did not understand yesterday they can understand today with sufficient effort.

Personal Action Steps to Success

A simple way to integrate study targets into everyday teaching practice is to issue regular Personal Action Steps for Success (PASS). The PASS targets may be captured in a proforma as the first page in student files, as illustrated, or utilizing the target or task setting feature of an online learning management system (LMS).

PASS			
Personal Action Steps to Success			
Date	Action	By when	Initials

Image 13.5

Most LMSs are intuitive to use and can link to a related assignment submission and later feedback. PASS targets may be issued to a whole class or to individuals and may be pre-planned or prompted at any point in a lesson in response to an observed learning difficulty or question. Simply invite the student(s) to enter the date in the left-hand margin, specify a target and set a deadline. The targets can be personalised in relation to support or stretch as appropriate with progress and completion monitored by mentors, as well as by the individual teacher(s).

Aim to advance progress by specifying precise SMART learning targets rather than bland aspirational goals e.g.

- Read pages 32 to 48 of the course textbook and write a short paragraph on the differences between inflation and deflation. Complete by next lesson.
- Watch the drfrostmaths.com video on algebra 1 and complete the linear equation examples. Ask for any further help on Thursday.
- Re-read the 'Proficiency scale' goal for score 2.0 and list the differences between a sole trader and a limited company in time for Tuesday's lesson.
- Label a diagram of the Stock Exchange and explain the difference between a bull and a bear market. Complete by next lesson.
- Watch the YouTube video, 'Origins of World War One' and create a list of long-term, medium-term and immediate causes of the outbreak of the war.
- Download the guidance handout entitled 'Correct use of the apostrophe' and read and correctly apply the possession and abbreviation rules in all future assignments.
- To stretch yourself visit the Future Learn website (www.futurelearn.com) and study the module on 'Persuasive Communication' for business. Remember to print the completion certificate and add to your CV.

This 'real-time' focus on setting whole class and precise personalised targets is very powerful because ultimately students who ignore the study suggestions will have to acknowledge that they have not helped themselves to learn. We immediately counter the hopelessness factor and 'I'm no good at . . .' argument because we have concrete evidence that improvement steps have not been attempted. Some of the actions might also encourage peer support by inviting a student to look at how X presented or completed the specified task and gained a high mark. Our aim is to stretch each individual to achieve his or her full potential with appropriately demanding targets. This is a key judgement to get right. Tilt too far one way and the pressure will become counterproductive and generate harmful stress, and too far the other way and we fall into the equally damaging trap of low expectations. The answer lies in encouraging students to apply self-regulated learning (SRL) strategies to reflect upon whether they are working to capacity and managing their time well. How much time does an individual student devote to study beyond the classroom? How much time do other students put in? Teenage social lives, the lure of peer group, watching a Netflix boxset, playing *Fortnite* and part-time jobs often fill a student's week more than independent study. Remind your students that being a student is their full-time job. For those at work, the standard working week in the Western world is thirty-seven to forty hours before any concept of overtime arises. Students should be encouraged to treat their course as a full-time job and to put in a minimum of thirty-seven hours per week: fifteen to twenty hours in the classroom and the remainder engaged in independent study and applying their PASS targets. Over time by pursuing the PASS approach and applying SMART targets, we can refine and further refine the performance of each student towards mastery and higher-than-expected learning outcomes.

SMART targets

Specific
Measurable
Achievable
Realistic
Time-bound

The acronym SMART in relation to writing objectives and target setting can be traced back to an article published in 1981 by the management consultant George T. Doran.[26] SMART targets have since been widely adopted by business and the world of education to drive change. It is a common observation that most objectives and targets set by teachers are not SMART and, far from driving change, contribute to no observable improvements. The former head of Harrow public school, Barnaby Lenon, described boys as "feckless, lazy and indolent" in his 2017 publication 'Much Promise'[27] (it worked in garnering media attention), and so if a target is not SMART and especially time-bound, it is unlikely to have any impact on progress and those boys will undoubtedly remain feckless, lazy and indolent. The examples of targets listed earlier fulfil the SMART criteria by being specific i.e. precise. They are also measurable, achievable within the time scale, realistic in relation to the study goals and lastly time-bound in terms of a 'by when' completion target. Our aim is to bridge gaps in student knowledge and understanding by using SMART targets to prompt beneficial study actions and to encourage and build self-regulation and metacognition. As necessary, question why some students have not fulfilled their study targets? Are there issues at home? Are there personal issues? Is it a misunderstanding? Is it poor organisation and time management? Is it forgetfulness or is it simply a lack of effort? Offer support as appropriate but reset the task and monitor completion.

Marzano's proficiency scales

Robert J. Marzano has published extensive studies on a wide range of effective teaching and learning strategies, and his recommendation for 'proficiency scales' offers teachers a clear platform for highly targeted study feedback and for students a way to measure their own progress and to set their own study targets. Marzano's 'Proficiency scale' presents the key study goals for a given topic within a scale of 0 to 4, moving from zero knowledge of the topic to low, average and higher knowledge/skill levels as illustrated.[28]

The descriptors entered in the proficiency scale are not quotations but provide a summary of Marzano's guidance. The approach is similar to the distinctions made between core knowledge, advanced knowledge and challenge levels in Chapter 4. The benefit is precision and clarity for both teachers and students. Lessons can be directed towards a specified score level or levels as appropriate, and students can measure their progress with the minimum target of 3.0. The proficiency scale informs whole class feedback on how far all are advancing and whether to slow the pace and take a step back or to step forward and move deeper. As individual students hit their personal 'ceilings,' teachers and mentors can provide additional support and guidance and ensure opportunities for collaborative peer practice to help each student to advance. Progress can be tracked with a simple chart to plot assessment

Score	Proficiency scale
4.0	A bullet point checklist of higher conceptual knowledge and skills reflecting the standards for high grade outcomes
3.5	Confirmation of success at score 3 and working towards score 4
3.0	Enter a bullet point checklist of the desired proficiency level i.e. the minimum target level for all students to achieve. Note any 'sticking points.'
2.5	Confirmation of success at score 2 and working towards score 3
2.0	Enter a bullet point checklist of basic foundation level factual knowledge and skills and note any 'sticking points.'
1.5	These scores offer graduated 'working towards' and partial 'with help' success statements.
1.0	
0.5	
0.0	No success even with help

Image 13.6

scores by placing the 0 to 4 scale on the vertical axis and the assessment points along the horizontal axis. After three or four formative assessment opportunities the students' charts will hopefully display rising evidence of personal progress. The teacher may also display averages for the class as a whole and offer feedback and/or re-teach particular aspects with whole class and/or set individual targets for improvement.

Employability skills

The regular application of study targets will hopefully drive high achievement, but all employers, even the local corner shop, raise a requirement for effective personal and employability skills. Our students should be aware that matching the entry standard for a particular profession or employment is only the start of the recruitment process. Once short-listed for a vacancy, qualifications become irrelevant if five other candidates possess the same or similar qualifications. The focus of a job interview is not on qualifications, but on evidence of effective social, personal and employability skills for confident interaction in the world of work and a global society. In 2017 the Sutton Trust applied the term 'life skills' to describe not just employability skills but the wider social skills and attitudes that contribute to personal advancement. Chapter 12 details the major employability skills with the recommendation for curriculum teams to define the generic and career specific employability skills valued by business and industry. The identified skills and qualities should inform targets for each student.

Personal development

Personal development is included as a category within target setting to promote the importance of participation in sporting, social, charitable and citizenship activities as highlighted in Chapter 11. It is not about formal targets, but rather highlighting opportunities and providing nudges and encouragement to engage with activities, wider enrichment and stretching students beyond their comfort zones. Well-being is significantly enhanced through active involvement in events, social engagements and team pursuits and may trigger a beneficial lifetime interest.

Make a list

Finally, the most effective target setting tool of all is a list. Write a list for the week ahead and pin it up in a visible location and it will help to combat procrastination. There is nothing more satisfying than ticking off items on a list as the first basic but highly effective step in developing SRL.

References

1 Eton College, *Aims*, www.etoncollege.com/EtonsAims.aspx?nid=7228fed0-c26f-4dd6-ae1d-db79bdcac748

2 Harris Federation, www.harrisfederation.org.uk/175/our-academies/academy/57/harris-academy-wimbledon

3 OECD, *Future of Education and Skills 2030, Conceptual Learning Framework*, OECD, pg. 2, https://www.oecd.org/education/2030/E2030%20Position%20Paper%20(05.04.2018).pdf

4 Hattie, John Professor, *Visible Learning for Teachers*, Routledge, 2012, pg. 78.

5 Ibid, pg. 50.

6 Ibid, pg. 44.

7 Social Mobility Commission, *State of the Nation 2016*, November 2016, pg. 14, www.gov.uk/government/publications

8 Willingham, Daniel T., *Why Does Family Wealth Affect Learning, American Educator*, Spring 2012, www.aft.org/sites/default/files/periodicals/Willingham.pdf

9 Waldfogel, Jane, For richer for poorer, *Times Educational Supplement*, 1st July 2008, pg. 22–23.

10 Scott, Stephen, *Sunday Times*, 24th August 2008, pg. 7.

11. Marshall, Paul, *The Tail, How England's Schools Fail One Child in Five – and What Can Be Done*, Profile Books, 2013, pg. 10.

12 Obama, Barack, *President, Back to School Event*, 8th September 2009, pg. 3, www.bbc.co.uk/education

13 Advisory Panel to Government Chaired by Rt. Hon Alan Milburn M.P., *Unleashing Aspiration: The Final Report of the Panel on Fair Access to the Professions*, HM Government, July 2009, pg. 30.

14 Commission on Race and Ethnic Disparities (CRED), *The Report*, CRED, 31st March 2021, pg. 70.

15 Ibid, pg. 31.

16 Institute of Education, University of London, *Effective Provision of Pre-School Primary and Secondary Education*, Executive Summary, July 2008, pg. IV, www.oie.ac.uk

17 Ibid, pg. 104.

18 Goodman, Alissa and Gregg, Paul (Editors), *Poor Children's Educational Attainment: How Important Are Attitudes and Behaviours?* Joseph Rowntree Trust, March 2010, pg. 22.

19 Willingham, Daniel T., www.danielwillingham.com/daniel-willingham-science-and-education-blog/the-debunking-of-hart-risley-and-how-we-use-science

20 http://news.mit.edu/2018/conversation-boost-childrens-brain-response-language-0214

21 Social Mobility Commission, *State of the Nation 2016*, November 2016, pg. 21, www.gov.uk/government/publications

22 The Literacy Trust, *Chat, Play and Read Campaign*, https://literacytrust.org.uk/news/chat-play-read-campaign-announced-encourage-learning-home/

23 Commission on Race and Ethnic Disparities (CRED), *The Report*, CRED, 31st March 2021, pg. 60.

24 Hattie John, *Visible Learning a Synthesis of Over 800 Meta-Analyses Relating to Achievement*, Routledge, 2009, Appendix B.

25 Ibid, pg. 66.

26 Doran, G. T., There's a S.M.A.R.T. way to write management's goals and objectives, *Management Review*, vol. 70, no. 11, 1981, pg. 35–36.

27 Lenon, Barnaby, *The Times*, 11th April 2017, www.thetimes.co.uk/article/ninety-nine-per-cent-of-boys-i-have-had-to-deal-with-are-lazy-fcd326vgv

28 Marzano, Robert J., *The New Art and Science of Teaching*, Solution Tree Press, 2017, pg. 12.

14

Personalised feedback

We commonly refer to teaching a class, but rather than a class, our focus should be on the individual students who all happen to be seated in the same room. Each individual is different, and the most effective feedback takes the form of a personalised coaching dialogue to help each student to achieve their full potential. Feedback is often regarded as an adjunct to teaching i.e. post-lesson marking and associated comments on students' assignments, but it is at its most effective as an embedded feature of every lesson to drive forward both individual and whole class high standards. Feedback advances learning by bridging the gap between individual starting points and a known standard. Timely feedback from a teacher can offer guidance that builds refinement upon refinement to the point of mastery. The example of Austin's Butterfly, as highlighted by the author and founder of EL Education (Expeditionary Learning School Consortium), Ron Berger, is regularly quoted in this respect. Austin was a first-grade pupil in Anser Charter School in Boise, Idaho, tasked with drawing a Western tiger swallowtail butterfly. His first draft was clearly a butterfly but not the Western tiger swallowtail butterfly his class was studying. Austin's classmates examined his draft and gave feedback on what they felt was missing. He listened to their feedback, redrafted the drawing and invited further feedback. The process of redrafting and feedback continued until all agreed that his sixth draft had produced a high degree of accuracy. Judge for yourself by googling Austin's butterfly and watch the video or find it as a resource on the EL website https://eleducation.org. The message is not so much about perseverance, but rather encouraging students to become receptive rather than defensive in relation to receiving feedback and to value and appreciate the benefits of constructive and helpful feedback. It raises the distinction between guidance and correction. Feedback that focuses on correction often demoralises and sparks defensive reactions, whereas feedback that offers positive suggestions for improvement encourages a positive 'can do' spirit. The goal is to shift the student/teacher relationship from *push* to *pull* whereby students not only seek feedback but act on the guidance received to close the gap between their performance and a programme standard.

DOI: 10.4324/9781003132783-18

The resulting dialogue may extend into dialogic coaching by applying Socratic question and answer to help students to question and judge their own work against the programme standards. Feedback in this context is no longer a passive process of receiving comments, but an interactive dialogue designed to stimulate the students' thinking and to encourage the development of self-regulation and metacognition. The dialogue may involve the whole class, small groups or individuals and with respect to reducing teachers' workloads feedback should be more about students recording rather than teachers writing feedback. Learning management systems (LMSs) can also reduce workloads by channelling feedback to individuals, groups or a whole class and by taking advantage of digital tools to annotate scripts with verbal, written, video or coded responses as appropriate. Online instructional design programmes are also transforming learning by embedding artificial intelligence (AI)–enhanced personalised feedback into the online programme with immediate further support or acceleration as appropriate e.g. Century.tech, Khanacademy.org and Tassomai.com for science. Regardless of the medium, feedback should adopt a step-by-step approach to progressively raise the challenge for each student with the aim of matching the programme standards in a process of continual refinement as exemplified by Austin's butterfly. The starting point is to ensure all students gain a sense of success within their first six weeks of starting a new programme.

Success in six weeks

We should never underestimate the anxiety most students feel at the start of a new programme. Within the first few lessons, the students will be silently absorbing the study goals, observing the actions and demeanour of their teachers, monitoring peer behaviour, silently questioning their prospects for success and finally, and most importantly of all, judging whether or not they feel they are fitting in and making friends. As early as the second week of attendance many students will conclude they are not and will switch off, raise behavioural challenges, play truant or drop out entirely. Within the UK 30,000 students typically drop out of their Post 16 college courses within the first six weeks of attendance (September to October). Some may join other programmes, but a significant number fall into the category of NEETs i.e. 'Not in Education, Employment or Training' at significant personal cost to their future life chances. The most common reasons for dropping out relate to a sense of isolation and a limited sense of progress. Students do not need to wait to receive feedback from their teachers to know if they are making progress or not. Students, as indicated, silently assess their own performance lesson by lesson and generate their own feedback. They reflect upon how far they have understood the lessons, whether their contributions appeared to be valued and how far they feel a sense of peer acceptance and belonging. Professor John Hattie notes,

> low classroom acceptance by peers can be linked with subsequent disengagement and lowered achievement . . . there needs to be a sense of belonging. . . .

the single greatest predictor of subsequent success is whether the students makes a friend in the first month.[1]

Six weeks is the maximum window, with four the optimum to ensure that every student receives positive feedback and not only a sense of progress but *knows* they are making progress. The goal is to draw the students into a dialogue to raise their awareness of the programme standards and the study targets they need to match. Macro feedback of this type sets a clear study agenda with the high expectation that all can succeed.

High expectations

Within the UK the link between high expectations and student progress was first significantly addressed in 2000 by the publication of the Hay McBer (now just Hay group) report entitled, *Research into Teacher Effectiveness: A Model of Teacher Effectiveness*. The Hay McBer report identified the importance of teachers projecting high expectations:

> expressing positive expectations of pupils – that they can and will learn and be successful – is one of the most powerful ways to influence pupils and raise achievement. It is one of the distinctive behaviours of high performing teachers who radiate confidence in their pupils and their potential and never give up on them.[2]

The words "radiate confidence" go to the heart of informal feedback in terms of teachers on a regular lesson-by-lesson basis, building and reinforcing the belief that all students can not only pass but achieve a high grade by fully engaging with the programme. This is not unrealistic. If students have met the entry requirements for a particular course or stepped up from a preparatory lower course, they should be capable of at least passing and in most cases stepping higher. Hay McBer warned against low expectations in relation to over-compensating for disadvantage i.e. not expecting too much from students from a poor neighbourhood or disadvantaged family background. This can manifest as teachers overlooking poor study behaviours, not challenging monosyllabic answers, tolerating students arriving in lessons ill-equipped to learn or non-participation in question and answers, etc. Unspoken 'feedback' of this type can offer students a license not to conform or to make an effort and will ultimately contribute to their underachievement. Hattie noted, "Having low expectations of the students' success is a self-fulfilling prophecy . . . teachers having expectations that **all** students can progress, that achievement for **all** is changeable (and not fixed), and that progress for all is understood and articulated."[3] Hattie's emphasis upon *all* is significant. Teachers often unconsciously display different expectations of students by conferring positive and negative halos through their body language and tone of voice i.e. warm, friendly informal relations with high-performing students but more perfunctory, formal and corrective relations with underperforming students. The classic jibe of 'teacher's pet' reveals that students are alert to differential teacher–student interactions. The unwitting attachment of positive and negative halos can, if unchecked, trigger the Pygmalion effect.

Pygmalion effect

In 1968 Robert Rosenthal, professor of psychology at Harvard University, published the results of a research study into teacher expectations entitled, *Pygmalion in the Classroom: Teacher Expectation and Pupils' Intellectual Development*. Pygmalion was a sculptor in a poem by the Roman poet Ovid who fell in love with a statute of a young woman. After praying to the gods, Pygmalion's wish was granted, and the statute was given the gift of life. Rosenthal's experiment investigated how far teachers unconsciously favour and hold high expectations of some students and the resulting impact on their progress. To test the proposition Rosenthal gave teachers in a participating primary school the outcomes of a fictional diagnostic test that identified some pupils, dubbed the 'late bloomers,' with a potential for high academic achievement. Subsequent assessment tracking revealed that the 'late bloomers' progressively gained higher marks from their teachers and outpaced their classmates. Rosenthal's research confirmed that teachers' subliminal behaviours can influence differential progression:

> when teachers expect students to do well and show intellectual growth, they do; when teachers do not have such expectations, performance and growth are not so encouraged and may in fact be discouraged in a variety of ways. Teachers give the students that they expect to succeed more time to answer questions, more specific feedback, and more approval: They consistently touch, nod and smile at those kids more.[4]

The research provoked considerable controversy, and although Rosenthal's scientific method was subsequently questioned, his basic premise was replicated by subsequent studies. In 1989 the educational researcher Kathleen Cotton published a meta-analysis of forty-six research studies into the impact of teachers' expectations and concluded, "The most important finding from this research is that teacher expectations can and do affect students' achievements and attitudes. Among the research materials supporting this paper, all that address this topic found relationships between expectations and student outcomes."[5] Cotton recorded the following (among many other) negative teacher behaviours in relation to students identified as low achievers:

- Paying less attention to low-expectation students than high-expectation students, including calling on low-expectation students less often during recitations.
- Seating low-expectation students farther from the teacher than high-expectation students.

- Interacting with low-expectation students more privately than publicly and structuring their activities much more closely.
- Conducting differential administration or grading of tests or assignments, in which high-expectation students – but not low-expectation students – are given the benefit of the doubt in borderline cases.
- Conducting less friendly and responsive interactions with low-expectation students than high-expectation students, including less smiling, positive head nodding, forward leaning, eye contact, etc.
- Giving briefer and less informative feedback to the questions of low-expectation students than those of high-expectation students.[6]

More recently in 2014 similar findings were reported by researchers engaged in reviewing student progress in preparing for General Certificate of Secondary Education (GCSE) maths and English examinations in the England:

> Some interviewees also felt that their teachers at school paid less attention to them because they were at a lower level in comparison to other learners. Maths learners in particular felt that their teachers were only interested in helping those who were already good at the subject in order to boost their grades further.[7]

The most recent confirmation of the Pygmalion effect arose from research undertaken by Stanford University in 2018. The researchers tested a group of sports students for the *CREBI* gene linked to stamina and gave some students, selected entirely at random, a low endurance test result, whereas others were informed they possessed the high endurance gene variant. The latter students outperformed the others on subsequent endurance tests. Students are perceptive and unintentional and informal negative feedback, if not corrected, can significantly damage progress because the relevant students soon switch off and become less inclined to cooperate further reinforcing and aggravating a negative relationship.

Teacher Expectation Project

Evidence that the opposite approach i.e. the conscious projection of high expectations can successfully promote deeper and more successful learning was demonstrated by the Teacher Expectation Project (TEP) developed by Professor Christine Rubie-Davies of Auckland University. The project initially focused on pupil progress in mathematics and reading and involved training teachers in techniques to translate 'high expectations' into specific classroom behaviours and actions:

- Using flexible grouping (rather than ability grouping)
- Creating a warm, positive class climate
- Using goal-setting to increase student motivation, engagement and autonomy, and improve teacher evaluation and feedback.

Rubie-Davies concluded that teachers who applied the above strategies gained marked increases in positive student engagement and subsequent progress:

> The evidence suggests that providing students with clear feedback on their learning goals, fostering intrinsic motivation and providing students with choices in the tasks that they complete, all appear to have marked effects on both student social-psychological and academic outcomes and these have all been found to be behaviors of teachers with high expectations for all their students.[8]

The recommendation for creating a warm, positive classroom climate has significant implications for teacher training to include coaching warm, upbeat communication skills in relation to body language, tone of voice, eye contact, smiling, affirmative head nods and regular circulation aimed at drawing all students into full participation. The Danielson Teaching and Learning framework, developed by the leading American educationalist Charlotte Danielson, offers similar guidance and identified teachers' communication skills as an element of 'distinguished' practice:

> Classroom interactions between the teacher and students and among students are highly respectful, reflecting genuine warmth, caring, and sensitivity to students as individuals. Students exhibit respect for the teacher and contribute to high levels of civility among all members of the class. The net result is an environment where all students feel valued and are comfortable taking intellectual risks.[9]

The TEP project concluded with a recommendation for ensuring that all students received clear feedback on how to improve: "Finally, the setting of specific, achievable goals for students, monitoring progress closely, and providing students with clear feedback about their learning provide students with clear directions for their learning and the focus is on mastering skills and learning."[10] The emphasis is upon feedback that offers *clear directions* by not only specifying *what* to improve but more importantly *how* to improve. This distinction underpins effective practice because the value of feedback lies not in benchmarking the standard of a student's work with a mark or grade but offering guidance for improvement.

To mark or not mark

One of the key principles that emerged from the Assessment for Learning research undertaken by Professors Paul Black and Dylan Wiliam was not to award any marks or grades and especially not in the early weeks of a new programme. They recommended reserving marks and grades for summative assessments because otherwise there is a tendency for students to focus on the grade or mark and to ignore the improvement guidance. This concept is not new. The *Board of Education Handbook for Teachers*, first published in 1904, provided the following guidance:

the essential point, however, is that the child should understand what is wrong and know how to correct it. This can never be secured if the teacher's revision goes no further than merely marking every mistake, without regard to its relative importance, and handing the exercise back to the child without comment.[11]

All students will need time to absorb the standard of working when joining a higher-level course or even a new course at the same level. Providing each student with 'how to improve' guidance provides an action agenda to follow, whereas presenting a student with a succession of percentage marks at a bare pass level reinforces a student's negative perception of their ability without offering any way forward. Black commented that low marks with no improvement guidance may generate frustration and the frustration may in turn prompt students to give up:

> The worst scenario is one in which some pupils get low marks this time, they got low marks last time, they expect to get low marks next time, and this is accepted as part of a shared belief between them and their teacher that they are just not clever enough. Feedback has been shown to improve learning where it gives each pupils specific guidance on strengths and weaknesses, preferably without any overall marks.[12]

Once students discover how to improve, the issue switches to ensuring that improvement actions are enacted. Ideally this will become self-regulating as students apply the specified improvements and discover a corresponding rise in positive progress.

Applying PACE

Clearly it is important to assess student progress and to offer benchmarks to inform feedback and to ensure students are aware of how far they are matching the relevant curricular standards. Opinions will vary as to the benchmarks to apply but PACE introduces four core measures:

Performance
Attendance
Coursework
Effort

The term performance relates to formal marked assignments, essays, tests or examinations. Attendance is a recording of individual percentage attendance while coursework relates to routine submission of day-to-day classwork, homework, and completion of specified online research tasks etc. The term 'effort' relates to the amount of effort and time being put into studying and this may be altered to 'extended learning' (perhaps for adult students) to mean the same thing but in a less challenging way. It is perhaps subjective but as detailed in Chapter 10, applying sufficient effort and perseverance is important and by raising the question students will often volunteer their own judgement. To implement PACE each curriculum team should agree a grading scale. Perhaps the most straightforward is A to D as follows:

A = excellent
B = Good
C – Satisfactory
D = Unsatisfactory

The criteria for the award of the grades should be agreed and set by each curriculum team to ensure consistency i.e. excellent might be 90%+ to reflect Bloom's mastery learning principles or to match a specified list of criteria. In relation to grading attendance it is notable that the average attendance rate for colleges is 84%, and many are content to set an attendance target of 90%. However, in the world of work employers expect 100% attendance and perhaps this should be the criterion for the award of a grade A. In addition, as learning beyond the classroom becomes as significant as learning within the classroom, attendance should encompass completion of specified online tasks by monitoring log-in records, and this may also raise an objective link to effort. By attaching PACE to each unit of study, it is possible to introduce a consistent and uniform system of continuous assessment with the potential, if wished, to replace formal summative examinations. Pace can be captured on one side of A4 or in electronic form for ease of access and updating by all staff. The completed record (as illustrated below) permits an 'at a glance' overview of individual progress and how far students are consistent in their formal test performances as against routine coursework. In addition, low grades for attendance and/or effort might explain low overall progress and provide a basis for feedback and study guidance.

CLASS PACE RECORD
Performance, Attendance, Coursework and Effort

Course		Subject	
Teacher		Date	

Student name	P	A	C	E	comments

A = Excellent, B = Good, C = Satisfactory, D = Unsatisfactory

Image 14.1

This PACE record is designed to capture progress for each individual unit of study, or alternatively, PACE might be applied twice per term to benchmark progress and inform feedback within each individual subject. An overall record of progress is also important to inform dialogue with personal tutors or mentors, and this can be captured as illustrated here.

TUTORIAL PACE RECORD
Performance, Attendance, Coursework and Effort

Course		Student	
Tutor		Group	

Autumn Term

Subject	P	A	C	E	comments
History	B	A	B	B	
English	C	A	C	D	

A = Excellent, B = Good, C = Satisfactory, D = Unsatisfactory

Image 14.2

To compete the overall record, simply repeat this table for winter and summer terms or alter to term one, term two, etc. As an alternative for grades A to D, consider the traffic light system of green, amber and red and colour the cells as appropriate with your own preferred standards and descriptors. Whether PACE or your own system of assessment is applied, the key is clarity and the agreement of common standards across a curriculum team. Otherwise, different teachers may apply their own standards and marking codes etc. Some might award a mark out of twenty, others a percentage and others a grade. Some might equally issue no marks or grades at all in line with the Assessment for Learning good practice. Some might correct spellings and grammar and perhaps deduct marks, whereas others might choose to ignore mistakes. If assessment and related feedback is to be effective, then a consistent standard is essential; otherwise, students may gain the impression that no standard exists beyond the whim of the individual teacher and in turn the danger of the Pygmalion effect.

Feedback model

Feedback is closely related to goals and targets, as illustrated, and involves both whole class and individual 'ways to improve' guidance based upon detailed curricular knowledge.

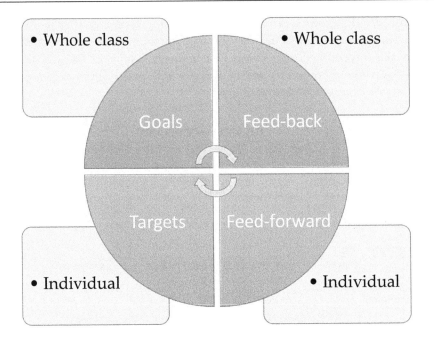

Image 14.3

Applying curricular knowledge

Great teachers apply their subject knowledge to the cognitive and skill demands of the relevant examinations or performance standards to inform purposeful and effective feedback. They are able to:

- Specify the performance difference between a distinction and a pass or a grade A and a grade E or the relevant grading structure,
- Visualise and model those different standards,
- Scaffold step-by-step support,
- Anticipate the common stumbling blocks,
- Intervene early to promote the progress of each student,
- Provide precise step-by-step personalised improvement guidance,
- Promote self-efficacy and inspire to target high grades.

The ability to guide and to help each student to step forward is the principal goal of feedback i.e. to predict and correct individual difficulties and misunderstandings. Rosenshine highlighted the importance of teachers' sign posting aspects of potential difficulty: "one characteristic of effective teachers is their ability to anticipate students' errors and warn them of possible errors some of them are likely to make."[13] The Sutton Trust equally underlined this facet of great teaching: "As well as a strong understanding of the material being taught, teachers must also understand the ways students think about the content, be able to evaluate the thinking behind students' own methods, and identify students' common misconceptions."[14] The influential Danielson Framework for effective teaching offers similar guidance: "Accomplished teachers understand the internal relationships within the disciplines they teach, knowing which concepts and skills are prerequisite to the understanding of others. They are also aware of typical student misconceptions in the discipline and work to dispel them."[15] The key is a timely intervention to counter frustration when a student hits a learning difficulty with respect to Vygotsky's Zone of Proximal Development as discussed in Chapter 10.

Whole class feedback

Whole class feedback should be an integral element of most lessons with regular feedback on overall progress, highlighting common errors and misconceptions and developing a clear, shared understanding of the performance standards. Consistency between teachers is essential, and curriculum teams should apply curricular knowledge and conduct a close analysis of the relevant examination standards to inform feedback. This should include the development of common marking schemes and/or Marzano-style proficiency scales as illustrated in the last chapter.

Individual feed forward

If we wish to secure higher performance, we should 'feed forward' more than we 'feedback.' Hattie reports, "students tend to be future-focussed rather than dwelling on what they have done beforehand and left behind."[16] Rather than identifying errors, it is more a question of converting the errors into specified improvement actions to be carried forward and addressed in future assignments. The Personal Action Steps to Success (PASS) proforma presented in the last chapter illustrates a practical way to feed forward. Dylan Wiliam warned against feedback that is too error focussed: "Unfortunately, in many cases, the feedback was not particularly helpful. Typically the feedback would focus on what was deficient about the work submitted, which the students were not able to resubmit, rather than on what to do to improve their future learning."[17] The American Psychological Association offers similar guidance:

> clear, explanatory and timely feedback to students is important for learning. . . . Students tend to respond better if feedback minimizes negativity and addresses significant aspects of their work and understanding, in contrast to feedback that is negative in tone and focused excessively on details of student performance that are less relevant to the learning goals.[18]

Less is more, and we should be mindful of cognitive load theory and not overwhelm students with a long list of corrections and/or improvement guidance.

In general, apply the 'rule of three' and feed forward a maximum of three improvement actions. The aim is to bridge the gap between a student's existing performance and the achievement of a higher standard.

Feedback competencies

The Danielson Framework for Teaching identifies four levels of competency in the provision of feedback.[19]

Level	Competency
Unsatisfactory	Feedback is absent or of poor quality. Students do not engage in self- or peer assessment.
Basic	Feedback to students is general, and few students assess their own work.
Proficient	Teacher feedback to groups of students is accurate and specific; some students engage in self-assessment.
Distinguished	A variety of forms of feedback, from both teacher and peers, is accurate and specific and advances learning. Students self-assess and monitor their own progress. The teacher successfully differentiates instruction to address individual students' misunderstandings.

Image 14.4

Danielson's hierarchy addresses actions by both teachers and students. At the lower levels of the scale, teachers' feedback is characterised as either entirely absent or too generic followed by stepping up to evidence of accurate feedback to groups and at the highest level of the scale evidence of a variety of methods of feedback and supportive feedback to individual students. In addition, the hierarchy addresses how far the students themselves engage in self and peer assessment, ranging from no engagement at the lowest level to students monitoring their own progress at the highest level. Danielson identifies feedback as an integral feature of the lesson: "The teacher is constantly 'taking the pulse' of the class; monitoring of student understanding is sophisticated and continuous and makes use of strategies to elicit information about individual student understanding."[20] The reference to 'taking the pulse' i.e. the regular monitoring of progress, is in accord with Rosenshine's guidance to gauge understanding and progress as the lesson unfolds. Rosenshine recommends regular pauses to 'check in' with the students during a lesson before moving forward:

Effective teachers also stopped to check for student understanding. They checked for understanding by asking questions, by asking the students to summarise the presentation up to that point or to repeat directions or procedures, or by asking students in they agreed or disagreed with other students' answers.[21]

Feedback from students to the teacher within the flow of the lesson is a very powerful driver of effective learning because it permits 'real-time' adjustments to the pace and development of new learning as noted by Hattie:

> feedback was most powerful when it is from the student to the teacher . . . when teachers seek or at least are open to feedback from students as to what students know, what they understand, where they make errors, when they have misconceptions, when they are not engaged – then teaching and learning can be synchronised and powerful.[22]

All students will find an aspect of new knowledge difficult, and therefore teachers need to promote a learning culture that routinely invites questions and helps all students to have the confidence to say, 'I don't understand . . . or Can you repeat . . . ? or I'm not sure how . . . ?' Essentially there is no gain in moving forward to the next topic or episode within a lesson if some or most students are still wrestling with an aspect of the new knowledge. Wiliam has written extensively on this issue and recommends the application of 'all response' question and answer strategies as described in Chapter 5 to capture feedback within the lesson. Ideally 'real-time' feedback should guide and steer our lessons. The ability to read body language and to 'hear' hesitancy is important, but of greater importance is reacting to hesitation to ensure that all are making appropriate progress and are growing in confidence lesson by lesson.

Feedback strategies

Marking students' work and providing improvement feedback is time consuming and places a restraint on how far each student can receive detailed personalised feedback, although this will alter once online personalised learning programmes (PLPs) are widely adopted. To reduce workloads and to more fully engage students with the curriculum standards, Wiliam recommends the following 'four quarters' marking policy.

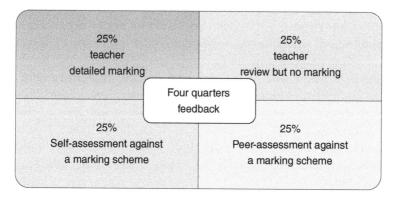

Image 14.5

The four quarters approach engages the students in thinking carefully about their work and applying the programme standards rather than simply receiving feedback.

- **Teacher marking** – Most teachers have their own shorthand, but perhaps the most straightforward marking code is a tick, a question mark, a cross and a circle. A tick indicates a good point and a double tick impressive. A question mark indicates a need to check for accuracy or clarity. A cross marks an error for correction and finally, a circle placed around a word, phrase or punctuation highlights an aspect of spelling, punctuation and/ or grammar (SPAG) for correction. In situations where errors are repeated throughout a student's work, the teacher should not mark each instance but rather specify a relevant improvement action. As far as possible build an online library of core topic information relevant to each topic and resources to support the SPAG basics. Refer the students to the relevant online resource with a suitable reference code. Most learning management systems (LMSs) also have the facility to return assignments electronically with oral or video feedback as previously raised. Alternatively, you can opt to mark a student's assignment on your computer and record a feedback video as you mark using a screen recorder like Screencast-o-matic. This is a free resource and is intuitive to use.
- **Teacher review** – Invite students to submit a specified assignment for reading and review ideally online as an electronic document. Skim read the students' work and identify and list the principal positives and negatives arising from the students' work for feedback to the whole class. Present and explain the key points to the class and invite the students to assess how far their script reflects the identified positives and negatives. Follow up by giving the students' time to write their own feedback commenting on aspects they think they managed well, aspects for improvement and what they might do differently in the future. This process may also generate beneficial peer sharing of different approaches to learning and identifying and correcting common misconceptions.
- **Self-assessment** – Discuss and issue marking criteria reflecting the exam board standards or a Marzano-style proficiency scale as detailed in the last chapter. List pertinent criteria down the left-hand column as illustrated below and invite the students to enter assessment comments and in the score column a tick, question mark or a cross. The completed forms should be handed in for teacher review and used to inform whole class or one to one discussion. Teachers should select a sample of the students' work to review the consistency and accuracy of the students' self-assessments, including any that raise a possible need for additional support or advancement.

Criteria	Comment	Score
Presentation and word count as specified		
Accurate SPAG*		
Introduction directly addresses the question and sets a clear direction for the answer.		
etc.		

Image 14.6 *Assuming the electronic submission of assignments, students should be advised not to submit an assignment with red or green underlining. Red indicates a spelling error and this should be checked and corrected, while green indicates a possible grammatical error. Ask the students to read the grammar correction and to rearrange their sentence, as appropriate, to see if the error is corrected. It is not perfect but over time will help students to think about their writing and key elements of good grammar can be a feature of all class feedback.

- **Peer assessment** – Ensure all assignments are anonymous and distribute at random to the students for assessment against a marking scheme as noted earlier. This is a useful technique because it allows students to read and examine other students' assignments often involving higher or lower standards than their own work. Discovering how other students approached the same assignment can be a significant revelation and deepen awareness of personal standards. Regularly extend the task into discussion by spacing out and listing the marking scheme criteria on flipchart paper. Post the flipchart paper on the classroom wall and invite the students to record their scores from their individual report sheets (as in the earlier example) onto the flipchart paper. This works best with coloured dots, in the traffic light colours of green, amber and red in place of the tick, question mark and cross. The result is a colourful display to inform discussion of the dominant areas of assessed strengths and weaknesses. A preponderance of red dots against a particular aspect should prompt examination and possible re-teaching. Padlet is a useful substitute for your classroom wall and will permit assignments to be posted and comments entered along with one or more stars
- **One to one** – Seek to build a positive rapport with each student by engaging in one-to-one planned feedback encounters at least twice per term but with many informal micro feedback encounters during lessons. Gain time for feedback appointments by devoting some lessons to individual, paired or group tasks. Alternatively, regularly end a lesson ten minutes early to gain time to coach an individual or a group over a particular learning difficulty. Ensure that one to one feedback is not just focussed on underperforming students because this will quickly taint feedback as a negative process. Feedback is about acceleration as much as support, and high-performing students should also receive one-to-one guidance in relation to stretch and challenge.
- **Small group** – Identify groups of students who are demonstrating the same misconceptions or alternatively displaying good progress. Issue appropriate feedback

to each group in relation to support or acceleration. The time for feedback to groups can be gained in the same way as for individuals as described earlier.

- **In-lesson feedback** – Draw feedback from the students in real time during the course of a lesson to inform the pace and direction of the lesson by using one of the many recap, recall and questioning strategies described in Chapter 5 and aim to build a learning dialogue. This is preferable to waiting to discover errors while marking students' work.
- **Hot and cold marking** – As an alternative to the earlier marking codes, regularly mark students' work by using a red highlighter pen (hot) on particular words or passages or sections that impress and blue (cold) on parts that could be improved. This reverses the normal association of red with errors. Clearly you need to be cautious with the ratio of red to blue or you will achieve the reverse of what you intend. Highlight in blue only one or two sections and invite the students to check and to self-identify, as far as possible, the reason for the highlight. This prompts the students to think about their work rather than simply presenting them with a list of improvements.
- **Carry forward** – Apply the 'rule of three' by specifying no more than three improvements to be carried forward into future work. Invite the student to copy the improvement point or points onto the top of their next assignment to 'carry forward' and demonstrate that they have acknowledged and applied the improvements.

Assessor one-to-one feedback

Apprentice and vocational programmes often involve workplace visits involving one-to-one feedback sessions to check and promote progress. An effective visit will involve:

- Venue (as far as possible) is suitable for a private discussion with no distractions.
- Clear goals i.e. an agenda for the session. Each visit should ideally be two-fold i.e. gaining feedback on progress and coaching an agreed aspect for improvement.
- A clear review of progress to date and seeking agreement on future, short-term SMART targets.
- Listen well – hear and respond to hesitancy.
- The ability to help the learner to evaluate their own performance and to set their own SMART targets linked to employer's requirements.
- Clear identification of skills/competency to be demonstrated.
- Ensuring appropriate balance between coaching and 'telling' exactly what to say or do. The individual must be able to independently display competence.
- Effective evidence collection of achievement of specified competency.
- Opportunities for the learner to raise issues of personal interest/concern – alert to safeguarding and to wider well-being.
- Coaching support to help overcome study or employment difficulties.

- Evidence of the learner addressing or being encouraged to address areas for improvement.
- Awareness of own limitations and when to refer to more expert guidance or personal support.
- Promotion of links with parents/guardians/employers to encourage support for learning and future career plans.
- Application of the relevant discipline code, as appropriate, in a firm but fair manner.
- Motivate to achieve full potential – confirm 'high expectation' SMART targets.
- Ending on a positive, warm upbeat note.

Lessons from Dunedin

The nature or nurture debate has a long history, but as indicated in Chapter 2, Plomin (2018) has confirmed that nature rather than nurture holds the dominant influence over our cognitive development:

> Genetics is by far the major source of individual differences in school achievement . . . environmental influence shared by children attending the same schools as well as growing up in the same family accounts for only 20 per cent of the variance of achievement.[23]

This appears to indicate that ability is fixed by inheritance and impervious to educational intervention. However, Plomin has emphasised that the polygenic scores (genetic markers) linked to educational outcomes and individual traits are probabilistic rather than deterministic. This is also the conclusion of the major Dunedin Multidisciplinary Health and Development Study. Dunedin is a small town in New Zealand and from 1972 to 1973 the development and life experiences of a cohort of 1,037 children were monitored, assessed and recorded from ages three to thirty-eight. This is a substantial more in-depth version of the famous ITV 7Up television series that charted the lives of fourteen British children at seven-year intervals starting from 1964. The Dunedin study not only involved 1037 children but introduced its first cognitive and socio-economic assessments at age three and thereafter every two years ages up to age fifteen followed by three years intervals up to age twenty-one and finally at five-year intervals into mature adulthood. The study has generated thousands of research findings and data sets and most can be accessed via the website (https://dunedinstudy.otago.ac.nz/). Alternatively, a highly readable summary of the major research findings entitled *The Origins of You* was published in 2019 by four of the research team's principal psychologists. The research revealed that those children with high polygenic scores correlated with educational attainment outperformed children with low polygenic scores at every step and not just in relation to higher educational attainment:

by age thirty-eight study members with higher polygenic scores were more likely than those with lower scores to be employed in more prestigious occupations, to earn higher incomes, to have accumulated more assets, to report fewer difficulties paying their bills, to rely less on social-welfare benefits and to have better credit scores.[24]

The researchers further reported, "even with educational attainment controlled the polygenic score still predicted adult attainment."[25] However, there is a significant difference between prediction and outcome, and the authors repeat Plomin's caveat that genetic inheritance is probabilistic rather than deterministic and more pointedly that biology need not be destiny. In this context the research identified that almost 60% of the links between genetic inheritance and educational attainment relate to cognitive ability, self-control and interpersonal skills and those elements are malleable.[26] Whereas our genetic inheritance is fixed, we can by appropriate nudges, interventions, experiences and opportunities influence and seek to mitigate a genetic predisposition to a particular behaviour or potentially life limiting trait. Mitigation might also become remission: "there is a reason to believe that it should be possible to counteract the effect of genes for limited life success with development interventions, to promote cognitive and non-cognitive skills and perhaps so much more."[27] This is a strategic gateway for education and highlights the importance of applying PASS targets and the provision of an opportunity rich curriculum, as detailed in Chapter 11.

Positive feedback for all

The feedback young people most often absorb from wider society is that academic achievement is the only measure that matters. The damaging impact of this perception was powerfully addressed by sixteen-year-old Ellie Chick in August 2018. At a time when the media was featuring and celebrating the successful exam results of high achievers, Ellie publicly revealed that her results fell within the 33% of the cohort who annually fail to achieve a single GCSE exam pass. Ellie posted her results on Twitter and addressed the following plea to the UK Secretary of State for Education Damian Hinds: "please don't forget about the 33 per cent like me in the education system, because we all have a variety of talents and just need an opportunity to use them! Reminder, I am kind, polite, funny, caring and adventurous."[28] Ellie may have underachieved academically, but she was an overachiever in gymnastics having won regional and national competition awards. Graham Bates OBE, JP, was one of many who responded to her tweet as follows:

> I am one of those who left school at 14 with no qualifications but now that I am 81 I can look back at many achievements.
> Businessman all my working life
> Borough Councillor 35 years chairing many committees

Mayor of Bedford 1973–74

Magistrate 31 years chairing courts

Appointed a Governor in 1966 and am still a Governor and Chairman of two schools

Chairman of two separate registered charities.

Made an OBE in 1988.[29]

Graham Bates is far from alone. There are many examples of successful people often managing global businesses without any formal qualifications. Feedback ultimately must reflect and keep pace with each individual's growth and development and to help all students to find a pathway that is personally fulfilling and rewarding. Harvard University's seven-point prescription for happiness included "find something you are really good at and do it as often as possible."[30] Our feedback should help each student to identify what they are good at with regular crossroads involving multiple directions and parallel highways rather than just a straight academic road terminating in formal written examinations. Feedback is about building and sustaining excellence, but excellence in all fields.

References

1 Hattie, John, *Visible Learning for Teachers*, Routledge, 2012, pg. 87.

2 BcBer, Hay, *Research into Teacher Effectiveness: A Model of Teacher Effectiveness*, DfES, June 2000, pg. 8.

3 Hattie, John, *Visible Learning, a Synthesis of Over 800 Meta-Analyses Relating to Achievement*, Routledge, 2009, pg. 35.

4 Rosenthal, Robert, *Pygmalion in the Classroom: Teacher Expectation and Pupils' Intellectual Development*, Harvard University Press, 1968.

5 Cotton, Kathleen, *Expectations and Student Outcomes*, Northwest School Improvement Service, November 1989, pg. 4, http://educationnorthwest.org/sites/default/files/ExpectationsandStudentOutcomes.pdf

6 Ibid, pg. 8.

7 Robey, Charlotte and Jones, Emily, *Engaging Learners in GCSE Maths and English*, Niace, February 2015, pg. 20, www.learningandwork.org.uk/wp-content/uploads/2017/01/Engaging-learners-in-GCSE-maths-and-English.pdf

8 Rubie-Davies, C. M., et al., A teacher expectation intervention: Modelling the practices of high expectation teachers, *Contemporary Educational Psychology*, 2014, pg. 5, http://doi.org/10.1016/j.cedpsych.2014.03.003

9 Danielson, Charlotte, *The Framework for Teaching, Evaluation Instrument*, 2013, pg. 35, https://www.nctq.org/dmsView/2013_FfTEvalInstrument_Web_v1_2_20140825

10 Rubie-Davies, C. M., et al., A teacher expectation intervention: Modelling the practices of high expectation teachers, *Contemporary Educational Psychology*, 2014, pg. 4, http://doi.org/10.1016/j.cedpsych.2014.03.003

11 Board of Education, *Handbook of Suggestions for Teachers*, Board of Education, 1927, pg. 110.

12 Black, Paul and Wiliam, Dylan, *Assessment for Learning, Putting It into Practice*, Open University Press, 2007, pg. 67.

13 Rosenshine, Barak, Principles of instruction, research-based strategies that all teachers should know, *American Educator*, Spring 2012, pg. 18.

14 Coe, Robert, et al., *What Makes Great Teaching? Review of the Underpinning Research*, The Sutton Trust, October 2014, pg. 2.

15 Danielson, Charlotte, *The Framework for Teaching, Evaluation Instrument*, 2013, pg. 7, https://www.nctq.org/dmsView/2013_FfTEvalInstrument_Web_v1_2_20140825

16 Hattie, John and Yates, Gregory, *Visible Learning and the Science of How We Learn*, Routledge, 2014, pg. 65.

17 Wiliam, Dylan, *Embedded Formative Assessment*, Solution Tree Press, 2011, pg. 120.

18 American Psychological Association, *Coalition for Psychology in Schools and Education, Top 20 Principles from Psychology for preK − 12 Teaching and Learning*, 2015, pg. 13, http://www.apa.org/ed/schools/cpse/top-twenty-principles.pdf

19 Danielson, Charlotte, *The Framework for Teaching, Evaluation Instrument*, 2013, pg. 74–75, https://www.nctq.org/dmsView/2013_FfTEvalInstrument_Web_v1_2_20140825

20 Ibid, pg. 75.

21 Rosenshine, Barack, Principles of instruction: Research based strategies that all teachers should know, *American Educator*, Spring 2012, pg. 16.

22 Hattie, John, *Visible Learning: A Synthesis of Over 800 Meta-Analyses Relating to Achievement*, Routledge, 2009, pg. 173.

23 Plomin, Robert, *Blueprint, How DNA Makes Us Who We are*, Allen Lane 2018, pg. 88.

24 Belsky, Jay, et al., *The Origins of You, How Childhood Shapes Later Life*, Harvard University Press, 2020, pg. 261.

25 Ibid, pg. 263.

26 Ibid, pg. 267.

27 Ibid, pg. 270.

28 Chick, Ellie, *YouTube*, Honest Opinion About GCSEs, www.youtube.com/watch?v=K3Q_4dhlZeU

29 Ibid, Bates Graham, *Comment Posted*, www.youtube.com/watch?v=LzMf-XwHZ6Y

30 https://www.health.harvard.edu/staying-healthy   /the-pursuit-of-happiness, 2017.

Challenge

15

Creative futures

Advances in our society arise from curiosity, observations, questions, hypotheses and experimentation rather than mere repetition, as intimated by Piaget: "the principal goal of education in the schools should be creating men and women who are capable of doing new things, not simply repeating what other generations have done."[1] Knowledge is not static and without the skills to apply, develop and step beyond the boundaries of what is currently known, our society and individuals would flounder. Our most successful companies and organisations do not stand still but actively seek and embrace change and innovation. A creative idea is popularly referred to as the 'best thing since sliced bread' in celebration of the first bread slicing machine designed and built by Otto Frederick Rohwedder in 1928. The machine was installed in the Chillicothe Baking Company in Missouri and was an instant success with people travelling from miles around to see it in action. Rohwedder's invention was the culmination of many years of development effort rather than a sudden eureka moment. The latter is the popular conception of creativity and often attributed to a brilliant mind, the outcome of exceptional imagination or simply happenstance, but the reality is more prosaic. A landmark study of 300 celebrated geniuses by Catharine Cox in 1926 failed to find any correlation between IQ and creativity. Lewis Terman's (1877–1956) longitudinal study of 1,528 children with an IQ of 140+, *Genetic Studies of Genius*, also failed to show any link between a brilliant mind and exceptional innovation, much to Terman's disappointment. As adults Terman's genius group all settled into comfortable academic careers but none of them produced any ground-breaking advances. Indeed, two children, William Shockley and Luis Alvarez, who were originally tested and rejected by Terman for inclusion in his genius group went on to separately achieve Nobel Prizes in Physics. In reality most advances do not arise 'out of the blue,' but like Rohwedder's bread slicing machine they are the product of in-depth research and/or deliberate practice over many years aided in many cases by the unconscious processing of a problem or issue. As noted in Chapter 2 we unconsciously absorb a wealth of information and images every day and often

DOI: 10.4324/9781003132783-20

during an idle moment or out walking or speaking with friends or drifting off to sleep disparate thoughts overlap and/or combine with information stored in our long-term memories to trigger an idea. Koestler described those random mental intersections between stimuli and a stored memory as bisociation associations, whereas Einstein described the brain's random wanderings and meshing of different thoughts as combinatory play. Steve Jobs, the creative force behind Apple, similarly remarked:

> Creativity is just connecting things. When you ask creative people how they did something, they feel a little guilty because they didn't really do it, they just saw something. It seemed obvious to them after a while. That's because they were able to connect experiences they've had and synthesize new things. And the reason they were able to do that was that they've had more experiences or they have thought more about their experiences than other people.[2]

Connecting things is the bedrock of creativity and requires knowledge and imagination, but focussed imagination with relation to critical thinking to resolve problems as they arise or to add value to existing products, services and processes, or most prized of all to develop new original products and applications. Our major challenge is to encourage our students to look beyond the narrow confines of the curriculum and to promote creative thinking in relation to personal interests, future career pathways and hopefully to help resolve society's major issues and challenges.

Why creativity

The present-day focus on creative thinking was largely prompted by the emergence of the global economy in the early 1980s. Countries like Japan and South Korea developed a reputation for high-quality design and reliability of their cars, televisions and consumer electronics. Cut price but highly attractive textiles, toys and household goods also entered the market from countries like Taiwan and Hong Kong. The scale of the competition threatened Western economic growth and prompted the United States to launch an urgent review of the school curriculum in relation to improving innovative scientific and technical skills. The resulting report, *A Nation at Risk: The Imperative for Educational Reform* published in 1983, identified the importance of developing a lifelong learning society and the need for schools to actively address higher standards: "Many 17-year-olds do not possess the 'higher order' intellectual skills we should expect of them."[3]

This was followed in 1991 by the first of a series of reports commissioned by the US Department of Labor to define the skill set required by the new and rapidly expanding technology orientated industries. The SCANS reports (Secretary's Commission on Achieving Necessary Skills) highlighted the significance of creativity as a key future skill for economic growth: "Creative thinking: Uses imagination freely, combines ideas or information in new ways, makes connections between seemingly unrelated ideas, and reshapes goals in ways that reveal new possibilities."[4] Within the UK similar conclusions were reached with the publication in 1999 of the government report, 'All Our Futures: "To enable young people to make their way with confidence in a world that is being shaped by technologies which are evolving more quickly than at any time in history."[5] The report chaired by the late Professor Ken Robinson identified the urgent need to develop the creative potential of young people across the curriculum "to ensure that the importance of creative and cultural education is explicitly recognised and provided for in schools' policies for the whole curriculum."[6]

The report's recommendations informed the 2005 Government White Paper 14–19, which introduced the Personal Learning and Thinking Skills (PLTS) initiative to embed employability skills, including the concept of 'creative thinkers' across the curriculum. This was followed in 2006 by the Vision 2020 report which included the learning goal "being creative, inventive, enterprising and entrepreneurial."[7] However, following a change of government, those initiatives waned and were not pursued. In contrast the highest-performing nations in the international Programme for International Student Assessment (PISA) tests – China, South Korea, Singapore, Finland and the province of Ontario – progressively shifted their focus away from exam results as the key educational outcome to promoting a personalised learning curriculum with an emphasis upon skills development, including creativity. In 2015 South Korea launched a new revised high school curriculum

> with an aim to nurture a creative and integrative learner, as part of the central goals to normalize public education. This curriculum focuses learning on key competencies that creative and integrative learners should acquire, such as self-management competency, knowledge-information processing skills, creative thinking skills, aesthetic-emotional competency, communication skills, and civic competency.[8]

The New Skills Commission in the United States equally stressed the importance of personal skills above and beyond exam results:

> The best employers the world over will be looking for the most competent, most creative and most innovative people on the face of the earth. . . . Those countries that produce the most important new products and services can capture a premium in world markets that will enable them to pay high wages to their citizens.[9]

The rapid rise of robotic and artificial intelligence (AI) applications across all sectors of society has spotlighted the significance of young people learning and gaining the confidence to create and innovate rather than copy and repeat. The World Economic Forum (WEF) elevated human traits above 'machines' as the winning edge in the future digital economy: "Proficiency in new technologies is only one part of the skills equation, however, as 'human' skills such as creativity, originality and initiative, critical thinking, persuasion, and negotiation will likewise retain or increase their value."[10]

Defining creativity

There are many definitions of creativity, but perhaps the most straightforward and succinct is Professor Robert J. Sternberg's description of creativity as "something original and worthwhile."[11] His definition can be applied at both the macro and micro levels of creativity commonly referred to as Big C and Little C:

- Big C – landmark inventions, discoveries and innovations that significantly advance knowledge or influence developments within a given field of study.
- Little C – everyday creative flourishes significant to the individual whether mastering the Floss, playing the piano, landscaping the garden, icing and decorating a cake, building a model railway, singing in a choir, etc.

The distinction between Big C and Little C is important because it recognises that everyone can be creative to some degree and that creativity is not simply about exceptional ability but also about personal growth and fulfilment.

The scale of the gap between Big C and Little C prompted Kaufman and Beghetto to propose a Four C model of creativity with the inclusion of two other distinctive phases of creative development:[12]

- Mini C – the ability of individuals to not only to receive and absorb new knowledge but to actively fashion and construct new insights into their studies or to develop and share original ideas. Mini C was defined by Kaufman and Beghetto as "novel and personally meaningful interpretation of experiences, actions, and events."[13]
- Pro C – the development of professional expertise to a notably high standard within a chosen field of study or employment e.g. craft, musician, artist, writer, architect, engineer, chef, etc.

The internet has heightened the visibility of Mini C and aspects of Little C beyond immediate family and friends by permitting many ordinary people to share their singing, writing, art, poetry, cartoons, cookery, sports, games, photography, videos, podcasts or simply musings and reflections via a blog or Twitter or Instagram or Tik Tok with the world. In relation to the latter sixteen-year-old Charli D'Amelio is Tik Tok's current highest attraction with 76.3 million followers and an astonishing 5.6 billion likes for her dance moves. Einstein's combinatory play has essentially shifted online, and many young people test, tweak and extend their ideas following online feedback or interactions in specialist online forums. The exposure may lead to employment, self-employment or simply immense personal satisfaction from engaging with like-minded people.

- Beth Reekles was fifteen when she posted a chapter-by-chapter release of her romantic novel, *The Kissing Booth* on Facebook. She gained 19 million followers and a book contract.
- Zoe Suggs while working as an apprentice in the design industry in 2009 established a blog to share her personal fashion and beauty tips. From a base of 1,000 followers in 2009 she now has over 12 million subscribers and over 1 billion video views.
- Jack Monroe was unemployed in 2015 when she started a blog 'Cooking on a Bootstrap' and posted a series of low-cost recipes. She won a book deal, published several recipe books, gained a newspaper column and enjoys regular appears on TV cookery programmes.
- Students engaged in a National Citizenship Service scheme in Exeter in 2018 improved donations to food banks. They designed 'foodbank shortage item' labels to be placed on relevant supermarket shelves to boost contributions of the items reported to be in short supply by the foodbanks. Both Sainbury's and Argos rolled out the idea, and donations to foodbanks subsequently soared and permitted shortage goods to be targeted for donations.
- Joe Whale, aged ten from Shrewsbury, is aka doodle boy for his unique and eye-catching doodle compilations on a wide range of themes. He has received many commissions for his artwork ranging from postcard size to whole wall murals. If you visit his website thedoodleboy.com prints range in price from £29 to £450.
- Nandi Bushell, aged ten, is an accomplished drummer who has been invited to play sets with major rock bands. You can catch her playing on YouTube.
- A group of high school girls in Los Angeles in 2017 developed a solar-powered tent for the homeless which folds into a backpack. The tent has integral solar panels used to power a light, multiple universal serial bus (USB) ports, a countdown timer and a sanitising ultraviolet light.
- Sixteen-year-old Nick D'Aloisio developed the app Summly and sold it to Yahoo for £20 million.
- At age eight Jaz Strzelecki monitored, catalogued and collected plastic waste from the beaches near her home in Pembrokeshire. At age nine she was appointed as the regional representative for the environmental campaign group for clean beaches, Surfers Against Sewage. Jaz publicises and manages regular beach clean-up days and associated challenge days for children.
- At age sixteen Liv Conlon decided not to pursue A-Levels and set up her own property furnishing company thepropertystagers.co.uk. The company specialises in furnishing empty flats and houses to a high specification as show houses or to help to sell an empty property or to furnish a rental property. In its first year of trading the company turnover was £30,000 but it now

comfortably exceeds 1 million pounds and rising. Liv employs a team of ten, including her mother and brother.

■ Fourteen-year-old Tommy Howard from Hawkchurch in Devon set up his own online toy retailing business in 2018 on eBay and currently fulfils an average of seventy orders per week while still at school.

■ Allie Sherlock started busking in her native Cork at the age of nine and today aged fifteen she is a regular on Grafton Street in Dublin. She has achieved a major following on YouTube with over 4 million subscribers and one of her most recent videos chalked up an astounding 44 million views.

■ At age seventeen Austin Russell dropped out of Stanford University having found the pace too slow and founded his own laser development company, Luminar, in his parents' garage. He successfully developed laser guidance technology for self-driving vehicles and now at the age of twenty-five in 2020 he is the youngest ever self-made billionaire worth, 2.4 billion dollars.

The category of Pro C, or professional expertise, acknowledges the ability of individuals to extend knowledge within their disciplines, often solving complex problems and adding significant value with innovative and original developments. Pro C creative thinking is all around us and regularly fulfils Sternberg's definition of 'original and worthwhile' but falls short of evidence of landmark breakthroughs that would qualify as Big C. Richard Fobes writing on the subject of creativity perhaps worded it best: "All innovations [begin] as creative solutions, but not all creative solutions become innovations."[14]

Creative thinking process

The Art of Creativity, published by Graham Wallas (1858–1932) in 1926, was the first significant study of creativity in relation to a process of critical thinking to engage with a problem and arrive at a solution. Wallace specified four major process steps as follows:

1 Preparation – a focus on the problem, conducting relevant research and generating as many different ideas as possible.
2 Incubation – Permitting a period of time to process and reflect upon the varied ideas
3 Illumination – isolating a possible solution
4 Verification – examining and testing the proposed solution.

Wallas's steps differentiated between generating ideas and identifying a solution, and this two-stage process was later defined and formalised by the American psychologist J.P. Guilford (1897–1987). In a much-quoted presentation to the American Psychological Association in 1950 Guilford distinguished between the importance of divergent and convergent thinking. The former related to the generation of as many imaginative, random free-flowing ideas and suggestions as possible and the latter to sifting, evaluating and testing the ideas to find viable solutions or original proposals. In 1967 Guilford devised the Alternative Uses Test as a test of divergent thinking by inviting participants to name as many alternative uses for an everyday object within two minutes e.g. a brick, a paper clip or a pencil. Ellis Paul Torrance (1915–2003) subsequently extended Guilford's test with a series of figural, oral and visual prompts designed to test an individual's propensity for creative thinking across four linked aspects:

- Fluency – the total number of ideas generated
- Originality – the rarity or novel value of each idea
- Elaboration – the number of additional added ideas
- Flexibility – the range of ideas across different categories

The 'Torrance Test of Creative Thinking' is widely employed in over thirty countries as a standardised measure of creativity. Elements of the Torrance Test often surface in the questions asked in job interviews e.g. if days had colours what colour would Wednesday be and why? It remains a matter of conjecture as to whether creativity can be fully measured, but perhaps the most straightforward test is the application of Sternberg's definition. In 1954 Alex Osborn, the originator of the term brainstorming, established the Creative Education Foundation with the mission "to spark personal and professional transformation by empowering people with the skill set, tool set, and mindset of deliberate creativity."[15] Osborn identified a similar process of creative thinking to Wallas and in later collaboration with Sidney Parnes developed the Creative Problem Solving (CPS) process. The Osborn-Parnes model has been widely adopted and has four stages and six process steps as follows:[16]

The subsequent debate within the educational community on the place of creativity within the cognitive hierarchy led to a revision of Bloom's Taxonomy.

Osborn-Parnes model	
Stage	Process
Clarify	Explore the vision Gather data Formulate challenges
Ideate	Explore ideas
Develop	Formulate solutions
Implement	Formulate a plan

Image 15.1

Bloom's Taxonomy revision

Benjamin Bloom's taxonomy was substantially revised by the educational psychologists Lorin Anderson and David Krathwohl in 2001. Krathwohl had collaborated with Bloom to write the original cognitive taxonomy as a guide to the setting of course and exam standards. Anderson had also enjoyed a personal connection with Bloom as one of his students. Their revision substituted verbs in place of the original nouns to emphasise an active process of thinking and reasoning but more significantly their revision replaced 'evaluation' with 'creating' as the highest form of cognitive development. In essence to evaluate is to judge or to assess something that currently exists whereas creating promotes originality. Anderson and Krathwohl defined creating as:

> Putting elements together to form a coherent or functional whole; reorganizing elements into a new pattern or structure through generating, planning, or producing. Creating requires users to put parts together in a new way, or synthesize parts into something new and different creating a new form or product.[17]

In other words, creating is about addition and adding something new, innovative and possibly unique.

Partnership for 21st Century Learning

The Partnership for 21st Century Learning (P21) was launched in 2002 to define and resource the development of 21st-century skills and published the 4Cs: Communication, Critical thinking, Collaboration and Creativity as the key employability skills, as detailed in Chapter 12. P21 defined creativity as follows:[18]

Think Creatively

- Use a wide range of idea creation techniques (such as brainstorming)
- Create new and worthwhile ideas (both incremental and radical concepts)
- Elaborate, refine, analyze and evaluate their own ideas in order to improve and maximize creative efforts

Work Creatively with Others

- Develop, implement and communicate new ideas to others effectively
- Be open and responsive to new and diverse perspectives; incorporate group input and feedback into the work
- Demonstrate originality and inventiveness in work and understand the real world limits to adopting new ideas
- View failure as an opportunity to learn; understand that creativity and innovation is a long-term, cyclical process of small successes and frequent mistakes

Implement Innovations

- Act on creative ideas to make a tangible and useful contribution to the field in which the innovation will occur.

These objectives identify the key steps underpinning creative thinking with a starting point of generating as many ideas as possible before refining and reviewing suggestions in collaboration with others to either solve a problem or to develop an original idea. The ability to develop creative thinking is endorsed by the American Psychological Association. Its top twenty principles for effective teaching and learning include "student creativity can be fostered."[19] The association recommends embedding creative prompts within the wording of objectives and instructions: "Varying activities by including prompts in assignments, such as create, invent, discover, imagine if, and predict."[20] Similarly school teachers in Singapore are encouraged to ask their students the following prompt questions:

> Teachers ask a set of three questions to get students curious about a topic. What do you see? What do you think about that? What does it make you wonder about? It's not about getting students to answer rhetorical questions but encouraging them to make careful observations and thoughtful interpretations in a specific context. This helps to stimulate students' curiosity and gets them to think more deeply about the topic.[21]

Big questions

The starting point for promoting and developing creative thinking is to stimulate interest in a chosen subject or career pathway by posing 'big' questions i.e. engaging with current issues and future challenges. Encourage a look to the horizon because the students in our classrooms will be in mid-career when many of us will be long since retired. What might they help to solve, design, improve or invent in future years or even before they leave school?

Image 15.2

The Organisation for Economic Co-operation and Development (OECD) identifies measures of the above type as transformative competencies as follows: "Creating new value requires critical thinking and creativity in finding different approaches to solving problems, and collaboration with others to find solutions to complex problems."[22] Look for opportunities for an interdisciplinary dimension to build an awareness of how different subject skills and knowledge interlock, complement and support each other. The XP college in Doncaster, UK, follows an 'expeditionary learning' curriculum and regularly sets the students 'big questions' to prompt deep and critical thinking and as catalyst for investigation

- What is my impact on the world around me?
- Why do we still need charity?
- How do we build a community?
- Should humans leave Earth?
- What do we need to know?
- Am I responsible for my own thoughts and deeds?[23]

The regular questions of this type are supported by a range of identified resources, and the students work collaboratively to arrive at and present their answers. Big questions might be incorporated into publicity leaflets, careers literature and initial induction courses. They can be displayed on posters in classrooms, corridors, the foyer or online or on social media to provoke discussion. Consider 'big' or 'challenge' question of the month with a prize for creative suggestions or solutions. Wherever possible link to current affairs because many students will have noticed a relevant TV documentary or YouTube video or have read the relevant newspaper article or post on social media. Find articles and videos of interest by visiting www.theconversation.com, the online academic journal or thoughtco.com or bigthink.com to find research and trends in your subject field or browse specialist YouTube channels:

- Google Zeitgeist
- Practical Engineering
- School of Life
- Veritasium
- Vox
- Everythink for Science

In addition, draw attention to any specialist journals held by the library or specialist websites or industry or university research to encourage independent study. Marzano commented: "the teacher draws explicit connections between content and the world outside school in order to make the content more exciting or relevant for students."[24] Our aim is to inspire and challenge by directing attention to real world and world class research as our ultimate answer to 'why learn?'

Deep Thought

To spark interest you might consider branding big questions as 'Deep Thought' named after the ultimate computer on the *Hitchhikers Guide to the Galaxy* television series that was asked, 'What is the answer to the ultimate question of life, the universe and everything?' After seven and a half million years of deliberation, Deep Thought famously answered 42. Start a lesson by posing a 'deep thought' question relevant to your subject that is a matter of debate or opinion rather than a straightforward answer. The aim is to promote 'deep thought' or critical thinking by encouraging students to develop confidence in forming and justifying opinions and to draw upon and apply their knowledge. Give your students thinking time in pairs or small groups and seek to build discussion and to encourage creative suggestions. You might select the video clip "The Answer to Life, Universe and Everything' on YouTube to provide some fun context.

DeepMind

Alternatively, you may consider branding 'big' questions DeepMind in honour of one of the world's most advanced computers operated by Google. DeepMind was designed by Demis Hassabis and was installed in the basement of Google's London headquarters near King's Cross. Hassabis was a chess prodigy at the age of seven, a programmer of top-selling computer games by the age of fifteen and is today the CEO of DeepMind (a Google subsidiary) which is at the leading edge of the development of artificial intelligence. DeepMind demonstrated its ability to 'think' rather than simply following a program by absorbing the rules of Go and playing several thousand games to perfect a strategy before defeating the world Go champion Lee Sedol in 2016. Creativity is still regarded as a purely human trait, but DeepMind is already demonstrating that given a problem to resolve it too may generate original solutions.

Applying RESOLVE

To fulfil Piaget's prescription, all students should be challenged to move beyond being the passive recipients of 'canned' knowledge by providing regular opportunities to think and reflect upon new learning. Our students need to realise their own potential to be originators and developers of new insights and original ideas. This involves introducing students to divergent and convergent thinking processes and, more importantly, to applying critical thinking with the aim of translating an idea into something of value. The following RESOLVE model incorporates the core elements of the Wallas and Osborn-Parnes creative thinking processes. It also applies the following definition and four characteristics of creativity published by Sir Ken Robinson:

"We therefore define creativity as: Imaginative activity fashioned so as to produce outcomes that are both original and of value.

- First, they always involve thinking or behaving imaginatively.
- Second, overall this imaginative activity is purposeful: that is, it is directed to achieving an objective
- Third, these processes must generate something original.
- Fourth, the outcome must be of value in relation to the objective."[25]

The RESOLVE model directs a robust process of ideation, evaluation, refinement and selection and extends to the often-omitted consideration of entrepreneurship as an optional end point of the creative process.

Random ideas
Evaluation
Select
Originality
Listening to opinions
Viability
Entrepreneurship

Step	Activity
Random ideas	Whether solo or as a group the aim is to brainstorm as many random ideas as possible. The term brainstorm was coined by the advertising executive Alex Osborn in 1938 as a means to maximise suggestions. He described it as process of using the **brain** to **storm** a problem. It is an urban myth that the term brainstorming is insensitive to people with epilepsy. The UK Epilepsy Society has confirmed that 93% of its members did not find the term derogatory or offensive so there is no need to 'thought shower.' Post-it notes work particularly well for solo brainstorming. Commit one idea per Post-it note and post on a wall or, if preferred, build a mind map on a whiteboard or flip-chart paper by placing the stimuli in a centre circle and radiating ideas outwards. Group brainstorming is more effective than solo brainstorming because people from different gender, social, cultural, ethnic and life experiences are more likely to cascade wider ideas. The standard approach is to appoint a leader to marshal the flow of ideas and a scribe to capture the ideas as they arise. The scribe should ideally capture one idea per Post-it notes to facilitate the later evaluation stage. Brainstorming should not involve any form of evaluation or judgement. Set a time limit with a timer. Seven minutes is the optimum time and within the time period everyone should jump in with as many ideas as possible. The participants should be encouraged to voice their ideas as soon as they bubble to the surface of their

Step	Activity
	minds no matter how wacky, fanciful or implausible. Brainstorming is all about the quantity of ideas rather than considerations of quality or feasibility. As Osborn noted, it is much easier to tone down a wild idea than to think up a new one. Once time has elapsed you can offer a further one or two minutes if participants are still in full flow. As an alternative to the group 'shout-out' you can instead issue all participants with Post-it notes and invite them to commit one idea per Post-it note and post on a wall. The group 'shout out' is preferable because hearing others' ideas might in turn spark additional ideas or 'piggybacking' as the participants bounce off each other. However, some people can be inhibited by the process and may be reluctant to voice an idea they think makes them sound stupid or silly. There is also the danger of dominant individuals hogging the process and the impact of the 'deference' factor if a boss or a key manager is in attendance. The anonymity provided by silently brainstorming on Post-it notes can help to generate ideas that might otherwise not be voiced. Once all ideas have been posted permit the group time to read the ideas made by others because it may spark further ideas. If tools like flipchart paper and Post-it notes strike you as not very 21st century then you might consider using apps like Brain Sparker or Ideament or Oflow to help prompt imagination and ideas. If you are brainstorming with others in different locations, then an app like Sync Space can draw all into productive simultaneous participation.
Evaluation	To evaluate all the ideas generated pin three sheets of flipchart paper on the wall with a large tick, a cross and a question mark as headings. Remind the participants of the overall aims and the nature of the problem by inviting some discussion around key questions like What are we trying to achieve? What extra value are we seeking? What image do we wish to project?, etc., as appropriate to the task. The purpose is to focus thinking around the overall aim. Next invite the group members to take turns selecting and reading a Post-it note aloud. The group exchanges opinions and decides whether to accept as a feasible idea worthy of exploring or to reject as not feasible or in between as a maybe. The Post-it note is allocated to the tick, cross or question mark flipchart paper as appropriate. After a short break invite the group to re-read the Post-it notes and to individually select and present a case for shifting an idea. Once any reordering has taken place, the group should focus on any Post-it notes remaining on the question mark sheet and transfer each one to the tick or cross sheet. Finally, set aside the rejected ideas on the cross sheet and focus all attention on the ideas posted on the tick sheet. Issue coloured dots in the colour of the traffic lights and invite everyone to go with their instinctive feel and to award a green, amber or red dot against each idea. Select the idea(s) with the largest number of green 'votes' to carry forward as possible solutions.

(Continued)

Step	Activity
Select	A period of reflection is essential before selecting and committing to any new idea or proposal. Wallas referred to it as 'incubation.' The time interval does not have to be extensive but should involve at least one period of sleep and ideally engagement in some physical activity e.g. playing a game, gardening, cooking, exercise, going for a long walk. This exploits the natural tendency of our brains to subconsciously mull over and process a new idea or proposal and engage in Einstein's combinatory play. Once the group reassembles the idea selected should be confirmed or modified or dropped entirely if some significant flaw has emerged.
Originality	Our thoughts and ideas are influenced by the endless stream of images, sounds and information we absorb on a daily basis. The musician Ed Sheeran was forced to settle two cases of alleged plagiarism when his songs 'Photograph' and 'Thinking Out Loud' were judged to draw heavily from earlier releases by Matt Cardle and Marvin Gaye, respectively. There was no suggestion of deliberate plagiarism, but rather an acknowledgement of the brain's subconscious store of memories bubbling to the surface during the process of composition. Brainstorming can equally trigger buried and subconscious memories and something that we think is original is not. Originality is at the core of creative thinking either as a wholly new novel development, innovation or solution to a problem or what was often referred to as mash-up i.e. a combination of existing ideas to create something new. Test for originality by considering what are the unique features of a new product or what extra value has been added or how will this development be of benefit? Does it share similarities with existing products or developments and check if it has been suggested or tried before? The consideration of taking out a patent may follow.
Listening to opinions	The law of unintended consequences often sabotages a new idea or development. In 2018 the British government, as part of its well-intentioned plan to reduce plastic pollution, encouraged supermarkets to replace single-use plastic bags with 'bags for life.' The latter were made of thicker and heavier-grade plastic and resulted in an increase in the production of plastic and plastic waste because too many shoppers bought a new one every shopping trip. Consequently before committing to a new idea, it is important to listen widely to opinions and views and to invite constructive criticism. Field-testing new products and new ideas on representative panels via specialist forums or more widely via social media can be highly beneficial in identifying flaws or gaining useful suggestions for improvement. Some of the famous product failures from not listening sufficiently include the 1957 Ford Edsel which was left in the showroom given a rising preference for smaller cars; New Coke 1985 failed the public's taste test; Kellogg's Breakfast Mates 1998 enclosed a small carton of milk, a plastic spoon and the cereal in a small plastic bowl all in theory to save time; Microsoft's Zune 2006 was regarded as a poor copy of Apple's iPod; and Google Glass 2012 overestimated the need for instant, literally in your face, connections with social media.

Step	Activity
Viability	Consider the financial viability of translating an idea into a successful product or service. Calculate all related costs and set a viable profit margin as well as considerations of ethical sourcing and environmental sustainability.
Entrepreneurship	The end point for many creative ideas is to recognise and act upon the commercial possibilities and to strike out as an entrepreneur. The definition of entrepreneurship provided by the business dictionary is "the capacity and willingness to develop, organize and manage a business venture along with any of its risks in order to make a profit."[26] The low start-up costs of the internet have not gone unnoticed and many young people you have never heard of before are successfully running their own businesses. At age eleven Jenz Oz has founded and manages the slick, professional lifestyle website for young teenagers www.icoolkid.com. Josh Valman started sending his product designs to companies aged just thirteen and today runs his own design company, RPD International (www.rpdintl.com). The twins Lauren and Sophie Chillock tripped across nut butter while touring in Australia and have since established their own successful range of nut butters (www.nuoifoods.com). Henry Patterson wrote a children's storybook at age ten and has since developed a full range of toys and products based on his characters (www.notbeforetea.co.uk). The websites https://startups.co.uk and www.entrepreneurer.com provide hundreds of case studies and supporting information for translating an idea into a business. The rising generation are very alert and open to the idea of self-employment: "A Gallup study (USA) showed that 77% of students in grades five through 12 said that they want to be their own boss, and 45% plan to start their own business. When we asked the same group if they believed they would "invent something that changes the world," 42% said "yes."[27] Finland's 2016 reform of its high school curriculum has introduced 'entrepreneurship education' as a key component of every students' study programme: "Entrepreneurship and an entrepreneurial mindset are something that can be learned. Their components are creativity, innovation."[28] This follows the European Union's 2015–2018 trial programme of offering students a practical experience of developing and managing a mini company while still at school. The mini company experience involved immersion in the full creative process of identifying and carrying forward an original idea to fruition as a business start-up accompanied by full guidance and support and concluding with a close down and evaluation of how to run a successful company. The outcomes and benefits of the trial may be accessed at icee-eu.eu. The 2018 OECD report, 'How to Build a 21st Century School System,' as highlighted in Chapter 11, included the observation, "The next generation of young citizens will create jobs not seek them and collaborate to advance humanity in an increasing complex world."[29]

An end goal of entrepreneurship also underpins Stanford University's recommended three-step process of creative thinking under the banner 'tangible thinking and involving, 'design thinking,': "The goal of Design Thinking is to find the sweet spot where what is technologically possible (feasibility), what makes money or meets business or organization goals (viability), and what people need (desirability) intersect."[30] RESOLVE adopts a similar approach and involves a step-by-step process of refining random ideas into a viable, costed proposal.

The creation of jobs, as indicated by the OECD, may represent the pinnacle of creative thinking, but for many creativity is simply about personal satisfaction and the sense of contentment they gain from pursuing and perfecting a particular skill or knowledge to a high standard. Not all creativity has to be Pro C or end in Big C.

Embedding creative thinking

The primary focus of our schools and colleges is to develop an opportunity-rich learning environment focusing on promoting Little C and Mini C. It is a process of planting acorns:

- Introducing case studies to seek solutions to realistic problems and apply the RESOLVE process of creative thinking.
- Invite Dragon's Den–style pitches as the culmination of the RESOLVE process.
- Introduce a Mini Company development project and apply the RESOLVE process.
- Suggest, design and organise community projects.
- Develop and manage a fundraising project for a named charity.
- Create a display or event to mark a major date in the calendar like Holocaust Memorial Day, International Women's Day, World Water Day, Human Rights Day or International Literacy Day, etc.
- Encourage critical appraisal of existing products, services and processes associated with relevant career pathways and invite improvements and forwarding of suggestions to relevant companies i.e. suggest a refinement to an existing product or pitch an idea for a new advert.
- Contribute to online forums or a blog or vlog own original music, poetry, art, recipes, crafts, apps, games, fashion tips, movie plots, drama, architectural designs, gardening advice, hair styles, makeup, toys, furniture designs, fitness programmes, childcare equipment, etc., whatever is relevant to the programme of study and personal interests.
- Take responsibility for and organise an outside visit, trip or residential experience.
- Take responsibility for and organise a programme of visiting speakers.

- Find and engage in a creative project with www.ideasfoundation.org.uk.
- Enter local, regional, national or international competitions.
- Highlight relevant winners of World Skills championships and consider competing.
- Recommend viewing of relevant TED talks and commenting on the research or ideas expressed.
- Select a free study programme from a leading university from one of the major online study portals e.g. www.futurelearn.com, www.open.edu/openlearn, www.edx.org or www.alison.com. Gain a certificate of completion. At the age of thirteen in 2018 Connell Cairns enrolled for a seven-week course in Astrospace Engineering offered by MIT and gained one of the highest-ever completion scores.
- For those interested in science and engineering try one or more of Sir James Dyson's creative challenges at www.jamesdysonfoundation.co.uk.
- Consider earning recognition for developing digital and employability skills by completing original projects with Inspiring Digital Enterprise Awards (iDEA) at www.idea.org.

Creativity is about challenge and empowering all students to develop a 'have a go' mindset. Research conducted by George Land (1932–2016) in 1968 revealed that creativity sharply diminishes with age as we become more inhibited in relation to imaginative expression. Land was contracted to develop a test of creative thinking by NASA to help inform their astronaut selection programme. Viewers of the movie *Apollo 13* will appreciate the lifesaving importance of creative thinking. Land's test proved to be a good predictor of creative thinkers, and in 1968 he commenced a longitudinal study of creative thinking by applying his test to 1,600 five-year-old children. The children scored 98% for their ability to generate a wide range of imaginative, original ideas. At age ten a retest revealed a sharp drop-off to 30% and a further drop to 12% by age fifteen. Land also tested 260,000 adults with an average age of thirty-one and reported their capacity for imaginative creative thinking as just 2%. The test for adults was repeated many times encompassing over 1 million adults and has replicated a steady 2% score for the capacity to be creative. Land's research perhaps lends credence to the late Sir Ken Robinson's view that schools kill creativity as articulated in his celebrated TED talk 'Do Schools Kill Creativity?' released in 2006. The number of views has surpassed 20 million and is still rising. As a part of his presentation Robinson remarked that a teacher asked a young girl who was busy painting in a primary classroom, "What are you painting?" The girl replied, "I am painting a picture of God." The teacher remarked, "But no one knows what God looks like?" To which the young girl replied, "They will in a minute." As the examples in this chapter illustrate, and contrary to many opinions, children are not only capable of thinking like a designer, a programmer, a scientist or a writer, etc., but can successfully translate their original ideas into action. Our challenge as teachers is to nurture and release creativity and to help fulfil Piaget's goal of ensuring that each generation is capable of 'doing new things.'

References

1 Piaget, Jean, https://quoteinvestigator.com/2014/06/04/education/
2 Farnam Street Blog, *Steve Jobs on Creativity*, https://fs.blog/2014/08/steve-jobs-on-creativity/
3 Report of the National Commission on Excellence in Education, *A Nation at Risk: The Imperative for Educational Reform*, April 1983, pg. 11, www.edreform.com/wp-content/uploads/2013/02/A_Nation_At_Risk_1983.pdf
4 U.S. Department for Labor, *Secretary's Commission on Achieving Necessary Skills (SCANS)*, 1991, www.sjsu.edu/faculty/chang/sped/scanskills.html
5 National Advisory Committee on Creative and Cultural Education, *All Our Futures: Creativity, Culture and Education*, May 1999, pg. 21, http://sirkenrobinson.com/pdf/allourfutures.pdf
6 Ibid, pg. 192.
7 DfES, *Vision 2020*, DfES, December 2006, pg. 10.
8 Korean Ministry of Education, *National Curriculum Priorities*, 2015, http://english.moe.go.kr/sub/info.do?m=040101&s=english
9 National Center on Education and the Economy, *The New Commission on the Skills of the American Workforce, Tough Choices or Tough Times*, pg. 5–7, www.skillscommission.org/wp-content/uploads/2010/05/ToughChoices_EXEC SUM.pdf
10 World Economic Forum, *The Future of Jobs Report 2018*, 2018, pg. 12, http://www3.weforum.org/docs/WEF_Future_of_Jobs_2018.pdf
11 Sternberg, Robert J., www.creative971.com/what-is-creativity-in-business/
12 Kaufman, James C. and Beghetto, Ronald A., *Beyond Big and Little: The 4C Model of Creativity*, 2009, https://pdfs.semanticscholar.org/f4fc/c5125a4eb-702cdff0af421e500433fbe9a16.pdf
13 Ibid, pg. 3.
14 Fobes, Richard, *The Creative Problem Solver's Toolbox: A Complete Course in the Art of Creating Solutions to Problems of Any Kind*, Solutions Through Innovation, 1993.
15 www.creativeeducationfoundation.org
16 www.creativeeducationfoundation.org/wp-content/uploads/2015/06/CPS-Guide-6-3-web.pdf
17 Wilson, Leslie Owen, *The Second Principle, Anderson and Krathwohl: Bloom's Taxonomy Revised*, https://thesecondprinciple.com/teaching-essentials/beyond-bloom-cognitive-taxonomy-revised/
18 Battelle for Kids, *Partnership for 21st Century Learning, Framework for 21st Century Learning Definitions*, Battelle for Kids, 2019, pg. 4.

19 American Psychological Association, *Top Twenty Principles from Psychology for Pre K12 Teaching and Learning*, 2015, pg. 14, http://www.apa.org/ed/schools/cpse/top-twenty-principles.pdf

20 Ibid, pg. 14.

21 School Bag, *Peek into the 21st Century Classroom*, 28th July 2017, www.schoolbag.sg/story/peek-into-the-21st-century-classroom

22 OECD, *Future of Education and Skills 2030, Transformative Competencies*, OECD Publishing, 2019, pg. 5.

23 www.xptrust.org

24 Marzano, Robert J., *The New Art and Science of Teaching*, Solution Tree Press, 2017, pg. 70.

25 National Advisory Committee on Creative and Cultural Education, *All Our Futures: Creativity, Culture and Education*, May 1999, pg. 30, http://sirkenrobinson.com/pdf/allourfutures.pdf

26 www.businessdictionary.com/definition/entrepreneurship.html

27 https://news.gallup.com/businessjournal/157925/don-fail-tomorrow-entrepreneurs.aspx

28 https://minedu.fi/en/entrepreneurship-training-and-education

29 Schleicher, A., *World Class, How to Build a 21st Century School System*, OECD Publishing, 2018, pg. 251.

30 Stanford University, https://tangible-thinking.com/what-is-design-thinking

CHAPTER

16

Future of learning

The future of learning is popularly forecast as online, self-access, autonomous learning, given the ease of access to online knowledge coupled with the ability of artificial intelligence (AI) to track and monitor progress. However, the sum of education is more than knowledge. The envisaged future of autonomous learning was fuelled by the development of massive open online courses (MOOCs).

MOOCs

The first MOOCs were developed by Stanford University in 2012 and offered the ability to study and learn without physically setting foot on the university campus and, as an added attraction, were entirely free. Over the past twenty years the rising generations have become accustomed to accessing free information from a Google search or Wikipedia, YouTube or a TED Talk, etc. MOOCs were a logical extension and have expanded rapidly and are now offered by 900 universities worldwide with a global enrolment in 2019 of 120 million students (excluding China) studying anything from a short one-week micro credential to a full degree programme. If you enjoy champagne perhaps the five-week champagne master programme is of interest and entirely free (www.champagne-mooc.com). Harvard University has enrolled more students on MOOCs than the total number of students who have attended the university in its entire 377-year history. The top five MOOC providers in terms of registered users in 2019 were:[1]

Coursera 45 million,
Edx 24 million,
Udacity 11.5 million,
Futurelearn 10 million.

Futurelearn.com is a consortium of UK universities managed by the Open University offering both paid and free online courses: "Our huge online library has

DOI: 10.4324/9781003132783-21

thousands of online ejournals, eBooks, databases and multimedia resources for you to tap into, 24 hours a day, seven days a week, whenever you need them and wherever you are."[2] MOOCs represent a huge success in extending access to high-quality education, but they have also exposed the limitations of online learning by underlining that learning is not simply about accessing information. Online learning in isolation has a low success rate. The very first MOOC offered by Harvard University in computer science in October 2012 attracted 180,000 registrations but fewer than 1% – around 1,439 of the registrants – completed. In 2017 the average completion rate for MOOCs was 13% and for many individual programmes as low as 5.5% far below the completion rates for traditional classroom-based programmes. The issue is the human factor i.e. sustaining personal motivation and self-regulation. This is not a new problem. The earlier traditional book- and TV-based distance learning programmes also suffered from high rates of attrition. Drop-out is a common problem across most aspects of personal development whether it is keeping to a diet plan or a new exercise regime; people start well, with good intentions, but quickly tail off. The low completion rate for MOOCs is at face value a negative but there is also a significant positive. Given the high number of enrolments, the small percentage of completers still represents a substantial number of people accessing a university education. Many of those completers may be housebound for a variety of reasons: in prison, in hospital, in full-time employment, raising a family or simply living in isolated communities remote from physical university access. MOOCs have successfully extended university education to people who would otherwise not have the time or opportunity.

SPOCs

To address the low completion rates, most universities improved their support systems and introduced small private online courses (SPOCs) to provide a more structured and regulated learning experience. The private aspect is not a pay barrier (although many do charge), but the introduction of a selection process to ascertain levels of motivation and evidence of a capacity to study. This will typically involve the submission of a 10,000-word assignment to test research and analytical writing skills. Most SPOCs also limit enrolment to around 500 students to facilitate realistic progress monitoring and support. Those measures succeeded in raising the average completion rates to 40% but still far below the completion rates for traditional on-campus programmes. The on-campus ingredient that makes the difference is collaboration because in all aspects of life we value shared endeavour, a sense of community and the opportunity for encouragement and support from peers and tutors when our motivation falters or we hit a hurdle. In essence education is about more than acquiring units of information. It is also, as detailed in Chapter 8, about enhancing personal development, warm human interactions, friendships and mutual support.

Try online learning

To experience and test your own resolve, why not try learning a foreign language wholly online? The following three apps are free and aim to build your proficiency in speaking a foreign language through short, daily practice. Select Duolingo or Memrise or Busuu and consider how well you make progress but also reflect upon your staying power in pursuing your new study option.

Role of the teacher

The expansion of MOOCs and SPOCs and the increasing wealth of information available online has renewed controversy over the future role of teachers. The controversy was first ignited in 1993, only two years after the launch of the internet, by the publication of the article 'From Sage on the Stage to Guide on the Side' by Alison King, associate professor of education in the University of California. King's article remains regularly quoted as a critique of the traditional teacher-led classroom:

> In most college classrooms, the professor lectures and the students listen and take notes. The professor is the central figure, the 'sage on the stage,' the one who has the knowledge and transmits that knowledge to the students, who simply memorize the information and later reproduce it on an exam – often without even thinking about it.[3]

The notion of teachers as guides provoked considerable controversy. The influential Professor E. D. Hirsch expressed concern that teachers might increasingly regard the presentation of subject information as unnecessary because "you can always look it up . . . or can you?"[4] This form of concern is not new but dates to the earliest days of educational debate. Plato recounted a story recounted by Socrates of a discussion between the Egyptian King Thamus and the god Theuth. Theuth offered Thamus the gift of writing, but Thamus rejected writing on the grounds that it would weaken rather than strengthen learning:

> Those who acquire it will cease to exercise their memory and become forgetful; they will rely on writing to bring things to their remembrance by external signs instead of by their own internal resources . . . they will receive a quantity of information without proper instruction, and in consequence be thought very knowledgeable when they are for the most part quite ignorant. And because they are filled with the conceit of wisdom instead of real wisdom they will be a burden to society.[5]

Hirsch's treatise is often misconstrued as a rejection of online learning, but Hirsch was not opposed to the internet. He was opposed to shallow, disconnected knowledge. His concern needs to be placed into the context of the early internet when many resources were of dubious merit and the answers to questions were often incomprehensible without wider contextual knowledge of the subject. Today few would deny that the internet has significantly evolved and offers authoritative subject resources, across all disciplines, both surface and deep. In this context King's description of teachers as a 'guide on the side' is not a diminution, but rather a refocussing of teaching skills away from presenting to evaluating information. This shift was acknowledged by the Education Training Foundation:

> Technology advances and more specifically the internet facilities a shift from thinking about teaching as providing information to thinking about learning and creating learning environments. This in turn creates a relationship shift between the teachers and the learners. The teachers' role is becoming one really of a coach and a facilitator guiding learners to take ownership of their learning.[6]

Across the professional world, whether sport, fitness or business settings, coaches are highly valued experts who guide and steer performance to a high level. Within educational settings a coach or mentor can also make a substantial difference to individual progress by not only pinpointing and correcting misunderstandings but also by boosting motivation. This has been recognised in the UK with the establishment of a National Tutoring Programme (nationaltutoring.org.uk) to help support pupils who have fallen behind during the coronavirus pandemic. An assessment of the impact of the scheme conducted by the Education Endowment Foundation (EEF) in February 2021 confirmed the benefits of one-to-one support and validated Bloom's mastery learning thesis as detailed on Chapter 2. The EEF reported that 96% of the pupils taking part in years 10 to 13 valued and benefited from the study support. Susskind, in reviewing educational strategies, confirmed the benefits of one-to-one tuition over the traditional classroom: "an average student who receives one to one tuition will tend to outperform 98 per cent of ordinary students in a traditional classroom."[7] The programme, as constituted, targets pupils requiring additional support, but coaching should, as in the professional world, also target challenge and excellence, as articulated by Mortimer Adler in 1982. Adler was the chair of the editorial board of *Encyclopaedia Britannica* and he placed 'intellectual coaching' at the heart of his Paideia Proposal for improving education. Paideia, from the Greek *pais paidos*, referred to the nurturing of a child and, more broadly, a holistic education for life. Harari referred to the classroom as 'bankrupt'[8] in relation to the expansion of online learning, but it is more a question of refocussing the classroom to address Adler's intellectual coaching as a key element in the future of learning. The guidance for education policymakers issued by the United Nations Educational, Scientific and Cultural Organization (UNESCO) in 2021 acknowledged "it is likely that teacher roles will change. . . . we know that teachers will need to build new competencies to enable them to work effectively with AI, and undertake appropriate professional development to foster their human and social capabilities."[9] As self-access online learning increases, teachers will gain more time and opportunities to address the performance of each individual and tailor appropriate support.

Future of learning

The following three core elements will place the individual at the heart of future learning and promote a fusion between the classroom and online learning.

Artificial Intelligence (AI)

Students will gain 24-7 access to authoritative, up-to-date knowledge libraries across all subjects reducing the need for teachers to produce their own resources and ending the lottery of poor as against high quality learning resources. Instructional design providers will supply highly attractive units of study employing expert opinion, text, video, photographs, quotations, research evidence, diagrams, charts etc., coupled with AI enabled embedded quizzes and gaming approaches to test and check learning and prompt additional support or acceleration. Teachers may also capture their own direct instruction presentations on video and take advantage of AI automated marking, communication and feedback tools.

The classroom will focus on the elaboration of online learning through involvement in regular paired and group collaborative activities, seminars, one to one tutorials and well-planned direct instruction to deepen and extend online learning, promote connections and the consolidation of new learning within long-term memory. A wide range of student reporting and presentation methods will promote life skills and help to hone the Four Cs of employability, Communication, Critical thinking, Collaboration and Creativity as our unique human signature.

Collaboration

Pedagogue

A personal mentor will restore the concept of the pedagogue as a life coach rather than more narrowly focussed on study support. The aim is to provide each student with a stable, positive anchor focussed on all aspects of their personal well-being with access to specialist support as required. The role will also encompass coaching good study and organisational skills and monitoring and supporting study goals. AI enabled chatbots will increasingly contribute to the provision of course information and provide students with support 24-7 with access to specialist agencies across a range of study, social and personal support issues.

Image 16.1

Artificial intelligence

Public awareness of AI was heightened in 2016 by the launch of Amazon's chatbot Alexa. Alexa, named after the famed Great Library of Alexandria (287 BCE), has extended its range of services and all via simple voice command. In 2020 Ofcom reported that 36% of twelve- to fifteen-year-olds in the UK interacted with a smart speaker in a rising trend.[10] Alexa can tell you the news, provide the weather forecast, read a book, play music, control smart devices, set timers, make phone calls, order a takeaway meal, control your TV and even tell you a joke. What was once the realm of Star Trek science fiction is today unremarkable, and for many children entering our classrooms, a norm. In addition, Alexa and similar chatbots like Apple's Siri and Google Home have unlimited capabilities as the Internet of Things (IOT) expands and more dramatically when cast in human form as a robot. The potential of the latter was dramatically brought to public attention in the UK on 21 June 2017 when the lifelike robot 'Sophia' was interviewed live on the breakfast time television programme, *Good Morning Britain*, by the broadcaster Piers Morgan. Sophia was able to maintain a conversation and coupled with appropriate facial expressions gave every appearance of being human. Sophia, developed by Hanson Robotics, is set for mass production in 2021 and will be marketed as a companion for the elderly or housebound and to undertake any customer-facing roles e.g. receptionist, librarian, shop assistant. Sophia is not alone. Robots in a variety of guises utilising similar chatbot technology are filtering into wider society:

- Pepper, a robot specialising in care and support for the elderly, created a stir giving evidence to a House of Commons Education Select Committee. Pepper warmly responded to questions, speaks twelve languages and, like Alexa, can answer any general knowledge question, tell a joke, play YouTube videos, place a telephone call, play music and provide the latest news, weather or summons help, etc., as requested.
- Kaspar, Moxie, Nao and many others are child-like robots designed to interact with and prompt social and language skills for children with autism.
- Andi is an avatar who manages and controls all aspects of recruitment by scanning applications, interviewing candidates via Skype and using assessments of speech and body language to produce a short list of candidates.
- Yuki is a robot teaching assistant who works in Philipps University of Marburg, Germany, to present aspects of lectures and seminars and to monitor student progress.
- Milton Keynes has 120 delivery bots trundling the streets from local shops to homes delivering all manner of items in large keypad-controlled containers. The bots designed and operated by Starship Technologies engage customers in cheerful conversation before confirming an order, releasing the goods and returning to base.
- The Henn-na Hotel in Sasebo, Japan is fully staffed by chatbot-enabled robots.

The YouTube video of Boston Dynamics robots dancing to 'Do You Love Me' was essentially a bit of fun but the more serious YouTube video '9 Most Advanced AI Robots' was watched by 3.6 million people in March 2020 and illustrated the potential of robotic technology. The fast pace of applications reflects the development of machine learning whereby many thousands of samples of speech or images or objects are uploaded to inform recognition and interactions. The ability of a chatbot to sustain a conversation with 100% speech accuracy and, more significantly, to pass the Turing Test was announced by Eric Horvitz, head of Microsoft AI in July 2017. Alan Turing (1912–1954) led the Hut 8 team of code breakers at Bletchley Park during World War Two and later challenged future computer programmers to design a computer that could successfully pass itself off as human during an online conversation. The Turing Test was first passed on 7 June 2014 when a chatbot successfully convinced ten out of thirty judges in the Royal Society in London that their questions were being answered by a thirteen-year-old Ukrainian boy called Eugene Goostman. The short duration of the interaction has been questioned along with the fact that only a third of the judges were fooled, but to fool any humans marked a significant milestone in the development of AI. Only two years later in 2016, Ashok Goel, a professor of computing science at Georgia Tech in the United States, developed a chatbot he named Jill Watson to handle all student enquiries regarding their study programme. The chatbot successfully answered over 10,000 enquiries without any student ever suspecting that Jill was not human. One student was so impressed by Jill's warmth and online interactions that he asked 'her' out on a date.

Ada leading the way

In 2017 Bolton College became the first UK college to 'employ' a chatbot or, more accurately, a digital assistant utilising IBM's Watson Conversation service. The digital assistant, pioneered by Learning Technology manager Aftab Hussain, was named Ada after the mathematician Ada Lovelace who worked alongside Charles Babbage and was credited as the first person to recognise the potential of computers to move beyond calculations. Hussain is leading the expansion of Ada's interactions with staff and students in three progressive development stages:

- **Stage one** – Ada is connected to all school/college digital databases, including student records, programme information, admin services, support services and wider sports, social and leisure information. This permits Ada to answer any enquiry on any aspect of a student's programme, including their personal progress, along with any information relating to college support, admin services or upcoming events.
- **Stage two** – Ada is authorised to draw upon appropriate data to update files, create records, generate reports, contact individuals, etc.
- **Stage Three** – Ada proactively issues information alerts, notifications of deadlines and prompts to action.

Ada will also play a leading role in supporting future teaching and learning by drawing on a comprehensive knowledge bank across every subject to answer students' questions:

> Teachers will be able to set up subject chatbots and compose answers to questions that are routinely asked by students about subject topics. Ada's subject knowledge will grow as more teachers contribute questions and answers to each subject chatbot. We hope that Ada will be a great resource for students; especially if hundreds or thousands of teachers sign up to teach Ada about their subjects. Students of all ages will have access to the Ada website. They simply select a subject chatbot and ask it a question. Ada will respond with answers that incorporate the use of text, images, links to resources and embedded videos. The service will be free to use by teachers and students.[11]

Once established, this resource will significantly 'level up' teaching standards by stepping beyond the knowledge and experience of a single teacher and create a stimulating range of resources as discussed in Chapter 9. Ultimately online knowledge banks of this type will extend and draw down expert knowledge beyond individual schools and colleges. The Singapore national Student Learning Space (SLS) is a central information hub for all schools in Singapore. The future is convergence as AI enhanced connectivity builds and identifies authoritative and public domain Open Education Resources (OER) to underpin high instructional standards.

Instructional design

Instructional design identifies a particular learning goal and offers AI-enabled step-by-step instruction with integrated assessment, progress monitoring, gaming approaches and corrective feedback, all within one carefully crafted package. Within business and industry, it has already transformed employee upskilling as knowledge increasingly becomes a packaged product. Each 'learning episode' or 'micro learn' is either stand-alone or a link in a chain towards higher learning goals and often released as an app. Leading providers like Edcast.com, Axonity.com, Grovo.com, Wranx.com or Lynda.com are ending the need for employers to send staff on external training programmes or to employ a consultant to train staff in-house. Axonify describes the benefits as follows:

> Simply put, microlearning is a technique for delivering content in small, focused, bite-sized chunks (from three to five minutes) several times per week, or even daily. . . . It's digestible chunks of everything your employees need to know, delivered based on what your employees current knowledge levels are, to build long-term knowledge retention.[12]

Grovo emphasises the application of the latest educational research:

> Our microlearning method uses learning best practices like spacing, interleaving, and repetition to help the brain move information from short-term

memory into long-term memory, where it can be more easily retrieved on the job.[13]

Whereas Wranx takes it a step further and in addition to selecting from fully developed programmes, offers to design bespoke programmes:

> We'll set about converting all of your training content into digestible drills, free of charge. Whether it's a brand handbook, new product specs, or just hard data, our **team of content writers** will ensure your material is made Wranx-friendly, ready for your employees to absorb and learn.[14]

Lynda.com now operates in partnership with the business platform Linkedin.com and provides an extensive range of training programmes. Instructional design is progressively entering mainstream education with services like uplearn.co.uk bypassing schools and colleges to directly target students with personalised learning support: "Our algorithm identifies your weak spots and focuses on those, until you're achieving A★ across every topic. Up Learn continuously evaluates your abilities, intelligently identifying what to study next."[15] The support provided does not simply relate to subject content but to AI-enabled intelligent tutoring systems (ITSs) i.e. responding to each individual's rate of progress by evaluating answers, repeating key information, retesting and offering further support or higher learning extensions. Services like Uplearn are expanding and setting a high bar for how teachers within schools and colleges coach and support individual students. The former master of Wellington College, Sir Antony Seldon, in his book The Fourth Education Revolution, has predicted that AI applications, including virtual reality (VR), will take the lead in guiding and delivering learning by 2030. VR offers the ability to explore and examine any object, process or place in full immersive 3D. Augmented reality (AR) takes it a step further by providing a full sensory experience involving haptic feedback. Google's 'Expeditions' or Gear VR or Daydream VR are fast expanding their educational content. Google cardboard viewers provide easy, entry-level, viewing with access to a library of over 700 virtual field trips. Within the gaming world Oculus.com leads the way with rich immersive virtual environments with significant implications for education as the technology becomes more widely adopted. However, it may be that less is more. There is a danger that the rich visual experience can overwhelm and produce sensory saturation and simply generate a 'wow' factor rather than any significant advance in learning. To secure a positive learning outcome, the learning purpose needs to be carefully planned to guide what the individual is 'looking' for and to confirm relevant progress.

Collaborative learning

People are social, and most students value interaction with teachers and peers in a confirmation that humanity cleaves to society rather than to solitude. Studying with others rather than in isolation helps to sustain motivation, deepen learning and build vital interpersonal and intrapersonal skills. Classrooms are and will remain the primary hub for learning but operating as dialogic classrooms. Collaborative tasks, as described in Chapter 8, will immerse students in a process of rigorous critical thinking to interrogate and question information and as appropriate extend into creative ideation and the presentation of high-quality learning outcomes e.g. oral, written, pictorial or digital formats. Classes will be fluid with the regular formation of small groups and teams to undertake different aspects of topic research jigsaw style or to pursue separate topics with interested peers drawn from different year groups and/or disciplines as appropriate. Rather than the single pace of a class, each group or team will set its own pace within a specified time window. Those trends are already evident in many schools and universities worldwide. The Hampton Park school in Melbourne offers an elective curriculum from Year Eight with three levels of study, explore, enhance and excel. Progression is by outcome rather than chronology and with collaborative working across the age range and disciplines. Ultimately the role of teachers will be enhanced rather than diminished by combining the following elements into inspiring and challenging sequences of learning.

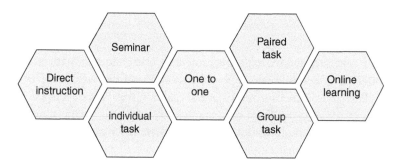

Image 16.2

The goal is not simply to engage but to drive high learning outcomes with a seamless learning flow from the classroom to online resources and back again.

Restoring the pedagogue

The Pedagogues of ancient Greece (as introduced in Chapter 1) were slaves with a responsibility for guiding children through life's travails to become confident, independent adults. The term mentor is perhaps the modern-day equivalent, although the terms personal or progress tutors are often preferred. Ideally, mentors should embrace the spirit of the pedagogue by stepping beyond the often narrow remit of assessment and attendance monitoring in favour of wider holistic personal development goals i.e. operating as a life coach offering positive advice and guidance and emotional support as illustrated:

Image 16.3

Mentors can mitigate disadvantage by providing every student with a positive anchor and offering unconditional support across all the earlier aspects of personal development. This holistic focus is important as children from disadvantaged homes underachieve at every measure from primary school Scholastic Achievement Tests (SATs) results, summative high school achievements, rates of university attendance and progression to professional employment.[16] However, all students – not just the disadvantaged – should have the benefit of a mentor. Students from all walks of life can hit personal challenges and make the wrong choices. Weekly meetings with mentors can offer valuable opportunities for concerns to be expressed and help to alleviate the stress and pressure many young people feel and especially in the age of social media. The highly successful Newham Collegiate Sixthform Centre in East London ensures that each student is attached to a high achieving volunteer mentor both as a role model and immediate source of positive support and guidance. Chatbots will also increasingly join human mentors in the near future as they evolve and step beyond immediate study related support to address lifestyle goals as predicted by UNESCO:

> it would not necessarily be difficult to leverage the capabilities of smartphones and related technologies to create an AI-driven learning companion that could accompany individual learners throughout their life . . . a learning companion would provide continuous support, building on the individual student's interests and goals . . . help them address their emerging goals and connect their learning interests and achievements, while encouraging them to reflect on and revise their long-term learning aims.[17]

The AI-enhanced chatbot, as indicated, would be a lifelong source of personal support and, once integrated with apps monitoring health, fitness and welfare, provide holistic personalised guidance.

The future of learning

The future of learning will be less convergent and more divergent as students take advantage of Open Education Resources (OER) and Intelligent Tutoring Systems (ITS) to set and achieve their own goals at their own pace. The future of knowledge may well be online, but the future of learning will be a stimulating and collaborative process of mentor-led questions, elaboration, feedback and challenge. Education is not a number, nor a grade, nor a single phase of life but a lifelong quest for personal fulfilment. In this regard the future of learning will ultimately rest not with the *Didaskalso* but with the *Paidagogues* and an education for life.

References

1   www.class-central.com/report/mooc-stats-2019/
2   Future Learn, www.open.ac.uk/courses/what-study-like/learning-resources
3   King, Alison, From sage on the stage to guide on the side, *Journal – College Teaching*, Taylor Francis, vol. 41, no. 1, Winter, 1993, pg. 30.
4   Hirsch, E. D., You can always look it up . . . or can you? *The American Educator*, 2000, pg. 2.
5   https://notaboutyouormewordpress.com/2011/12/31/king-thamus
6   Liogier, Vikki, www.et-foundation.co.uk/supporting/support-practitioners/edtech-support/digital-skills-competency-framework/
7   Susskind, Daniel, *A World Without Work*, Allen Lane, 2020, pg. 159.
8   Harari, Yuval Noah, *21 Lessons for the 21st Century*, Jonathan Cape, 2018, pg. 266.
9   Miao, Fengchun, et al., *AI and Education Guidance for Policy-Makers*, UNESCO, 2021, pg. 18.
10 Ofcom, *Children and Parents, Media Use and Attitudes*, Ofcom, 2019, pg. 5.
11 Ada Subject Question and Answer, www.aftabhussain.com
12 https://axonify.com
13 www.grovo.com
14 www.wranx.com
15 www.uplearn.co.uk
16 Department for Education, *State of the Nation 2019: Children and Young People's Wellbeing*, Department for Education, www.gov.uk/government/publications
17 Miao, Fengchun, et al., *AI and Education Guidance for Policy-Makers*, UNESCO, 2021, pg. 19.

Index

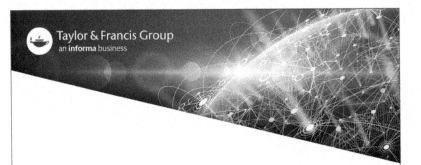

Lightning Source UK Ltd.
Milton Keynes UK
UKHW032149291221
396367UK00007B/59